I0810136

IMAGES
of America

NEW BRITAIN
VOLUME II

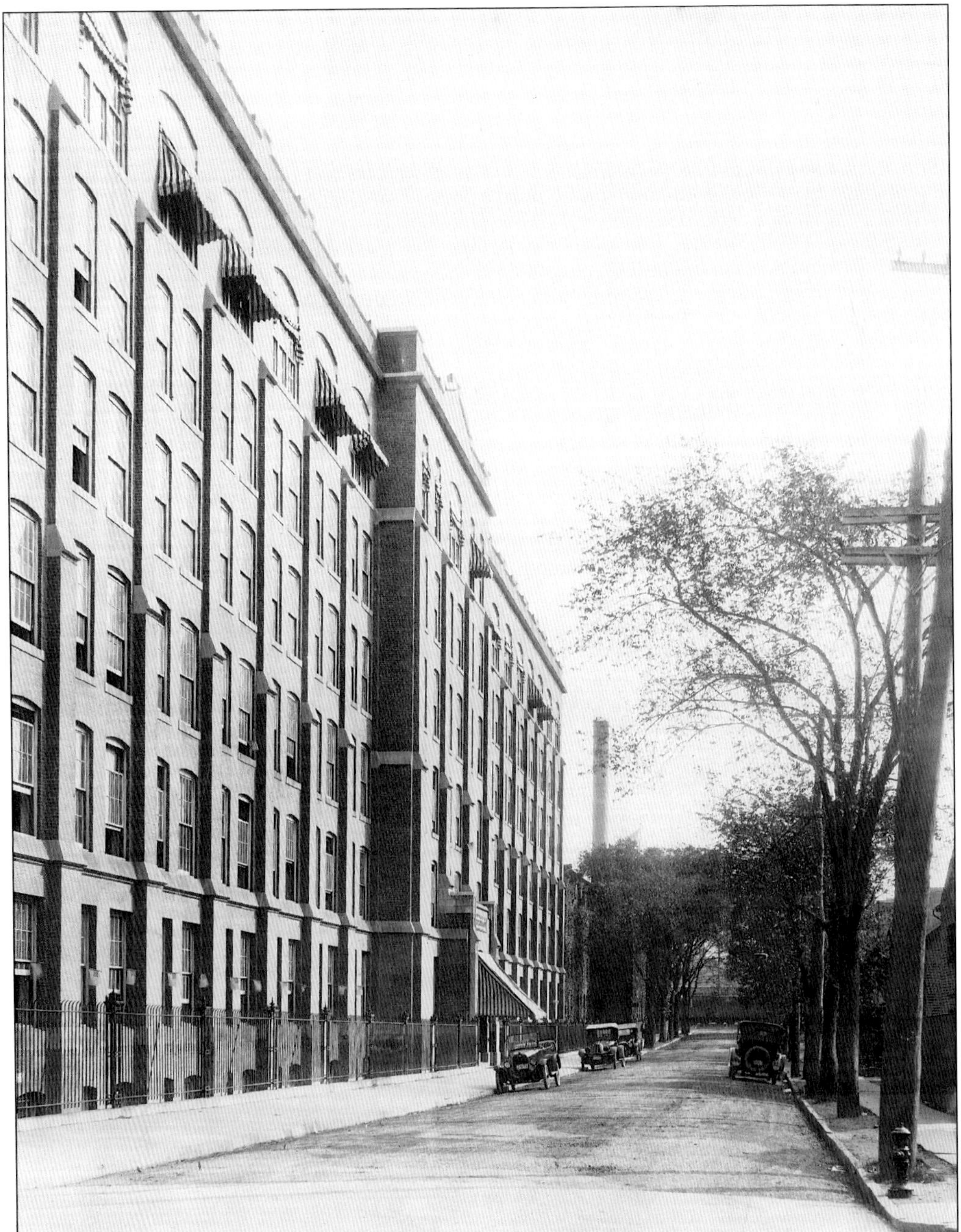

The Landers, Frary and Clark Manufacturing Co. on Center Street. Although this building designed by Davis and Brooks has been gone for decades, the products manufactured here are still in high demand. From food choppers to percolators, the "Universal" trademark is recognized worldwide. While some people find these products desirable as collectibles, others still delight in using them in their homes—a testament to their high quality. (Local History Room, NBPL.)

IMAGES
of America

NEW BRITAIN
VOLUME II

Arlene C. Palmer

ARCADIA
PUBLISHING

ISBN 978-0-7385-5706-9

Published by Arcadia Publishing
Charleston, South Carolina

Printed in the United States of America

Library of Congress Catalog Card Number: 2007939580

For all general information contact Arcadia Publishing at:
Telephone 843-853-2070
Fax 843-853-0044
E-mail sales@arcadiapublishing.com
For customer service and orders:
Toll-Free 1-888-313-2665

Visit us on the Internet at www.arcadiapublishing.com

To the staff of the New Britain Public Library and D.J.P. . . . as ever.

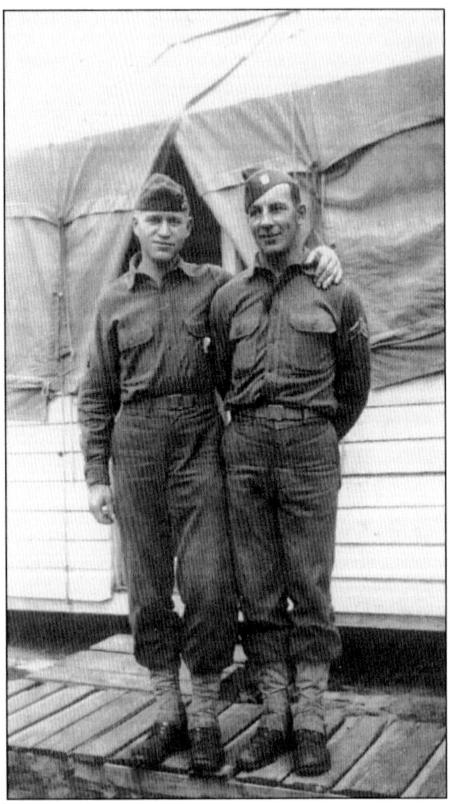

Sgt. Henry J. Szczesny. Pictured here with Richard Zapor, Sgt. Szczesny lost his life in the Pacific during World War II. The Bank Street garage is named in his honor. The Washington Street garage is named after another World War II veteran, John N. Badalato. (Alfred "Fritz" Casella.)

Contents

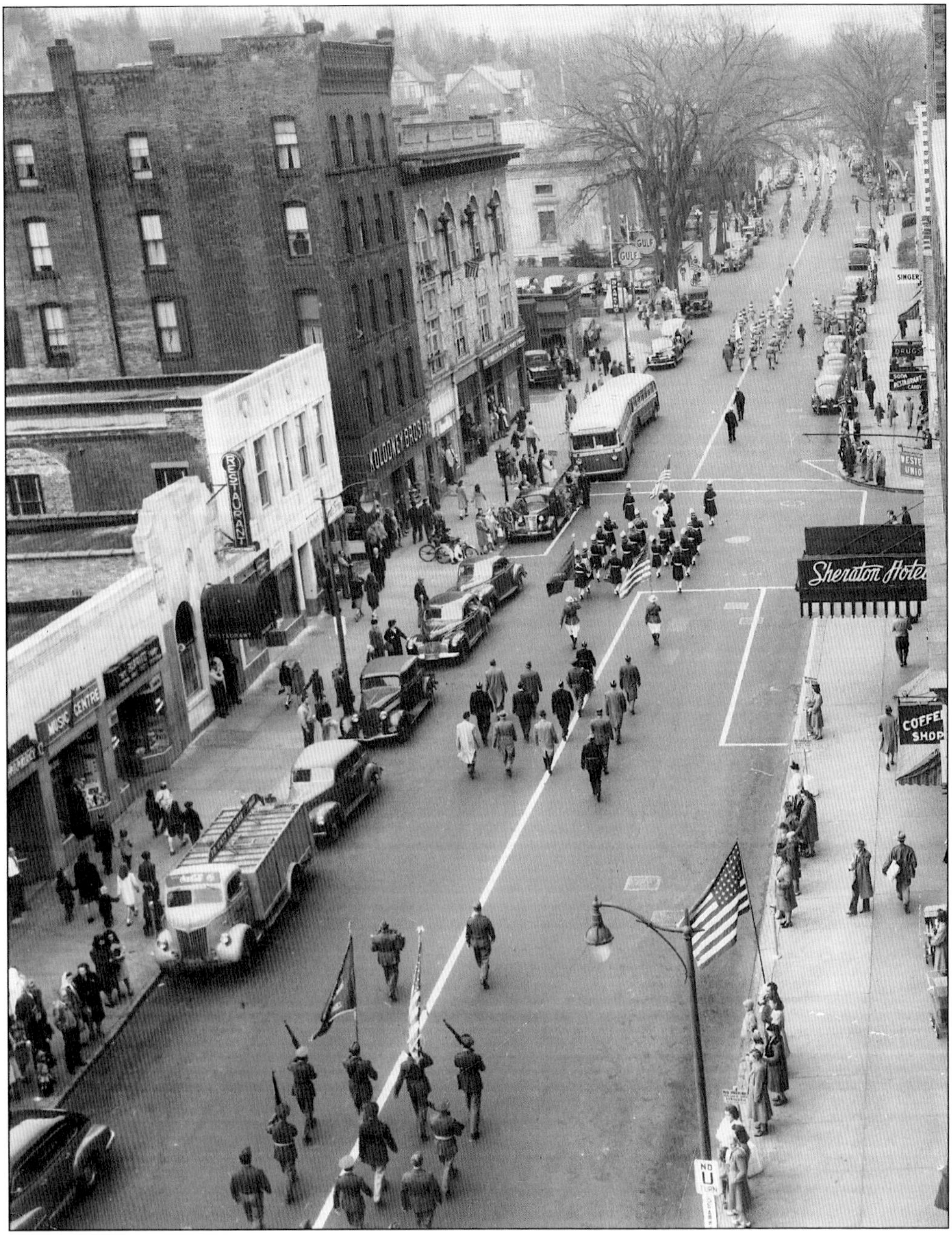

An Armistice Day parade going up West Main Street. New Britain has always been known for its celebrations. From the colorful circus parades held in the late nineteenth century, to the parades on Memorial and Veterans Day honoring military personnel, the city turns out en masse. Note the marquee advertising the Sheraton Hotel. Originally this was the Hotel Burritt, a name that was reestablished in later years. (*Herald* photograph file.)

Introduction

When we look for a place to live, there are basic questions we have to ask. We may consider where the city is located, what the educational system has to offer, where we will worship, and how we might entertain ourselves when we are not busy at work. It is with this perspective that the second volume of *New Britain* in the Images of America series was compiled. The book photographically examines aspects of who, what, when, where, why, and how. This year New Britain celebrates the 125th anniversary of its incorporation as a city. These photographs illustrate the diversity of culture, civic pride, and the determination of a populace to succeed through wars, depressions, urban renewal, and the decline of industrialization. At the June 1996 Main Street USA festival, citizens voted for a city slogan. "New Britain: A City For All People" was the winner. An apropos title for a city that embraces all nationalities, races, and creeds.

The final chapter of this book is devoted to those who have served both city and country. From the Revolutionary War up through the Gulf Conflict, the men and women of New Britain have defended their nation and what the current mayor, Lucian J. Pawlak, calls the "Home of the American Dream." There are also hosts of residents who generously contribute their talents to city organizations. Whether it is helping the less fortunate at the Friendship Center or helping someone learn English through Literacy Volunteers, citizens have demonstrated their compassion. It is impossible to recognize every church, civic, and social organization existing in the city. Those not mentioned are due to lack of space, not lack of importance. Names have been recorded as accurately as possible.

With the increase in modern technology, the world has become smaller. We can routinely order merchandise via television's "infomercials," "talk" to people worldwide via the Internet, and even check on the local library's bestsellers, via a computer with a modem. New Britain has survived for 125 years as a city that recognizes the worth of its people. It is therefore imperative that we take the time to reflect on simpler times, when people took precedence over machines.

Arlene C. Palmer
June 1996

Acknowledgments

Many of these photographs were borrowed from the William F. Brooks, K.A. Larson, and Paul Manafort collections, and the general collection of the Local History Room at the New Britain Public Library. Sincere thanks to the following for use of their materials and support: Gordon Alling; Eugenia Chrisoulis Banios; Frances Bauer; Geoff Bell; Virginia Blanchfield; Mr. and Mrs. Irving Blomstrann; Mr. and Mrs. William Bonney; Michael Borselle; Douglas Boyea; Ann Bova; Judith Weld Brown, *The Herald*; Lynn Gorecki Budnick; Joan Eumendi Budnick; Laurene Buckley; Alfred Casella; Nancy Clark; Robert Clinch; Mr. and Mrs. Stanley Dabkowski; Paul Dabrowski; Rick Daddario; John D'Amato; Alan Daninhirsch; Philip Davidson; Mr. and Mrs. Sid DeBoer; Fred Dickson; Orlando Dolce; Leslie Eza; The Elks; Mr. and Mrs. Ben Firestone; Frank Fraprie; Ted Fusaro; Mary Grip; Ray Greene; Mary Higgins; Mr. and Mrs. Ed Honeyman; Brenda Hedenberg; Mark Johnson, Klingberg Center; Junior League; Mary Jaronko Marut Karwoski; Barbara Kirejczyk; Albert Larson; Ed LeMire; Jeff Louis; Paul J. Manafort; Patricia McKeon Marinelli; Helen McInerney; Artemese Blanchette McKeon; Charles McKeon; John Melechinsky; Bernie Muraca; Al Nadolny; Deborah McKeon Nelson; Mark Newman; the New Britain Symphony; Alainie Nevilas; Mary O'Brien; Lillian Padula; Daniel J. Palmer; Katherine Petruff; Deborah Pfeiffenberger; Nancy Redling; Russell Robinson; Frank Rocco; Ada Seaman; Elizabeth Scalise; Flossie Morris Sfiridis; Saul Sibirsky; Reverend James Simpson; Carolyn Tibbetts; Katherine Tullai; the Ukrainian Educational Center; Peter Veleas; Marie Ruschkowsky Venberg; Ray Venberg; Margaret Knight Verzulli; Sam Volvo; Katherine Nadolny Wasel; John Westergom; Dale Whalen; Eleanor Hahn Zaleski; and Mr. and Mrs. Sidney Zucker.

A very special thank you to former Fafnir Bearing Co. photographer Fred Hedeler, for his donations and expertise, and also to my "right hand," Christine Cocores Balint. Without her contacts and support this book could not have been compiled. Finally, special nods to City Planner Sarahjane Pickett, and Richard Youngken of Newport Associates, whose attempts to heighten awareness of the city's architecture are an inspiration to all.

One

Who Are We?

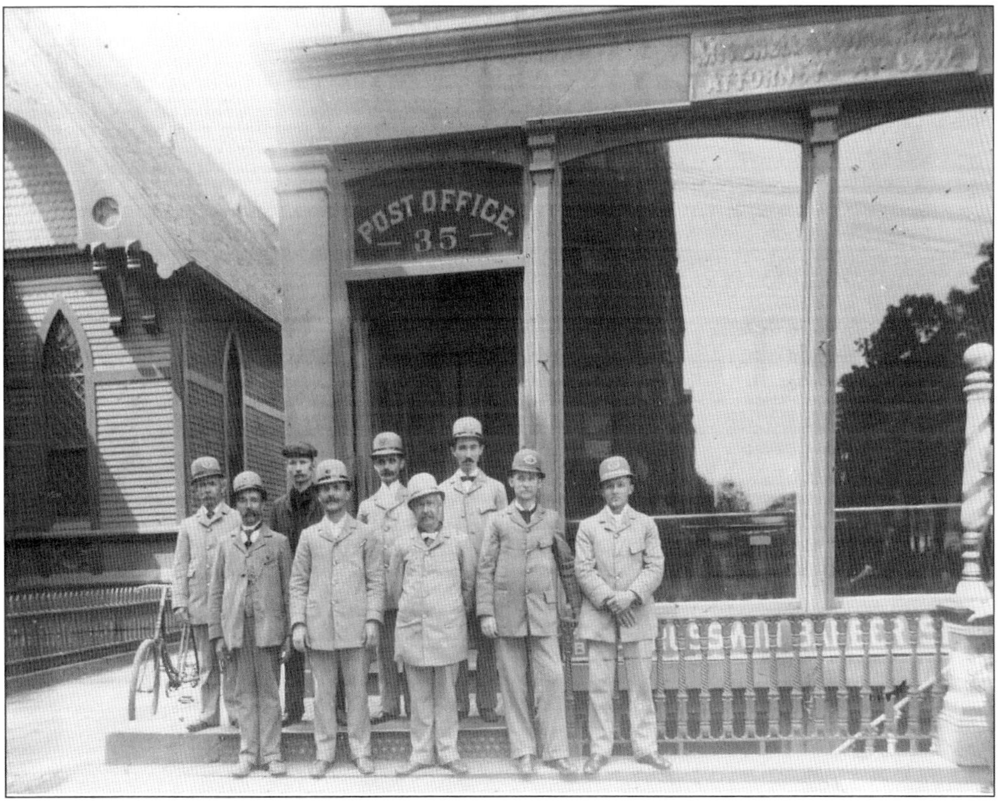

New Britain mail carriers in front of the old post office at 35 West Main Street, *c.* 1900. Old St. Mark's Church is visible on the left. On the New York City Post Office there is an inscription often affiliated with the postal service: "Neither snow, nor rain, nor gloom of night stays these couriers from the swift completion of their appointed rounds . . ." The spirit of this inscription reflects the spirit of the people of New Britain throughout its history. (Local History Room, NBPL.)

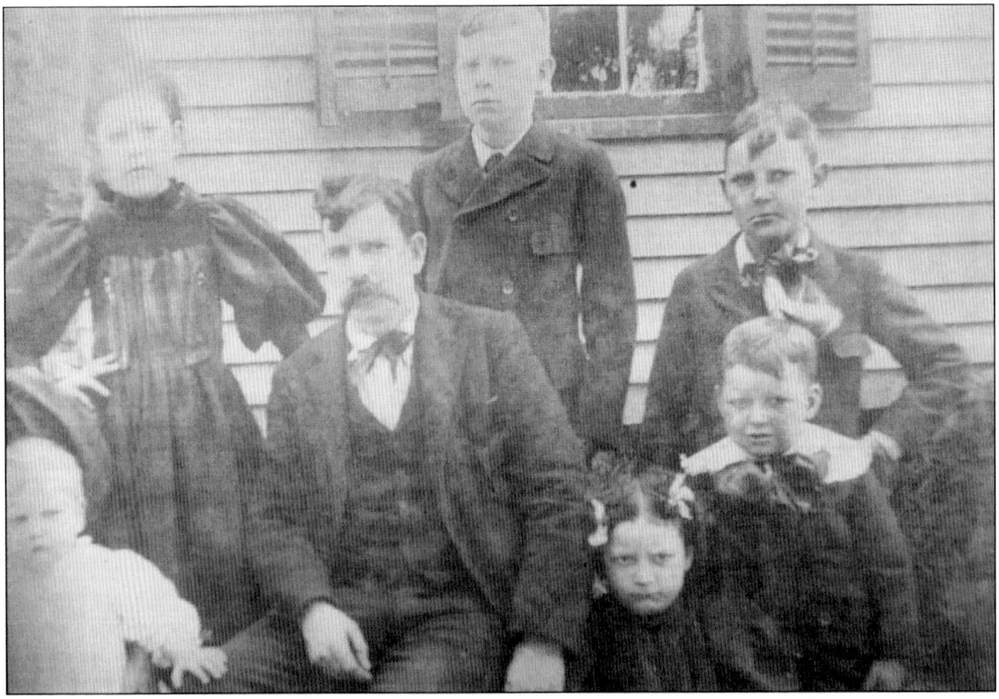

A McKeon family portrait. The Irish were among the first immigrants to settle in New Britain. Although most of this family moved to surrounding towns, Charles McKeon, standing behind his father, remained in the city, primarily in the south end. (Artemese Blanchette McKeon.)

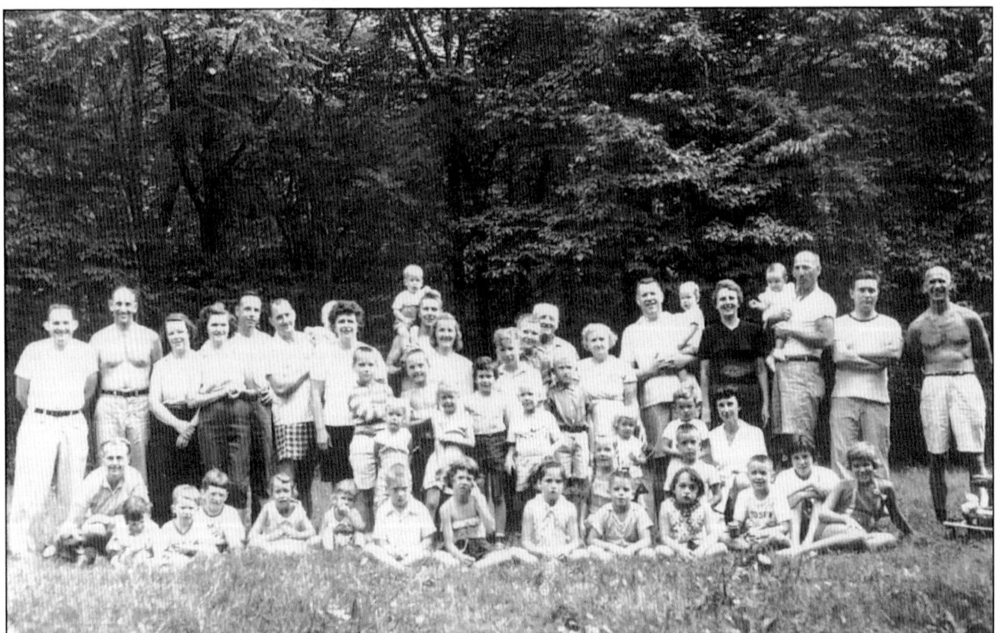

Descendants of Charles McKeon. This photograph was taken at a fire department family picnic held in Stanley Quarter Park in 1960. A direct descendant, Edward McKeon had five children, many of whom still reside in the area. (Artemese Blanchette McKeon.)

Merwin Stanley Hart, at age two-and-a-half in 1893. It was not unusual during this era for little boys to be clothed in dresses, wearing their hair long. (Local History Room, NBPL.)

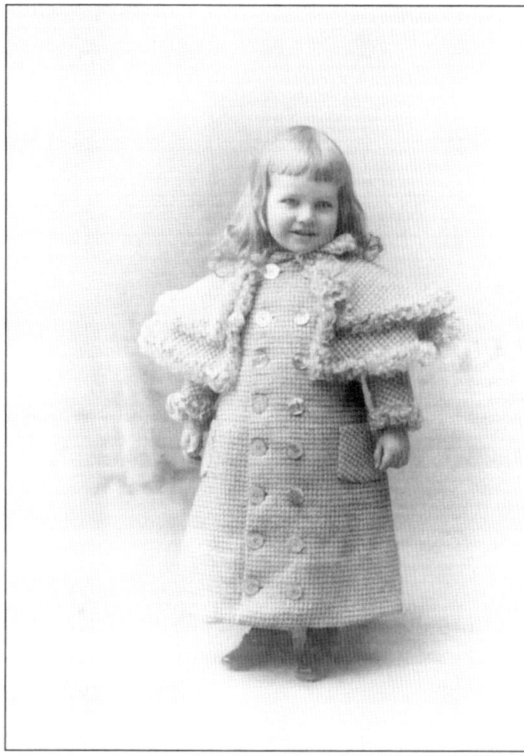

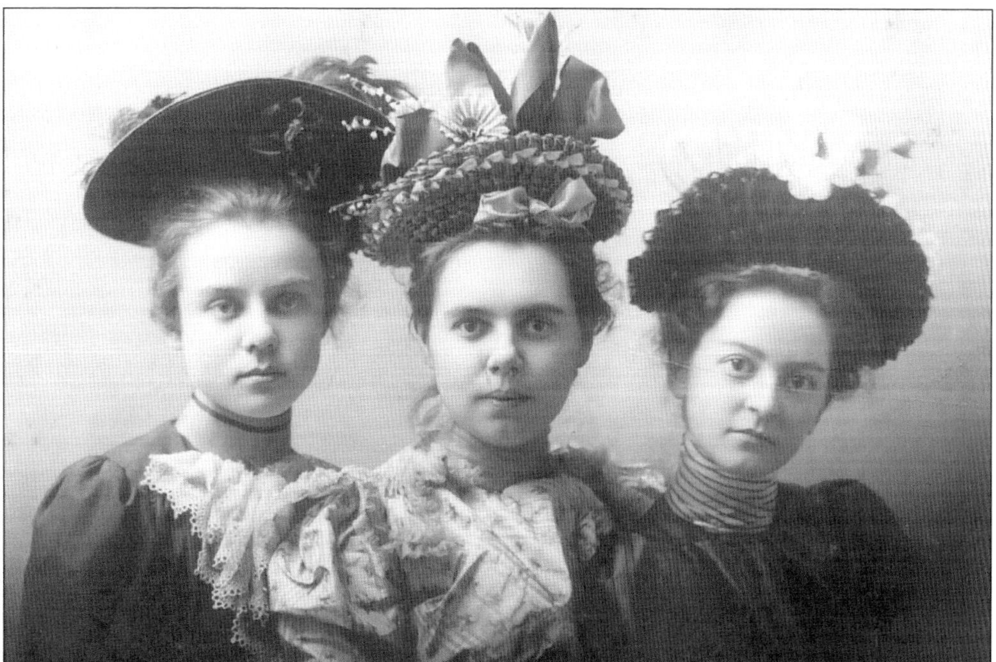

Close friends. Maud Coles, Mary Miles, and Lottie Geer pose in what must have been chic hats. Unlike portraits today, in those days, most people did not smile for the camera. (Local History Room, NBPL.)

Reverend John Klingberg and his family. As he proceeded home on May 20, 1903, Reverend Klingberg, pastor of Elim Baptist Church, was stopped by Policeman Charles M. Johnson and told of three destitute boys. Having retraced his steps and collected the children, Reverend Klingberg took them home and told his wife, "These are new additions to our family." This marked the beginning of what would become the Klingberg Family Center, often called, "The Children's Home." The sign on the cover of this book, which translates to "God is the Provider of all things," indicates the importance of the Klingbergs' faith. (Klingberg Family Center.)

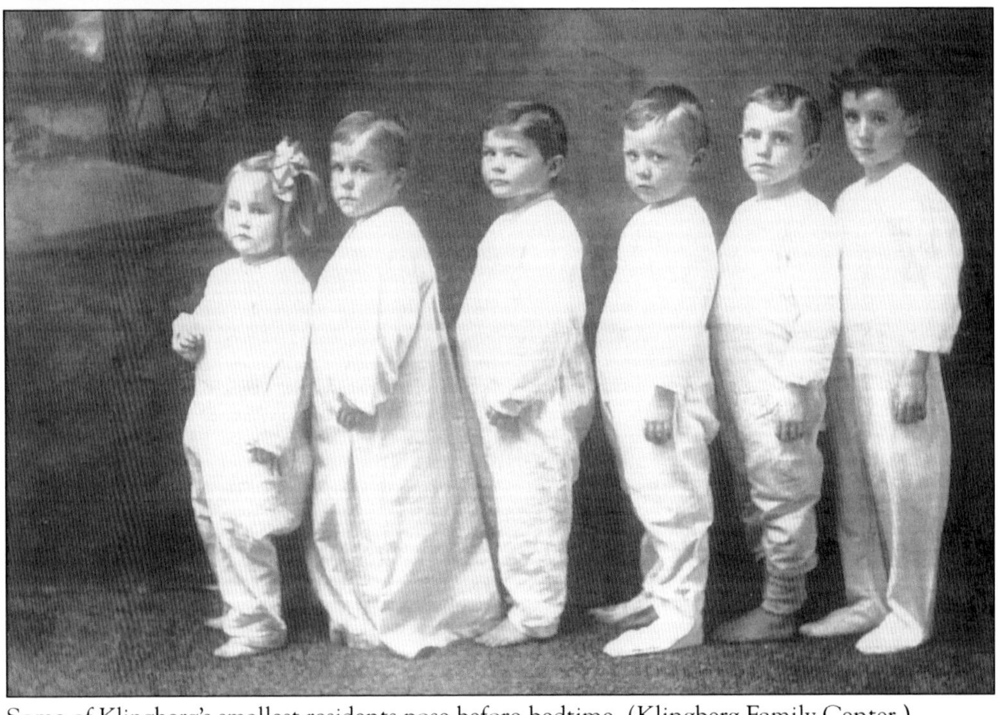

Some of Klingberg's smallest residents pose before bedtime. (Klingberg Family Center.)

The 1954 mayoral debate between Edward B. Scott (standing) and John L. Sullivan (seated). Mr. Scott, noted for his wit and gentlemanly demeanor, and Mr. Sullivan, described as colorful and feisty, were both tireless workers in community affairs. (Local History Room, NBPL.)

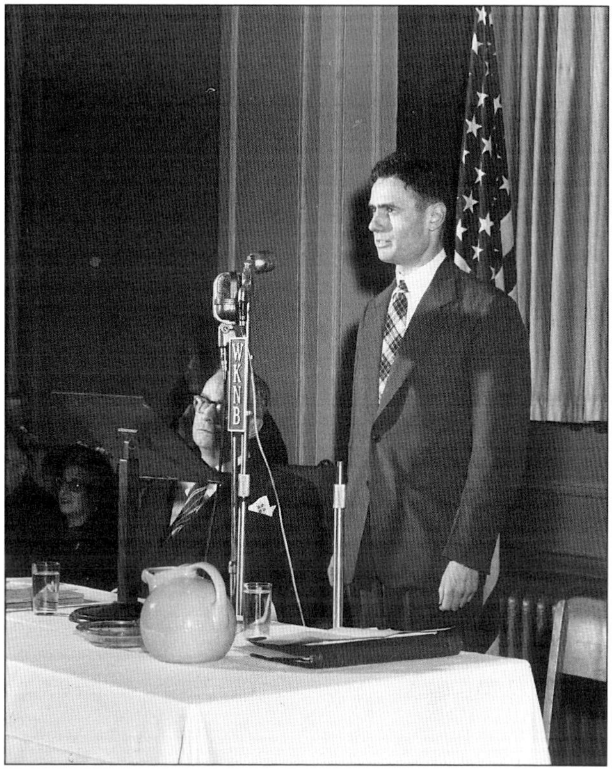

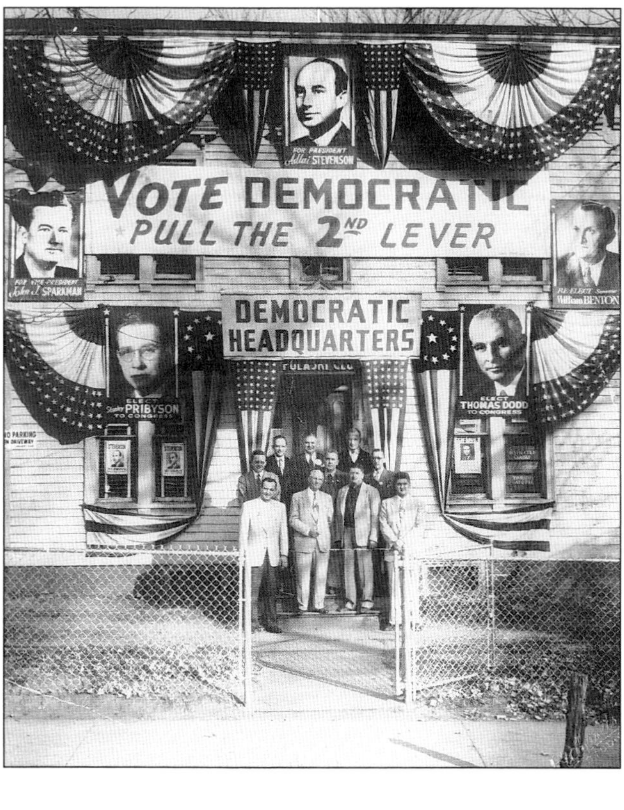

The sentiment of the Pulaski Democratic Club in 1952. The main purpose of the organization, which dates back to the early 1930s, was to foster involvement of the Polish community in government. Minutes show that as the club developed, its activities were both social and political. (Mary Jaronko Marut Karwoski.)

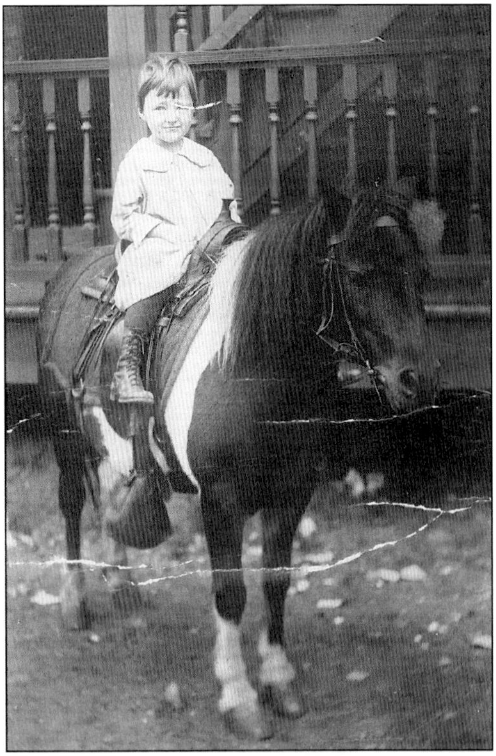

Christine Cocores Balint with pony at 123 North Street in 1925. In the 1920s, a local photographer roamed the city with his pony, enticing parents to memorialize their children on horseback. (Christine Cocores Balint.)

The family of Nguyen Quee Tuan from Vietnam. The family is shown here settling into their new American home while Father Reilley of St. Joseph's Church looks on. In 1975, the church sponsored the family, formerly of Saigon. Upon arrival, as they were driven through the city, Mr. Tuan commented, "It is beautiful." (*Herald* photograph file.)

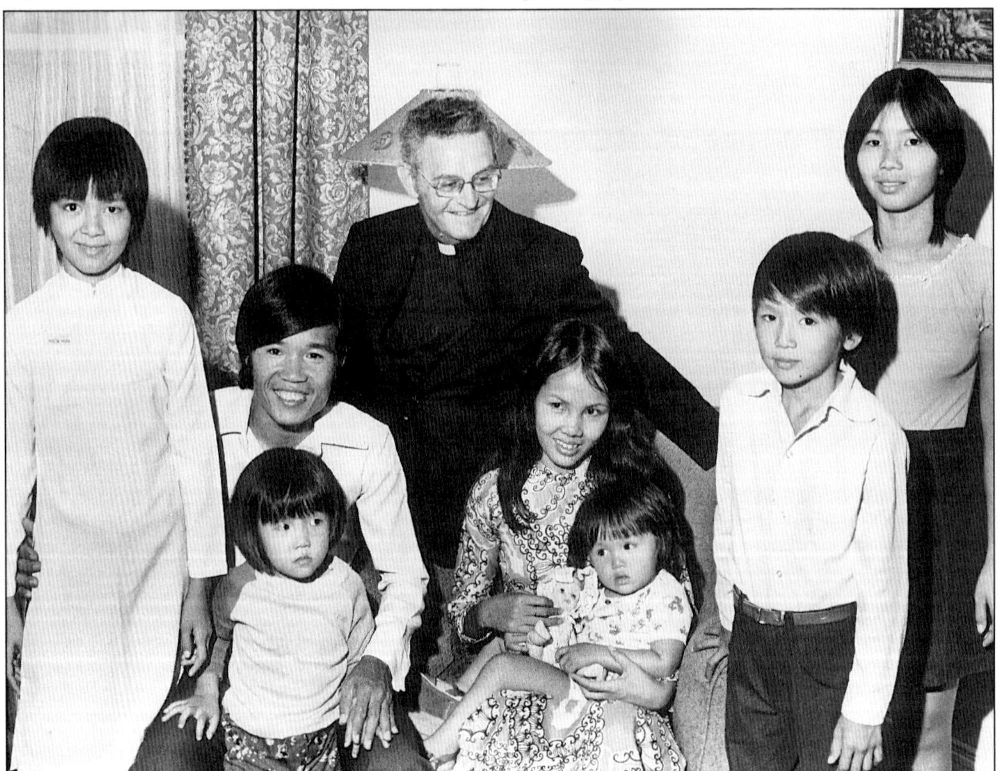

The Frederick G. Platt residence. Currently the home of a law firm, this home at 25 Court Street was restored to its former beauty in the 1980s. Among other achievements, Mr. Platt, president of New Britain Machine and the New Britain Lumber and Coal Co., was instrumental in the development of New Britain General Hospital. For many years, this structure served as storage for the Kolodny Brothers Hardware Store. (*Herald* photograph file.)

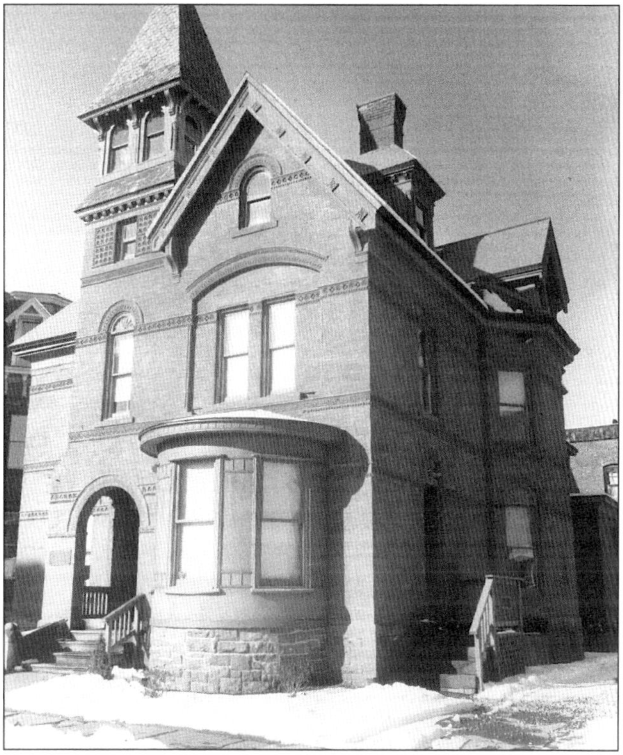

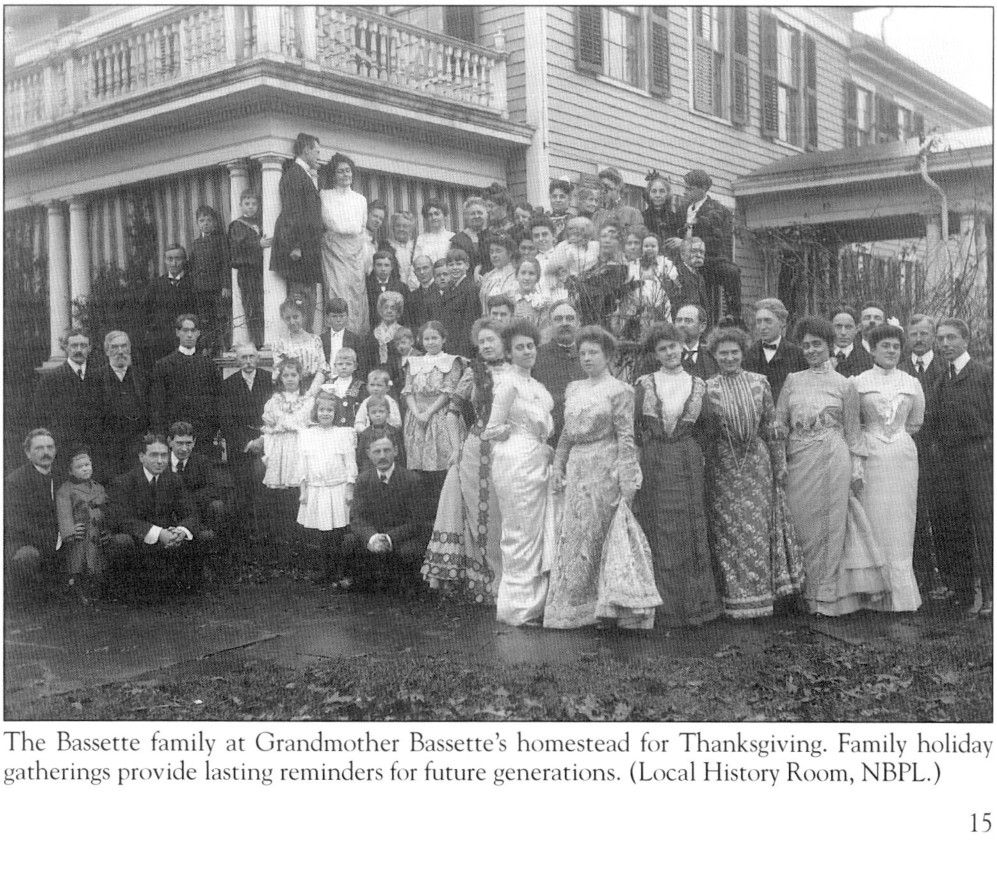

The Bassette family at Grandmother Bassette's homestead for Thanksgiving. Family holiday gatherings provide lasting reminders for future generations. (Local History Room, NBPL.)

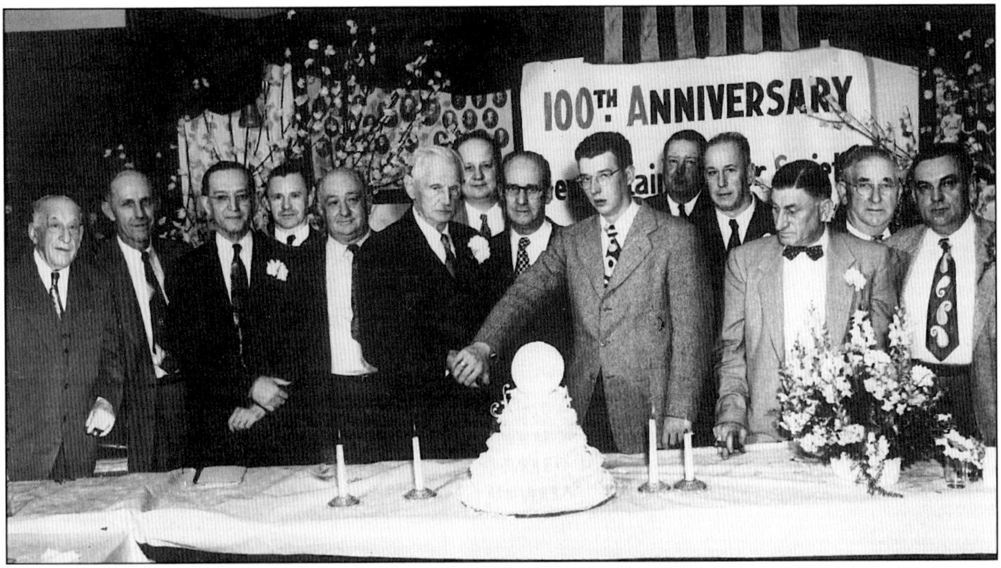

A dinner at the Donau Club on Arch Street. This event was part of the festivities commemorating the 100th anniversary of the Turner Society. On April 25, 1853, twenty-nine members formed the Sozielerturnverein. Membership peaked *c.* 1912 with 250 members. By the 1950s the society was opened to anyone who shared an interest in social talk and singing. (Fred Hedeler.)

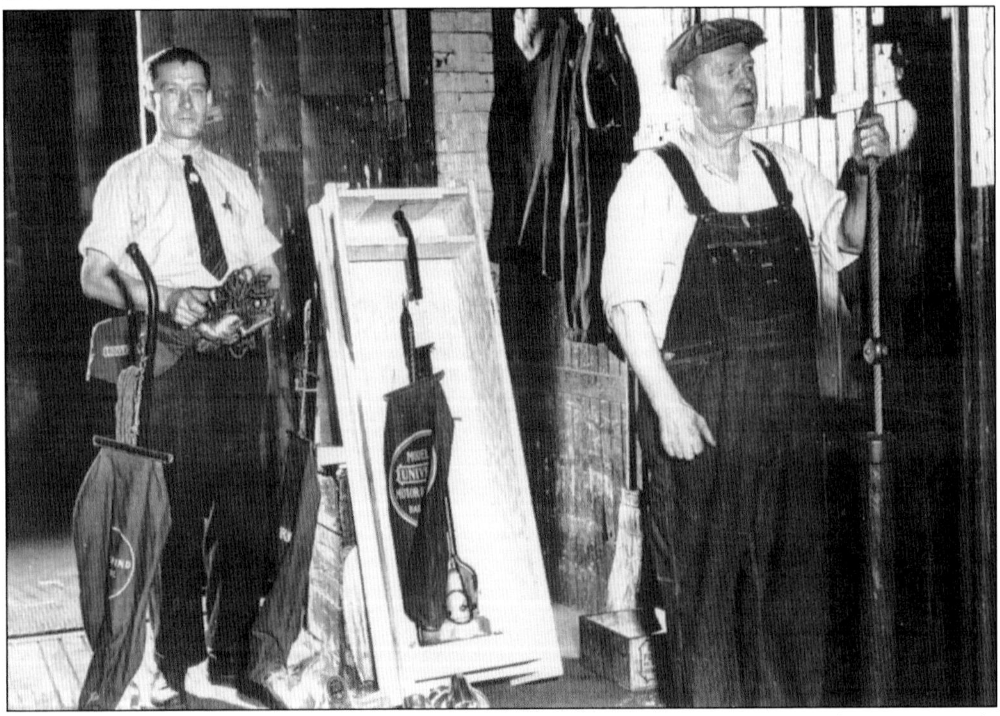

Longtime employee Julius Sabottke (right) and another unidentified worker with a "Universal" vacuum cleaner. Products manufactured by Landers, Frary and Clark and other local industries are preserved and displayed at the New Britain Industrial Museum. Mr. Sabottke's granddaughter is one of the museum's founders. (Lois Lynch Blomstrann.)

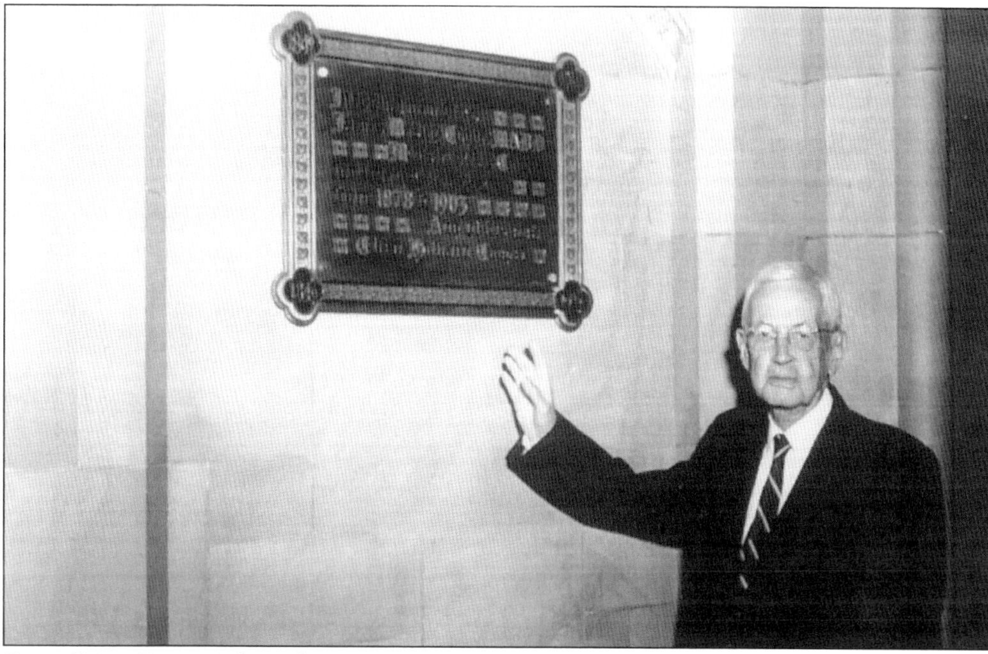

One of New Britain's finest historians, Oliver Wiard, in the South Congregational Church. A graduate of New Britain High School and Yale, Mr. Wiard was multi-talented—an architect, artist, historian, and musician. Upon his death at age ninety-five in 1974, it was noted that his demise was "the passing of an era." (South Congregational Church.)

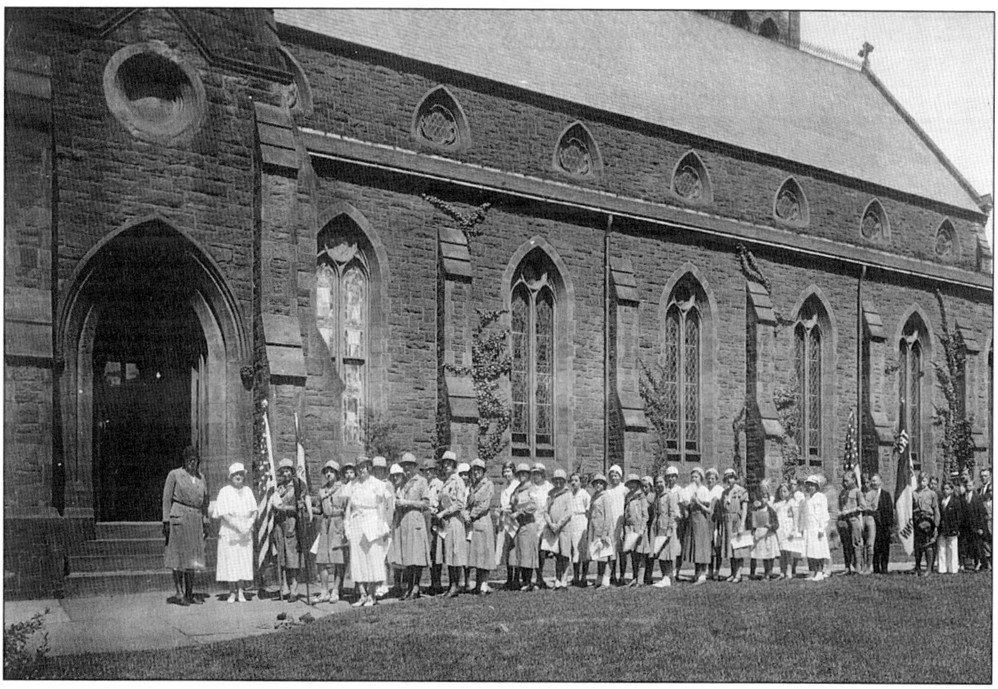

Girl Scout leader Mabel Bonney and her troop at South Church in the 1930s. Scouting has taught leadership skills and enriched the lives of all ages since its inception. (South Congregational Church.)

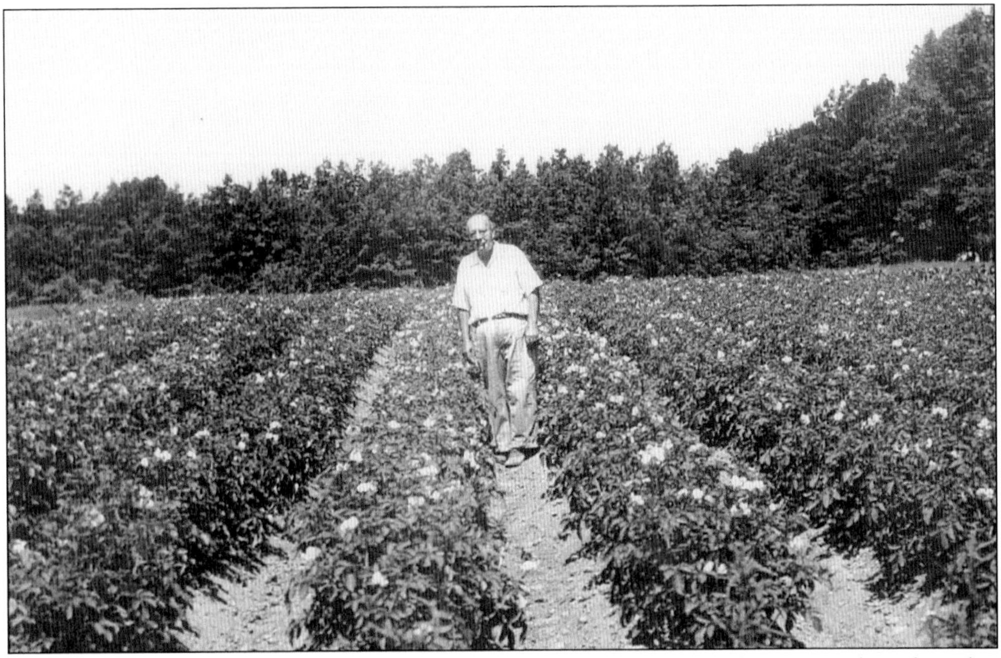

Bronislaw Jaronko. Mr. Jaronko often helped his neighbors by distributing produce from his immense garden. Shown here in the midst of his potato field on Slater Road, he epitomized generosity and reminds us of a time when extensive gardens, open fields, and being a good neighbor were commonplace. (Mary Jaronko Marut Karwoski.)

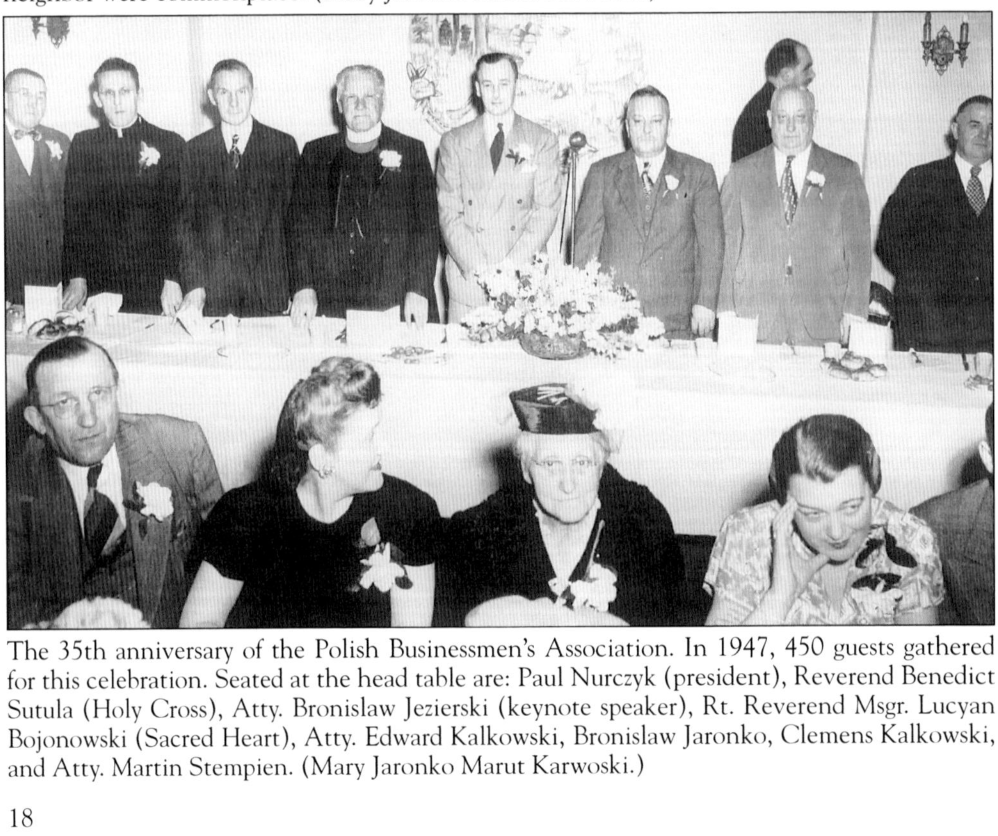

The 35th anniversary of the Polish Businessmen's Association. In 1947, 450 guests gathered for this celebration. Seated at the head table are: Paul Nurczyk (president), Reverend Benedict Sutula (Holy Cross), Atty. Bronislaw Jezierski (keynote speaker), Rt. Reverend Msgr. Lucyan Bojonowski (Sacred Heart), Atty. Edward Kalkowski, Bronislaw Jaronko, Clemens Kalkowski, and Atty. Martin Stempien. (Mary Jaronko Marut Karwoski.)

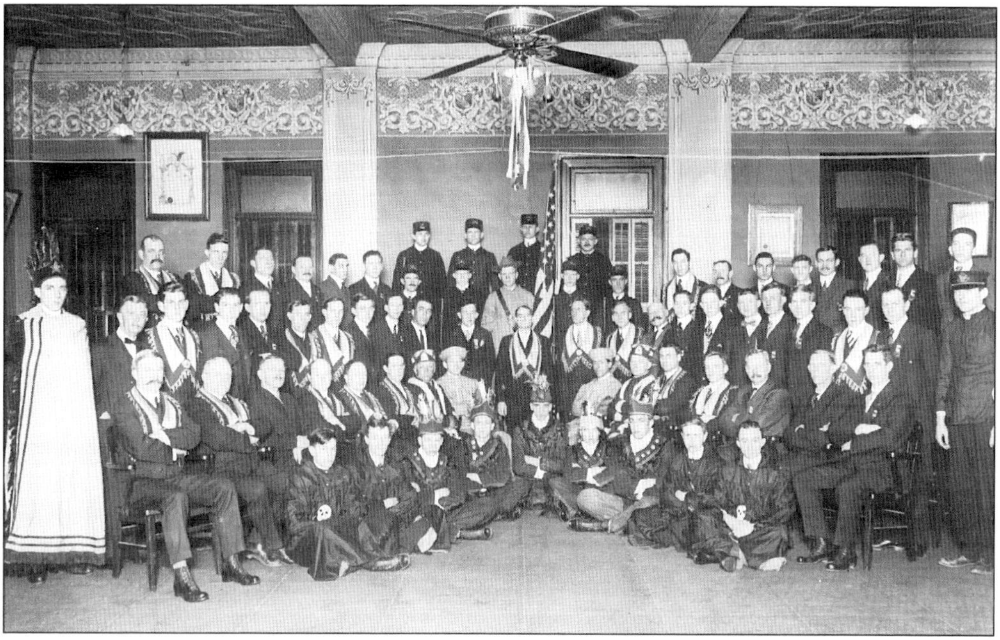

The Mattabassett tribe, Improved Order of Red Men. At seventeen, William E. Venberg (third row, fourth from right) was one of the youngest members of this group. Founded in 1890 with one hundred charter members, this tribe was one of the oldest in the state. Freedom, friendship, and charity were the ideals they pursued. (Marie Rushchkowsky Venberg.)

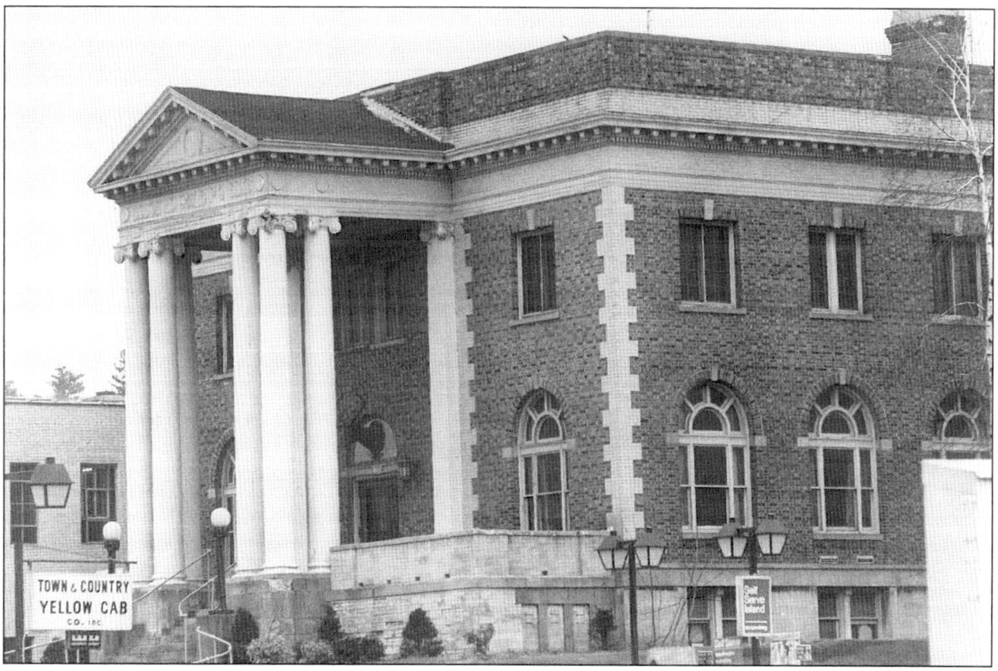

The BPOE building on Washington Street. This handsome building was designed by architect Walter P. Crabtree. It has been home of the Benevolent and Protective Order of the Elks Post #957 since its dedication on March 27, 1913. The post has been in existence since March 28, 1905. (Local History Room, NBPL.)

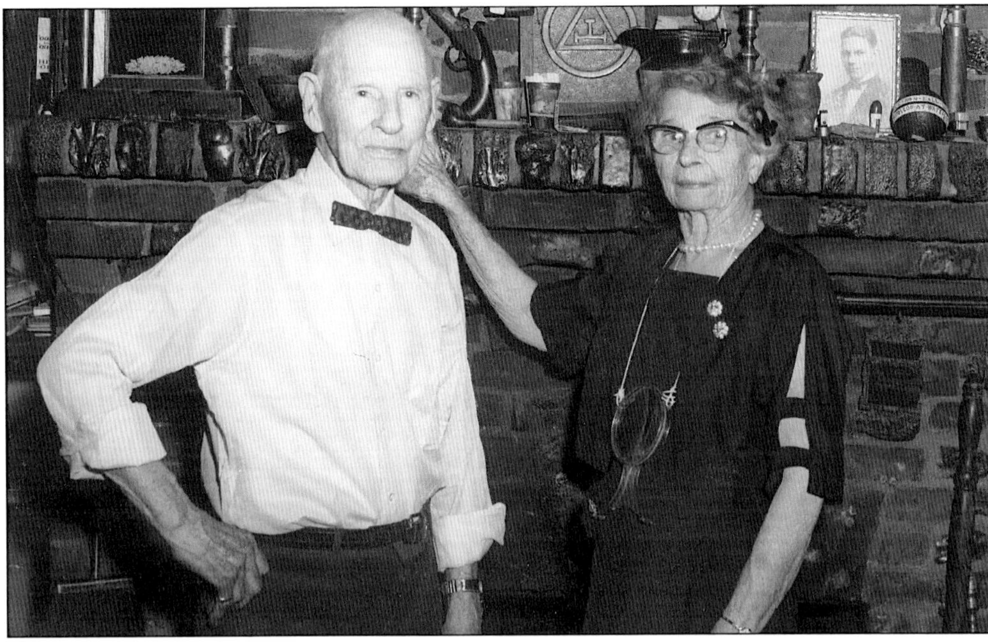

Mr. and Mrs. George H. Wells. The couple is shown here in 1968 as they celebrated seventy-one years of marriage. A lifelong resident, Mr. Wells started his coffee and tea business in 1892. Always a lover of history, he preserved the records of the GAR Post #11 and served as past commander of the Sons of Veterans of the Civil War. (*Herald* photograph file.)

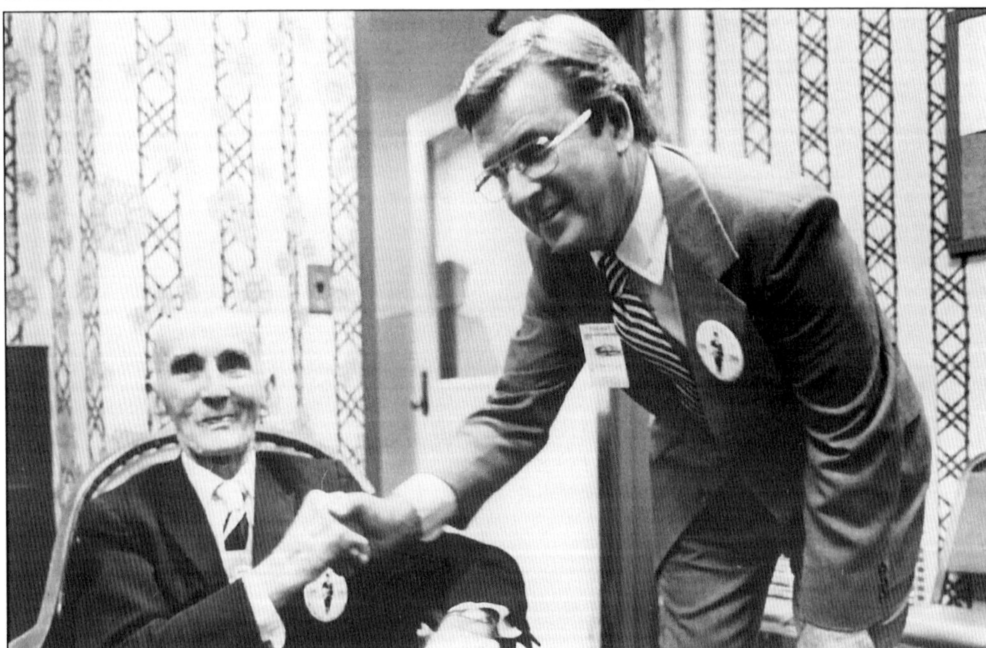

Horace I. Hart (left) in 1980. When this photograph was taken, Mr. Hart had just made New Britain history as the oldest living *Herald* newspaper carrier. In 1989, Mr. Hart passed away at the age of 104. He spent most of his life at his father's home on Arch Street, which was demolished the year following his death. (*Herald* photograph file.)

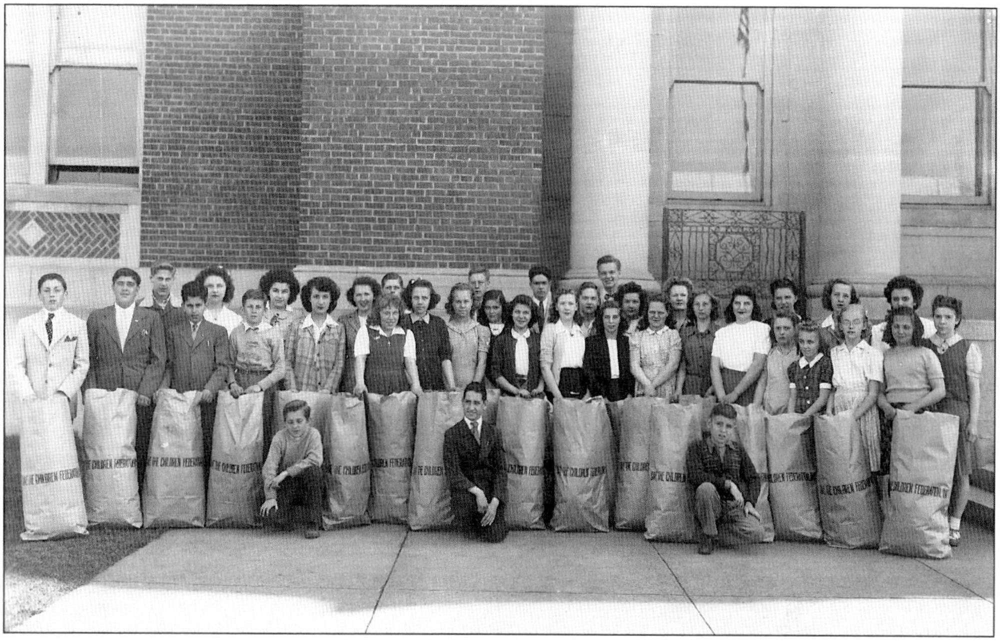

Students from the Roosevelt Junior High School. This group collected clothing for the Save The Children Federation in April 1944. Two representatives from each homeroom proudly display some of the thirty bags they filled. (Local History Room, NBPL.)

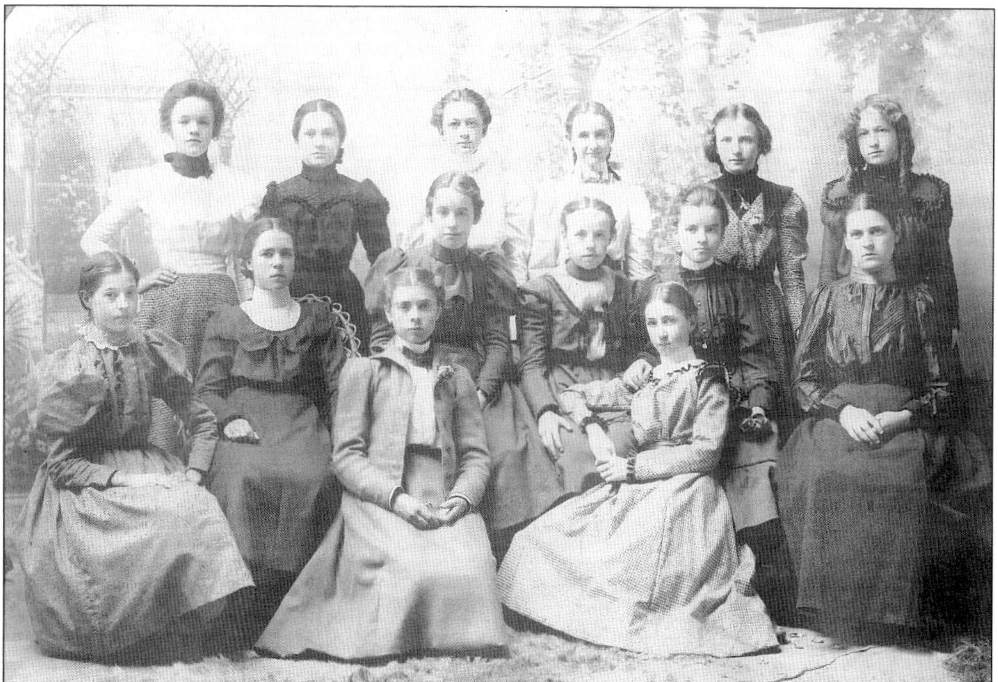

The 1899 graduating class of St. Mary's School. Appearing solemn and thoughtful, the class sits for a portrait. In the early 1860s, the church itself was used as a classroom where lessons were taught in the pews. By 1878, a parish school had been built and the Sisters of Mercy arrived to teach. (Mary O'Brien.)

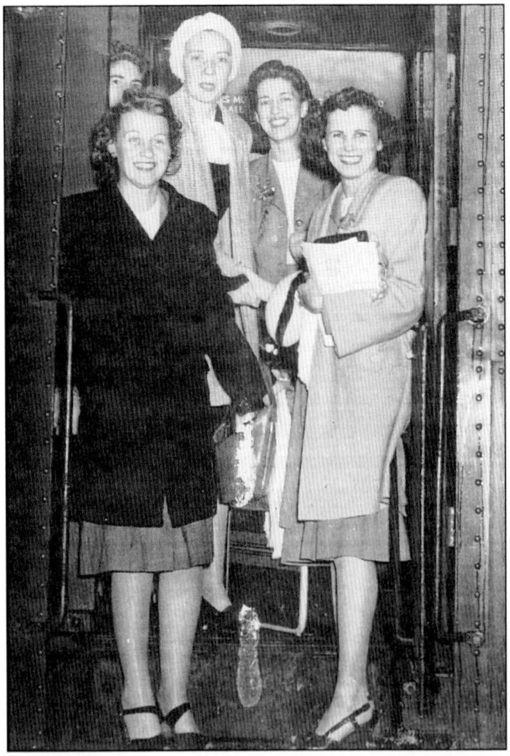

Members of the Landers, Frary and Clark Girls' Club on a trip to New York. Pictured from left to right are: Julia Grezorzek, Mary Shepanski, Helen Spring, and Sally Grigutis. (Helen Spring McInerney.)

Pam Sivilla, Nancy Clark, Marg Hackney, and Julie Vobalas. These young women were all members of the Fafnir Girls' Club. They are shown here preparing to tape a session with WKNB-TV in 1955, promoting the civic activities of the club. (Nancy Clark.)

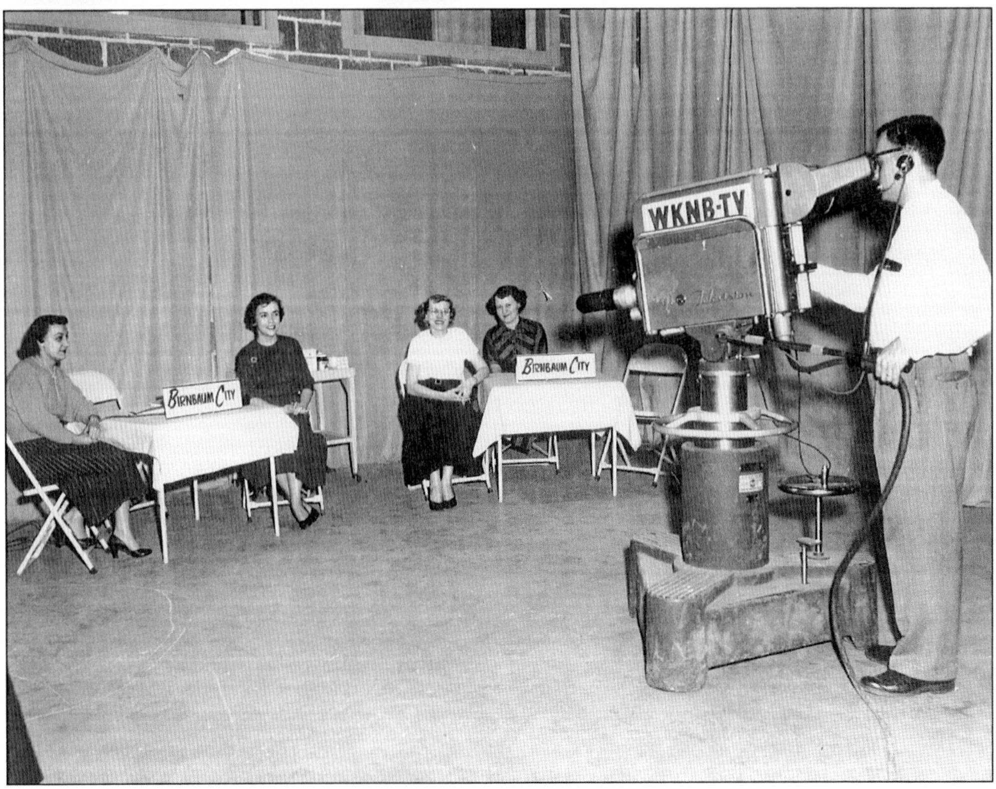

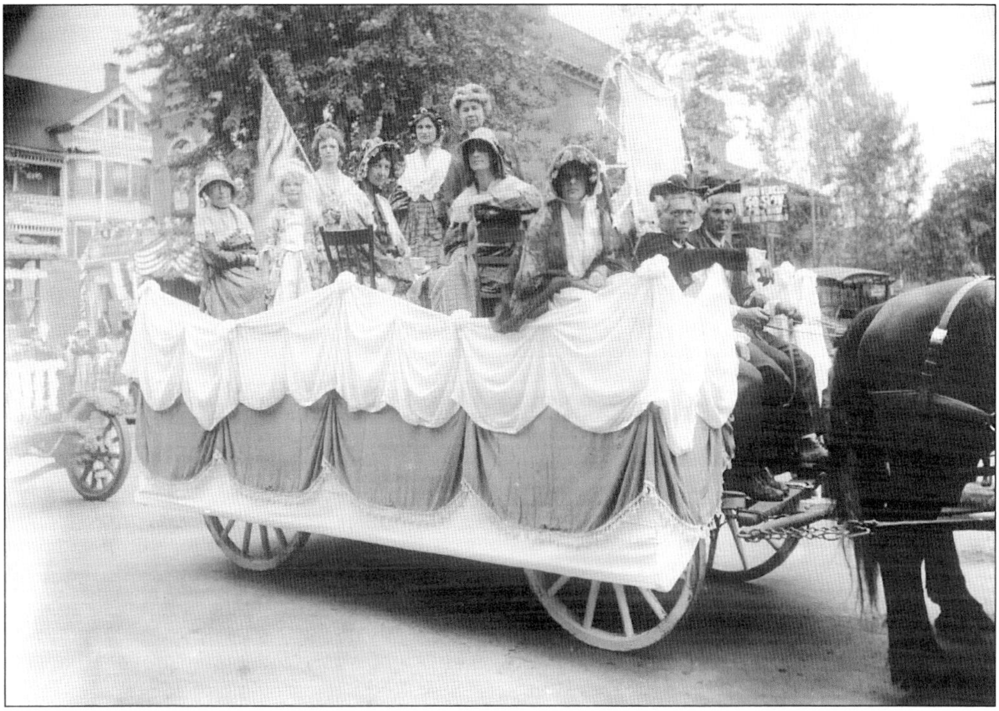

Ladies from the Daughters of the American Revolution on a decorative float. In November 1994, the local chapter celebrated its 100th anniversary. Named for Esther Cowles Stanley, mother of Revolutionary War Captain Gad Stanley, this organization promotes education and patriotism. (Local History Room, NBPL.)

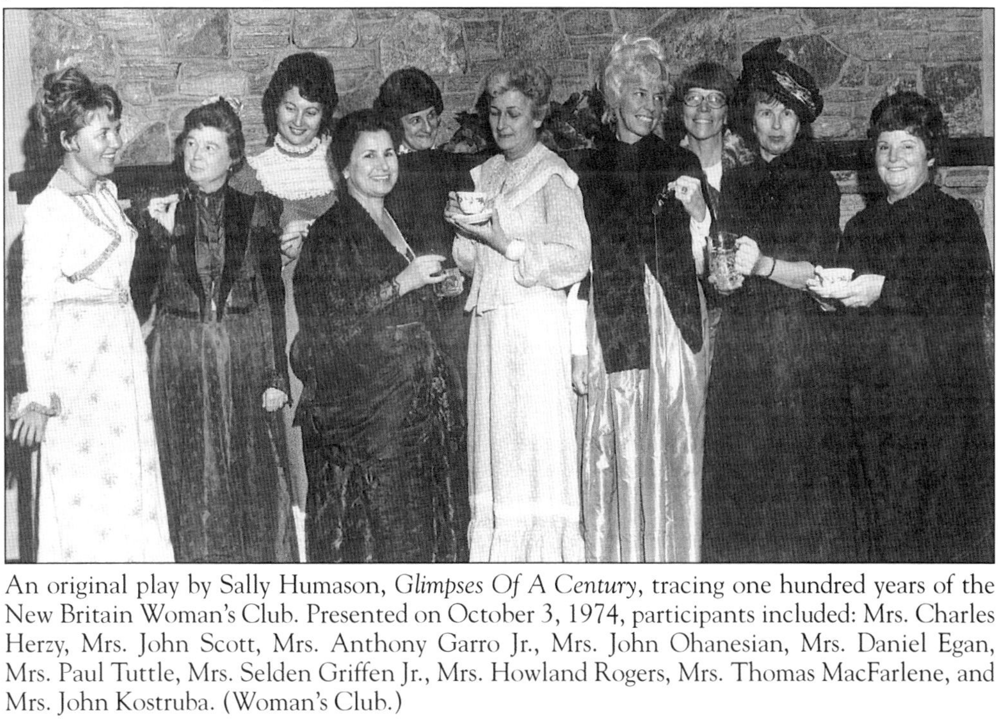

An original play by Sally Humason, *Glimpses Of A Century*, tracing one hundred years of the New Britain Woman's Club. Presented on October 3, 1974, participants included: Mrs. Charles Herzy, Mrs. John Scott, Mrs. Anthony Garro Jr., Mrs. John Ohanesian, Mrs. Daniel Egan, Mrs. Paul Tuttle, Mrs. Selden Griffen Jr., Mrs. Howland Rogers, Mrs. Thomas MacFarlene, and Mrs. John Kostruba. (Woman's Club.)

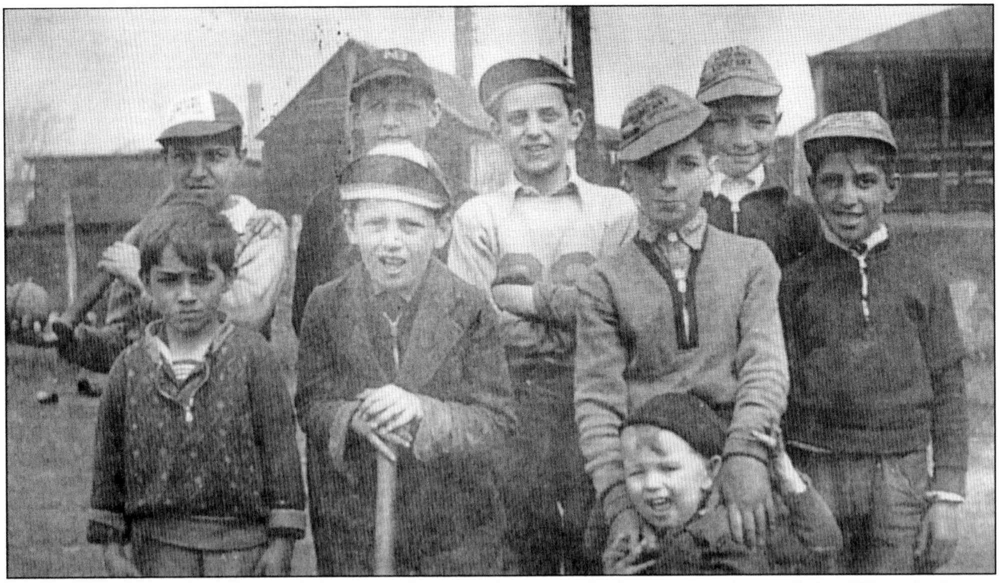

Members of the Church Street gang. The top photograph shows members of the Church Street gang in 1935, flanked by the Union Manufacturing Co. and the Skinner Chuck Co. With names like Borselle, Daversa, George, Alex, and Casella, it was evident members transcended ethnic bounds and formed lasting friendships. By 1942, Americans were engaged in war, but as pictured below, this did not preclude a gathering near the Railroad Arcade in New Britain. Forty years later, distance had not severed old ties. Some came from California and others only from across town, as 150 members held a reunion and renewed friendships that had been formed in the east end. (Sam Volvo.)

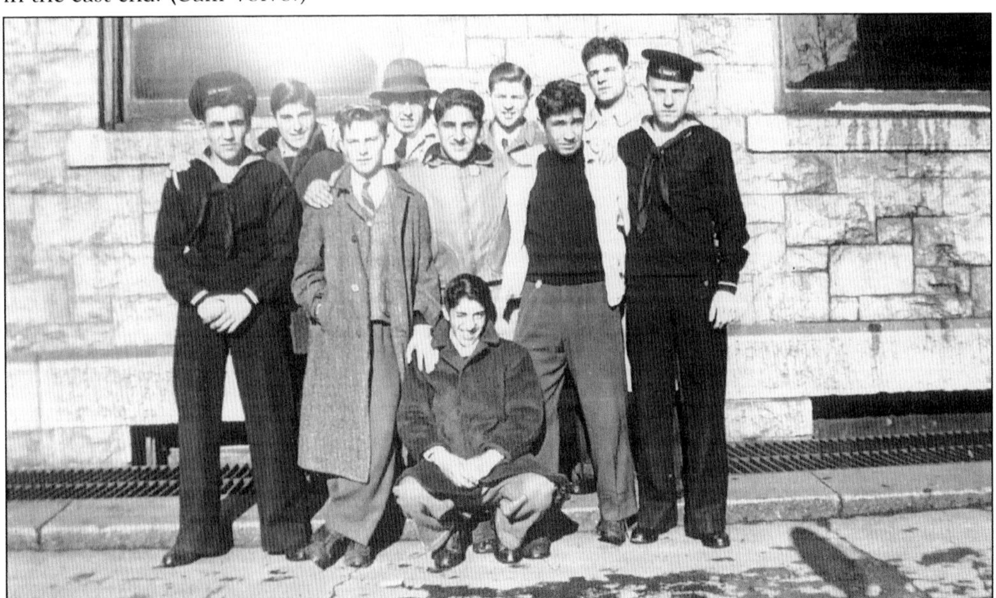

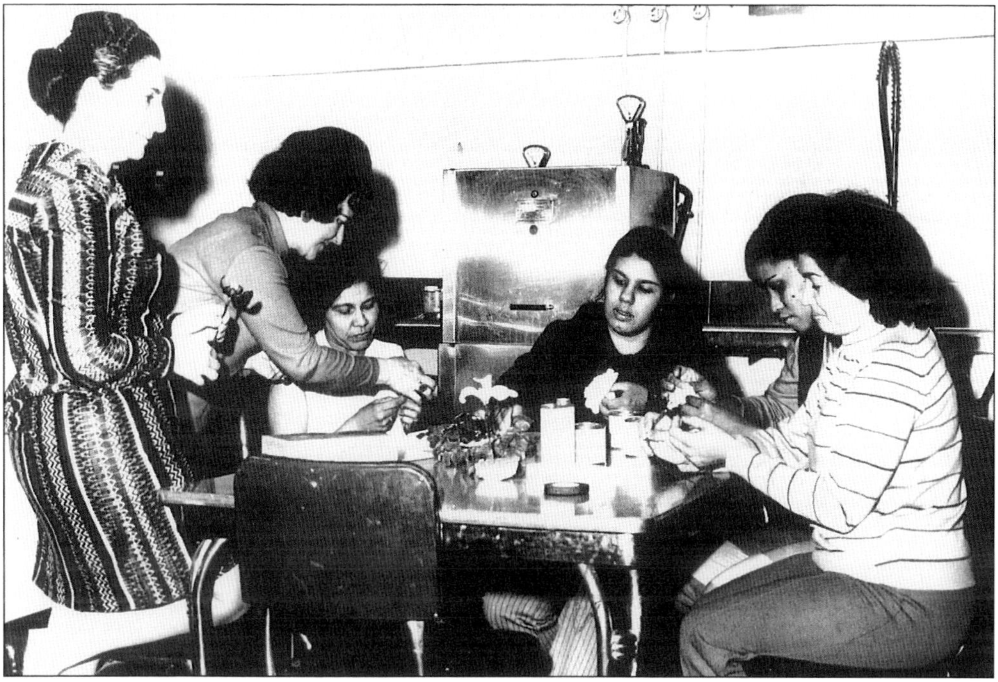

The Spanish Speaking Center. Since its inception in 1964, the Spanish Speaking Center has played a vital role in New Britain's Hispanic community. One of its driving forces, Lola Mondoruza (second from left), is shown helping in an arts and crafts class. Always upbeat and positive, this social services director's departure in 1976 left a void in the community. (Spanish Speaking Center.)

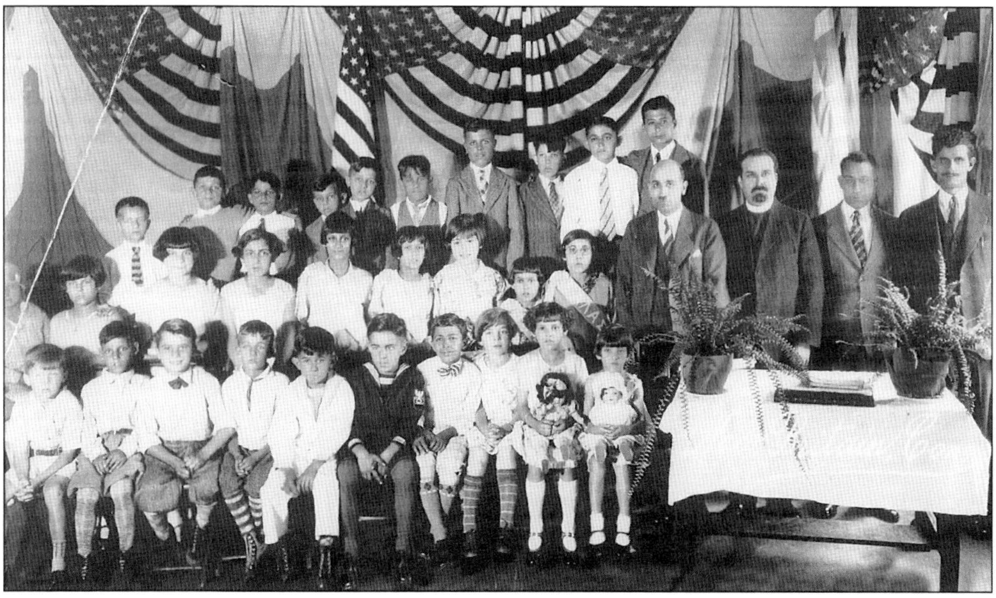

Children from a local Greek school. With their spiritual leader, Reverend Kaisaris, in attendance, these children ended their year with exercises held on July 21, 1929. Some of these students, with names like Dimos, Zissis, Meligonis, Calos, Chrisoulis, Kondonellis, Contaras, Cocores, and Apostalon, are still active in the Greek community today. (Peter Veleas.)

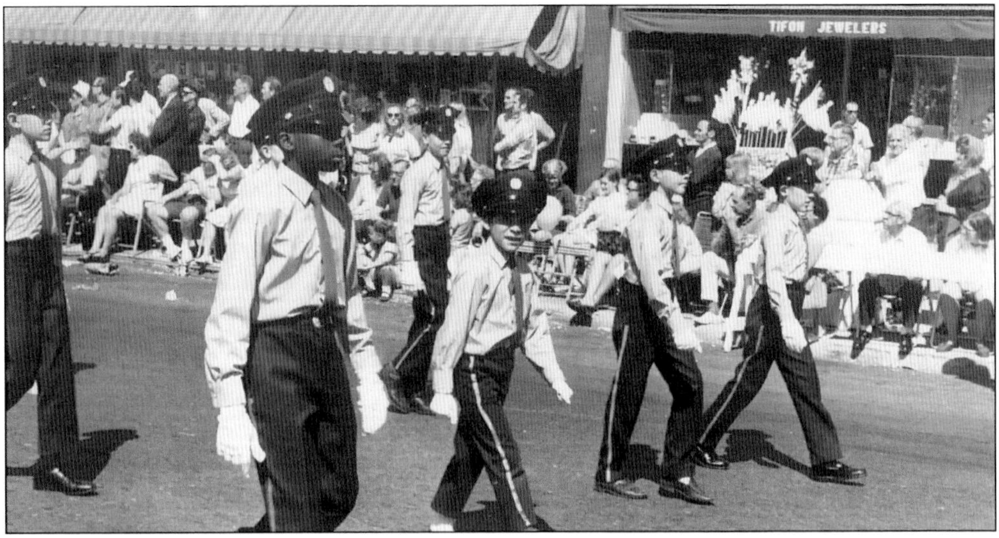

The Police Athletic League's (PAL) junior policemen on Memorial Day in 1969. The League's pledge, which reads in part, ". . . I will at all times conduct myself in a manner that will bring credit to P.A.L., to my city and my country . . ." emphasizes the strong values members pass on to the city's youth. (Local History Room, NBPL.)

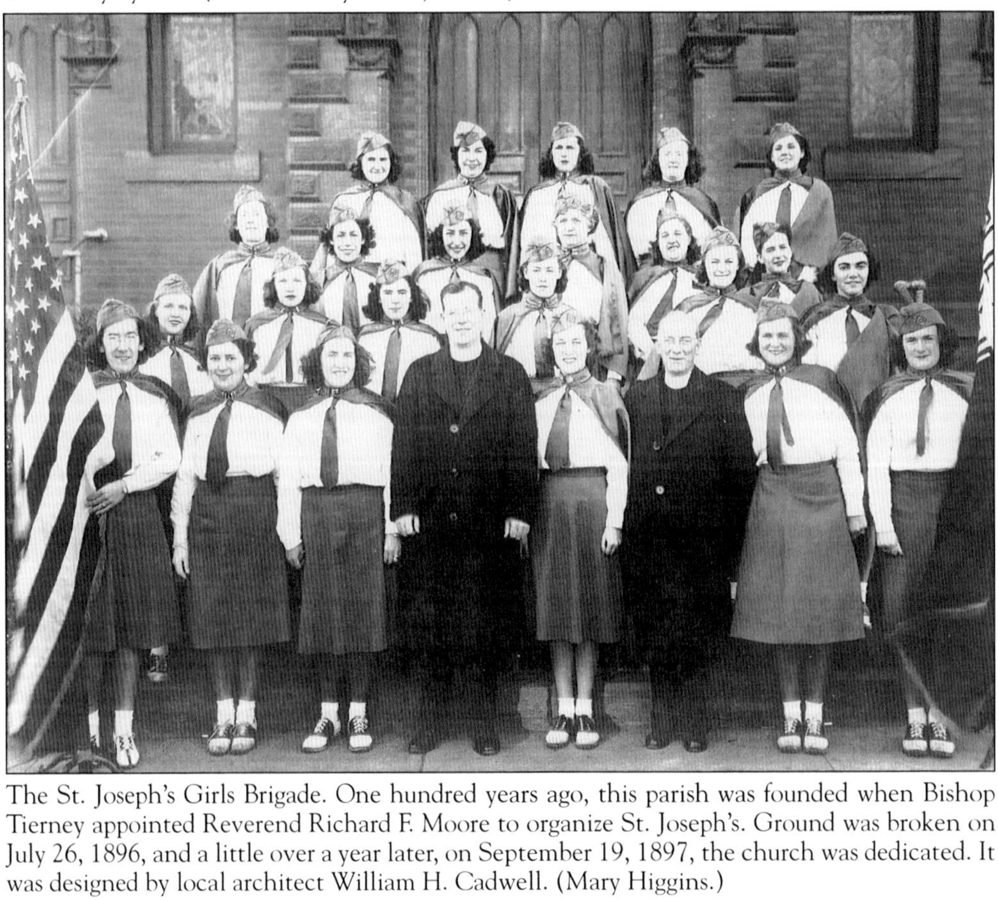

The St. Joseph's Girls Brigade. One hundred years ago, this parish was founded when Bishop Tierney appointed Reverend Richard F. Moore to organize St. Joseph's. Ground was broken on July 26, 1896, and a little over a year later, on September 19, 1897, the church was dedicated. It was designed by local architect William H. Cadwell. (Mary Higgins.)

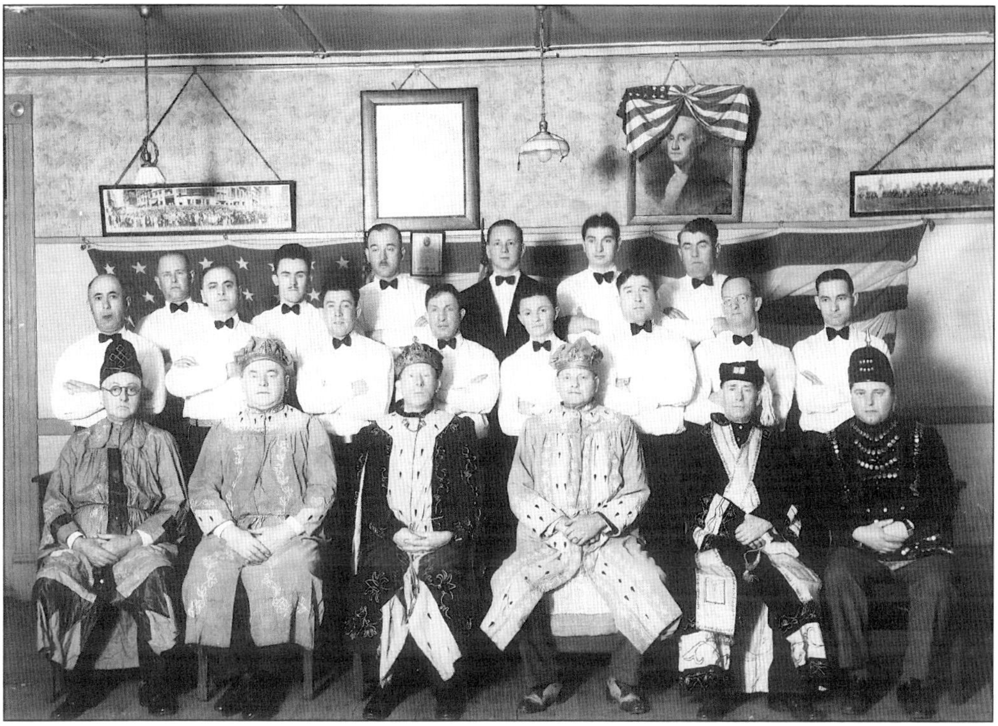

The New Britain Lodge, Loyal Order of the Moose, organized on June 22, 1911. By the mid-1950s this club had become one of the largest lodges in the state. In 1953, forty-five charter members organized the New Britain chapter, Women of the Moose. The charitable work of the lodge has aided hundreds of children and the elderly. (Local History Room, NBPL.)

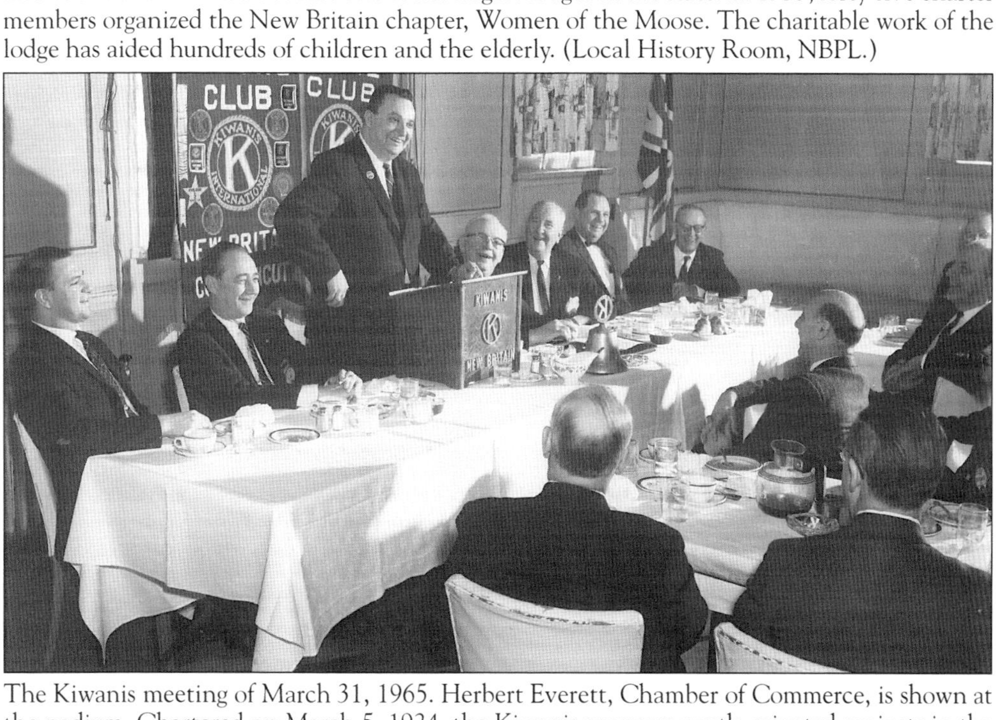

The Kiwanis meeting of March 31, 1965. Herbert Everett, Chamber of Commerce, is shown at the podium. Chartered on March 5, 1924, the Kiwanis sponsors youth-oriented projects in the community. The club's first female member, Judith Greco, joined in 1968. (John Melechinsky.)

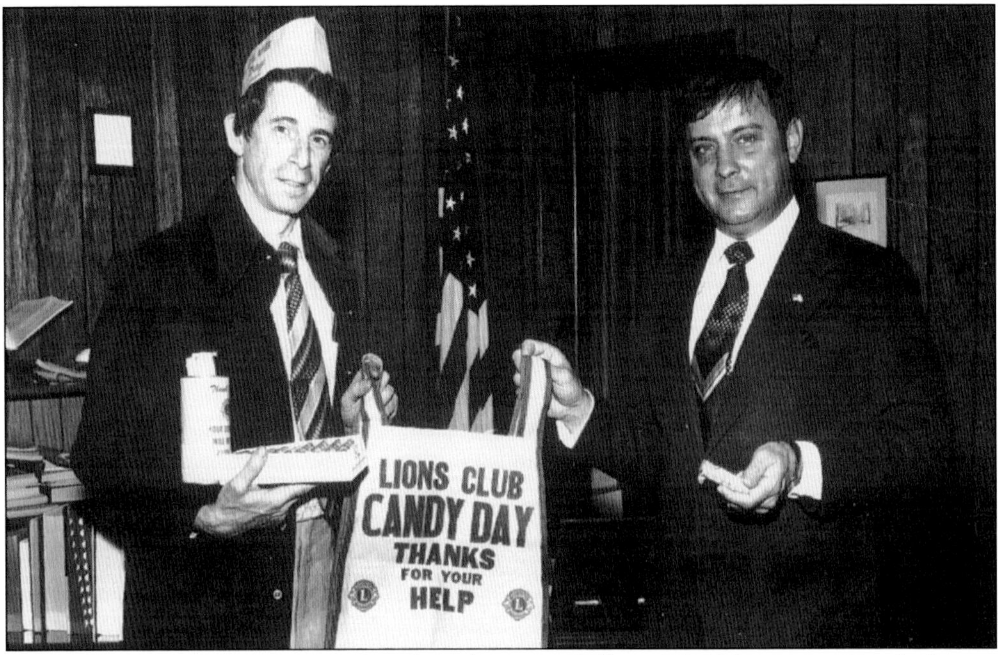

Lions Club President Alan Daninhirsch with Mayor William J. McNamara on Candy Day in 1977. Proceeds from the drive aided the Connecticut Lions Eye Research Foundation. This is now called Light Saving Day. The Lions Club of New Britain has received recognition from two presidents, Herbert Hoover and Ronald Reagan. (Lions Club.)

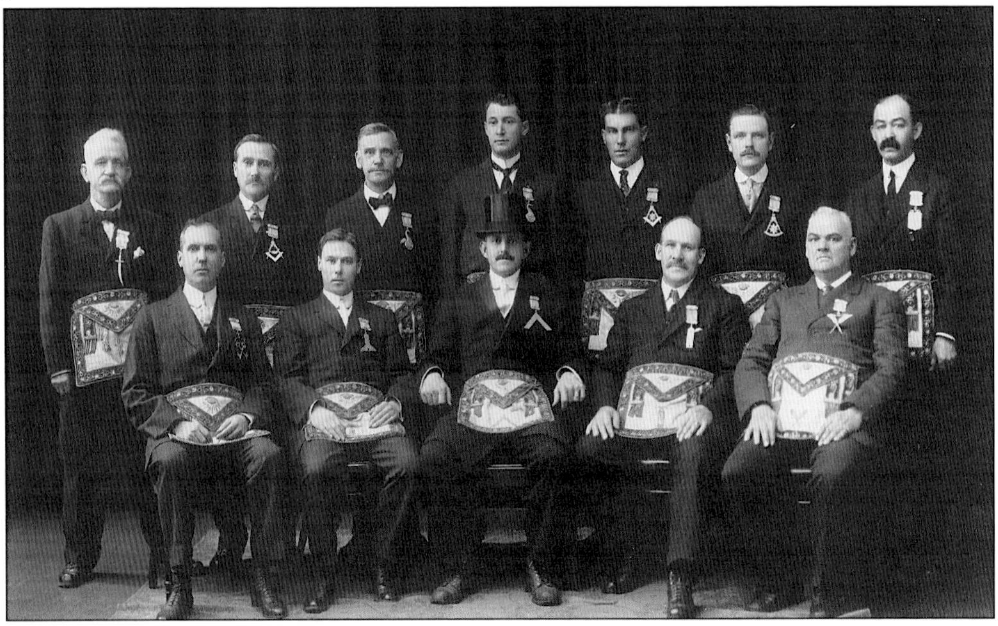

Members of one the area's oldest organizations (founded in 1791), Harmony Lodge #20 AF & AM. This December 1915 photograph shows: (front row) G. Boyer, L. Dyson, R. Dixon, C. Wigglesworth, and W. Rawlings; (back row) E. Haslam, F. Dohrenwend, J. Hill, F. Goodrich, G. Norton, C. Munson, and F. Goddard. The Masonic women's organization, Martha chapter of the Eastern Star, was formed in 1876. (Local History Room, NBPL.)

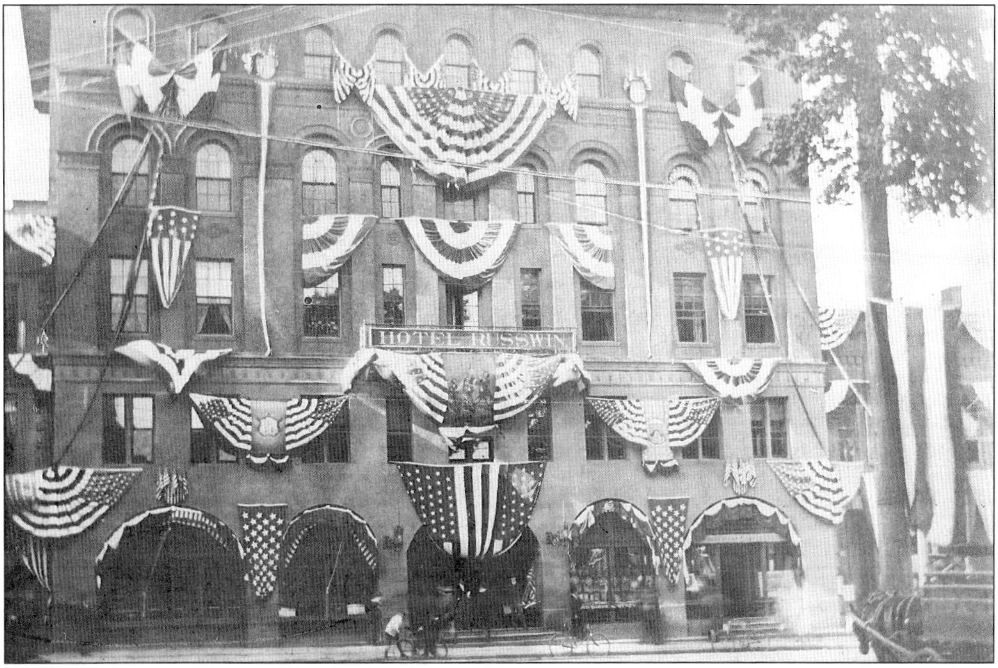

The Hotel Russwin, elaborately decorated for the dedication of the Civil War monument in 1900. Designed by Joseph Morrill Wells of McKim, Mead and White, it opened for business in 1886 and was converted into City Hall by 1909. Extensive renovations took place between 1990 and 1992. (Local History Room, NBPL.)

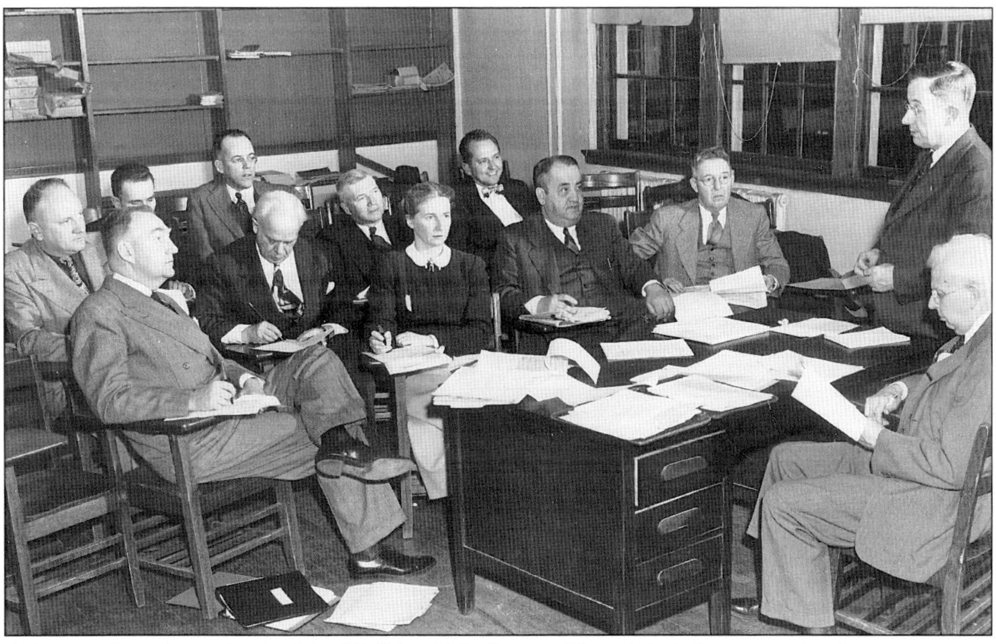

A finance board meeting in City Hall in 1971. Among New Britain's most endearing citizens was Ernest T. Brainard (first row, second from the right). Considered the nation's oldest stockbroker, he was still working up until his death in 1990, three weeks shy of his 100th birthday. (Local History Room, NBPL.)

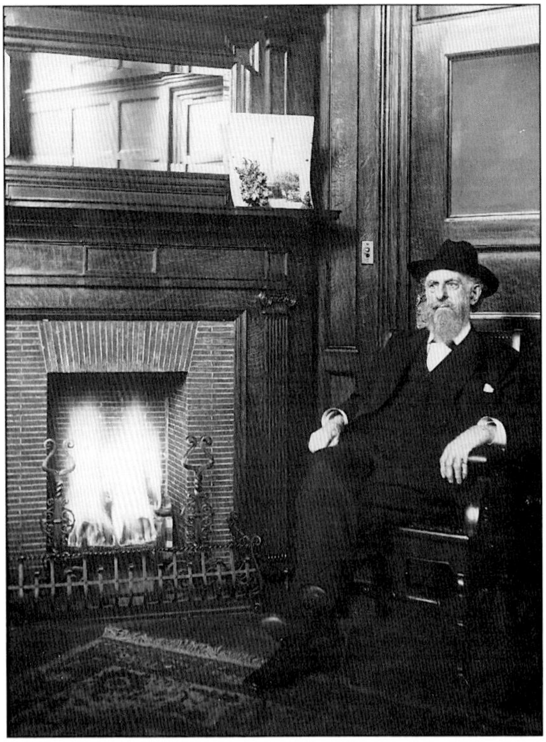

Philip Corbin, one of the city's leading industrialists. On November 4, 1910, his death was eloquently reported in the *New Britain Herald*: ". . . as the shadows of evening began to fall yesterday, Honorable Philip Corbin, dean of New Britain's captains of industry and the leading citizen of the Hardware City, closed his eyes upon the scene of this life and opened them to the blessedness of the world beyond." (Local History Room, NBPL.)

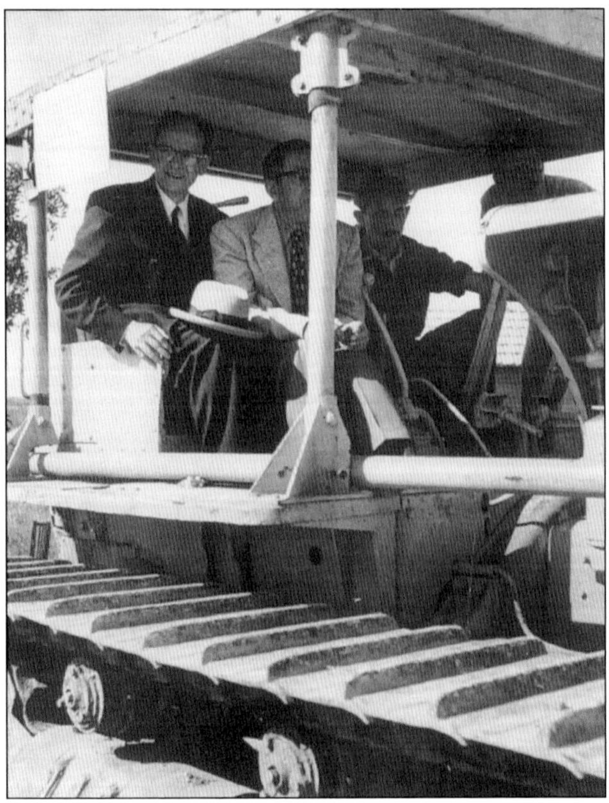

Dr. Morris S. Dunn. Dr. Dunn is shown here atop the tractor he helped purchase for the citizens of Palmach Tzova, a kibbutz in Israel. A local dentist for forty-five years, Dr. Dunn spearheaded the effort to raise $25,000 for the machine. In 1948, long before our current "sister cities" program began, this kibbutz was adopted by Connecticut Zionists and called Nachlat. (Libbie Dunn Zucker.)

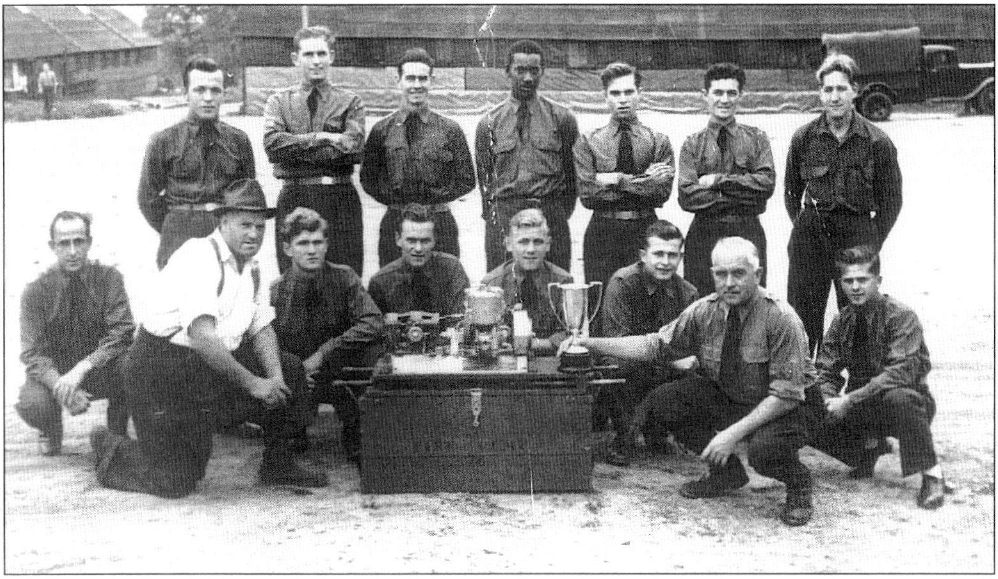

Local members of the Civilian Conservation Corps (CCC). Originated as part of Roosevelt's New Deal program in 1933, this program had over 500,000 participants nationwide. It offered people an opportunity to work during the Depression years. The men lived in military-style barracks while constructing dams, building roads, and working on forestry projects. (Mary Jaronko Marut Karwoski.)

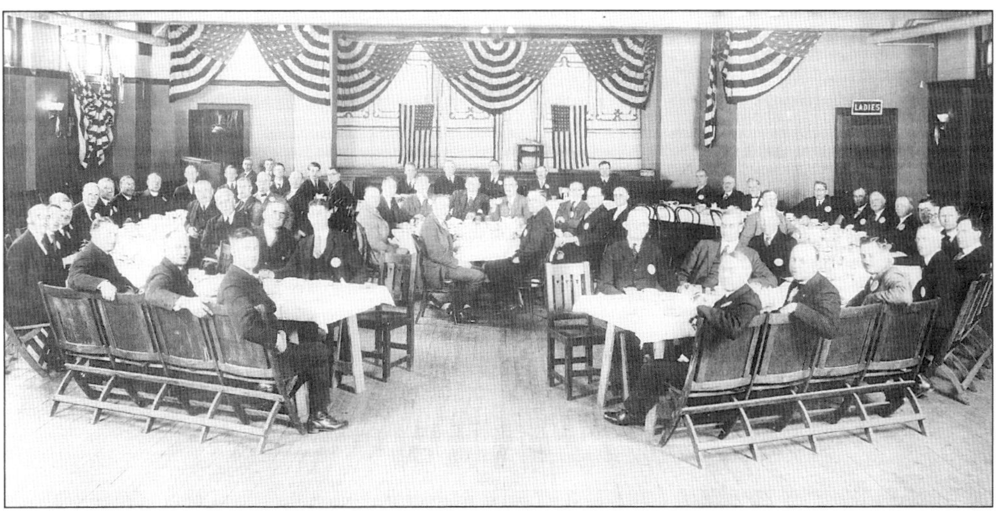

The first meeting of the New Britain Rotary Club in 1921. Original members included well-known men like Delbert Perry, Max Unkelbach, Frank Traut, W.L. Hatch, and Bernard Gaffney. Seventy years after its inception, the Rotarians elected their first woman president, Donna Piretti. (Rotary Club.)

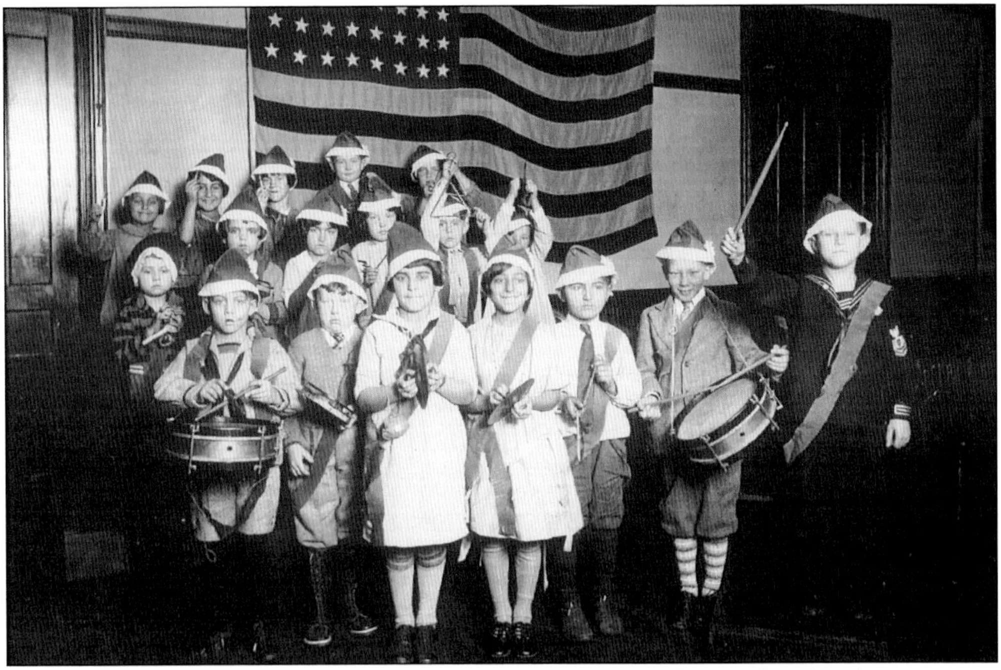

The primary band from South Church, 1926. Music has always played a large part in the city's history. This band was led by Wilton Haffey (far right with the baton). (South Congregational Church.)

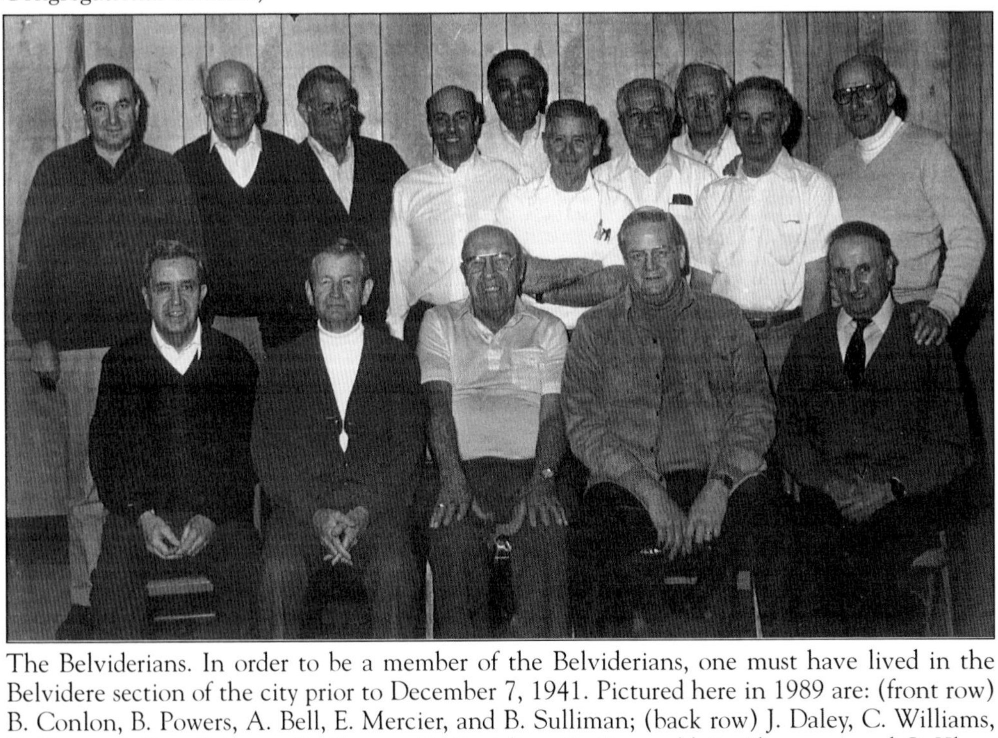

The Belviderians. In order to be a member of the Belviderians, one must have lived in the Belvidere section of the city prior to December 7, 1941. Pictured here in 1989 are: (front row) B. Conlon, B. Powers, A. Bell, E. Mercier, and B. Sulliman; (back row) J. Daley, C. Williams, H. Funari, J. Rao, P. Lucas, R. Greene, H. Davidian, D. Fitzgerald, S. Chapman, and C. Klett. (Ray Greene.)

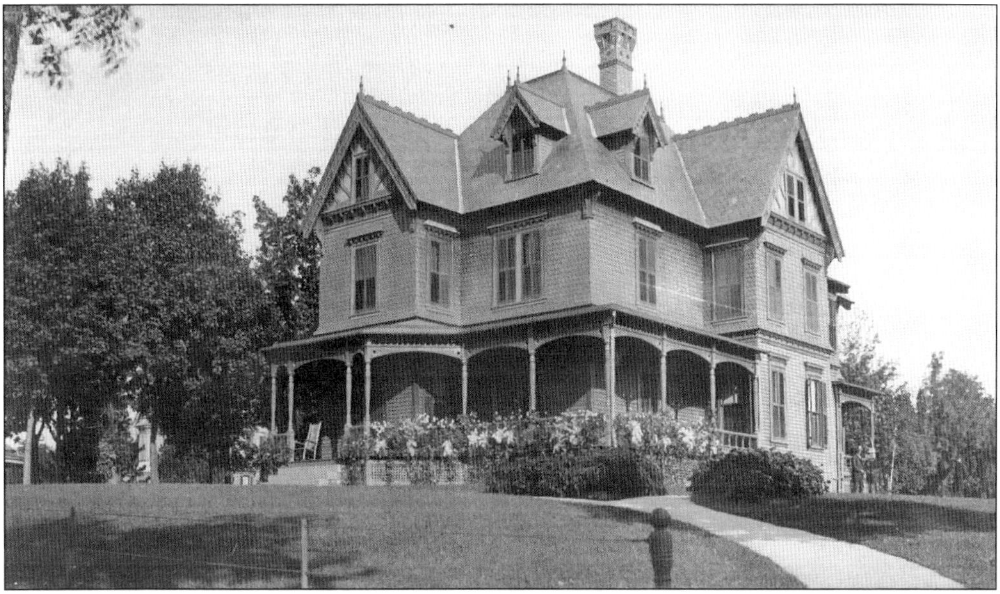

The former home of the Whittlesey family, on the corner of Grove Hill and West Main Street. Frederick Whittlesey's successful business would develop into McMillian's Department Store. After his death in 1916, his daughters, Mary and Frances, maintained the home, which was renown for its beautiful gardens. Today this building houses the Bordiere law firm. (Local History Room, NBPL.)

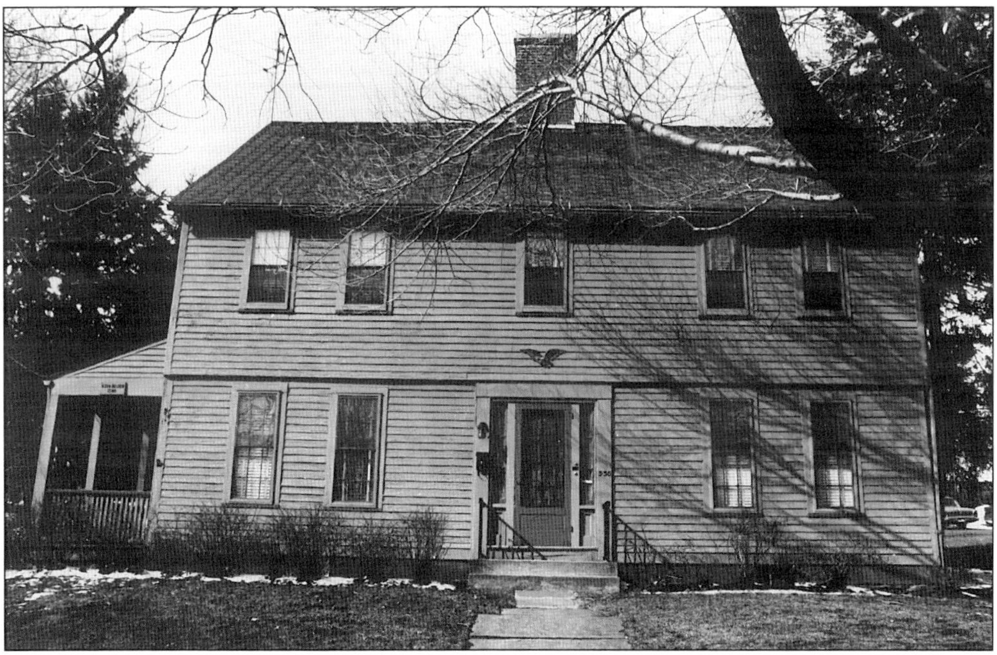

The Ezra Belden house at 530 East Street. This is the oldest house standing in New Britain. Built in 1746, it is occupied by the eighth generation of Belden descendants. Originally, the house stood on a 60-acre tract of land. (Local History Room, NBPL.)

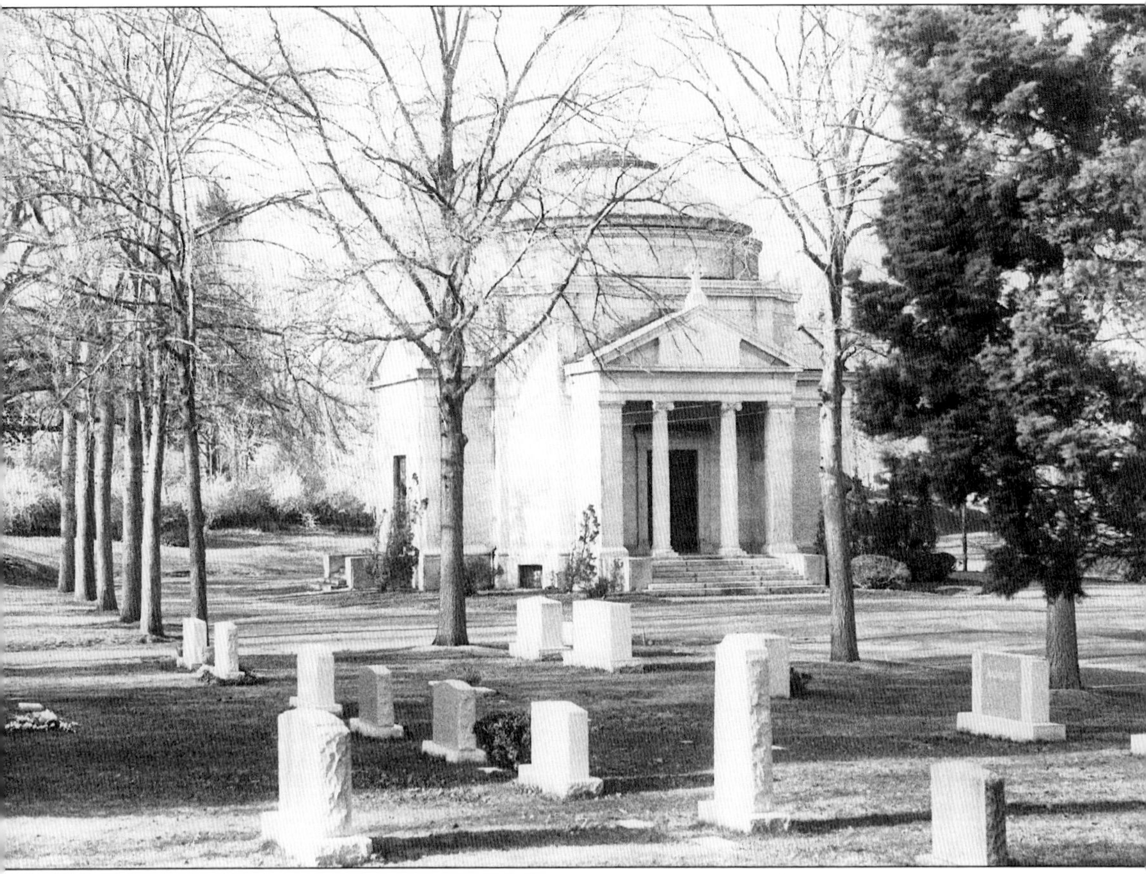

The Erwin Chapel at Fairview Cemetery. This chapel is one of the beautiful memorials located in the city. Erected in 1900, the chapel was refurbished and rededicated in 1974. One of the city's treasures, it was named after industrialist Cornelius B. Erwin and built five years after his death. Erwin's bequests to the city were plentiful, and included monies for the construction of the public library, the Erwin Home, the Civil War Monument in Central Park, maintenance funds for Fairview Cemetery and Walnut Hill Park, and this chapel. (Local History Room, NBPL.)

Two

What We Did for Fun

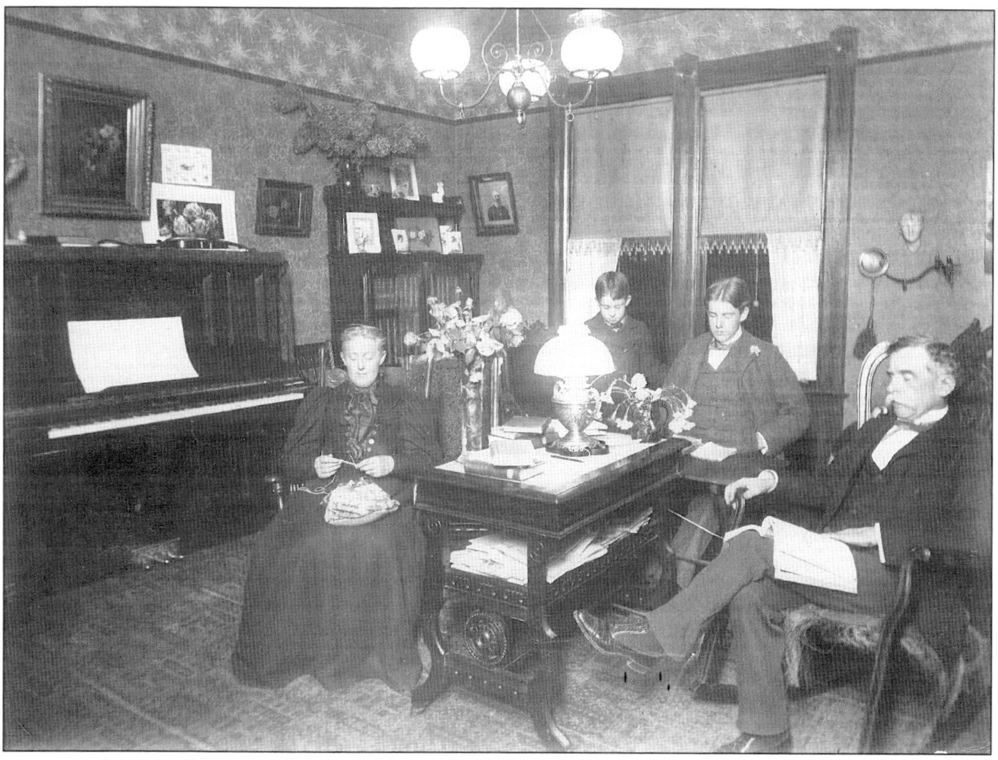

Laura Noble Copley, Merwin, George N., and George D. Copley in their parlor at 23 Park Place. Long before electronic advancements, evening entertainment centered around reading, music, and handiwork. This chapter offers a sampling of what residents did for enjoyment. (Local History Room/NBPL.)

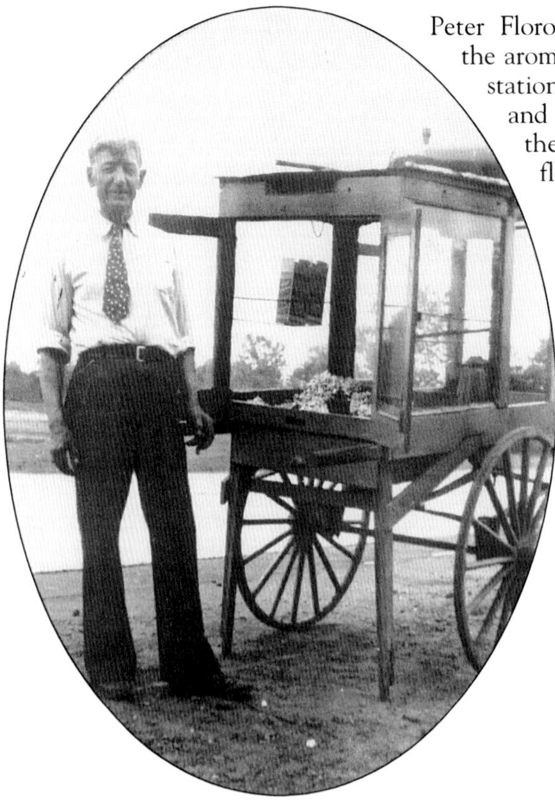

Peter Floros. New Britain's "popcorn man" knew the aroma of fresh popcorn was hard to resist. He stationed his cart on the corner of West Main and High Streets, near the public library, thereby insuring the business of a constant flow of customers. (Alainie Nevilas.)

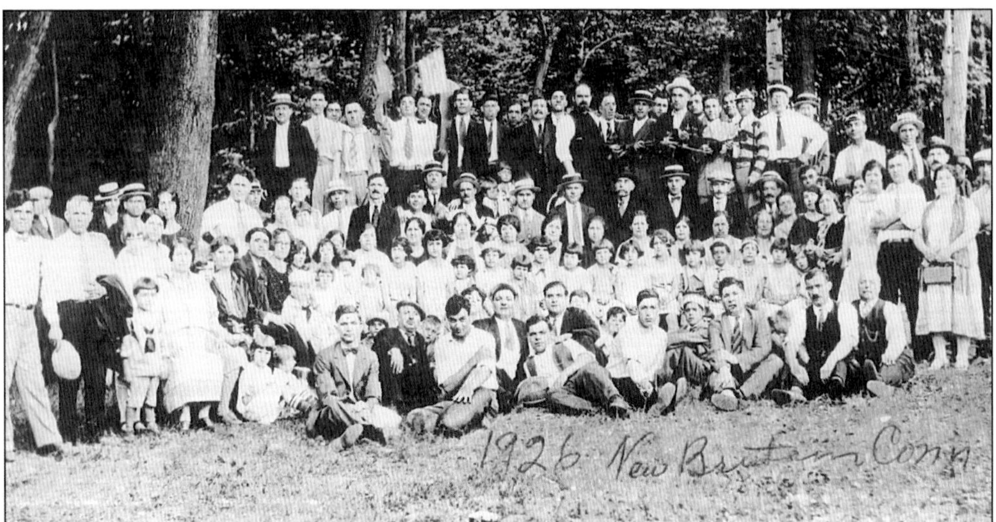

A picnic gathering. A popular form of socializing, picnicking is as *en vogue* today as it was when this group from New Britain's Greek community gathered for a repast in 1926. (Eugenia Chrisoulis Banios.)

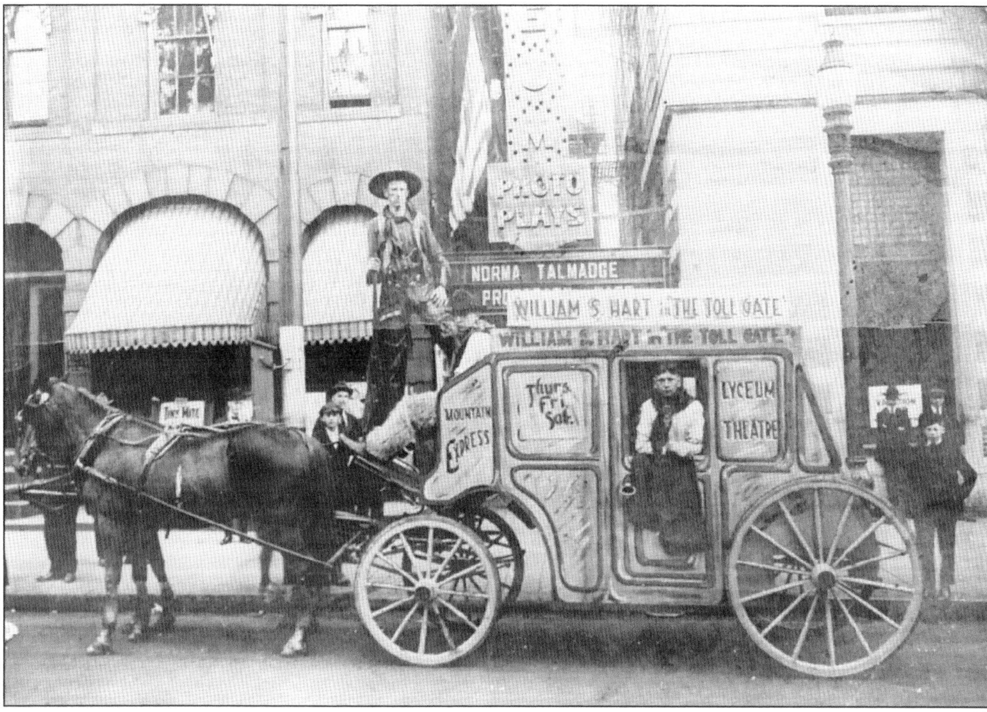

The old stagecoach in front of the Russwin Lyceum. This stagecoach provided great advertising space for the theatre. Parades and Wild West shows, such as the one shown here, drew large crowds to the downtown area. (*Herald* photograph file.)

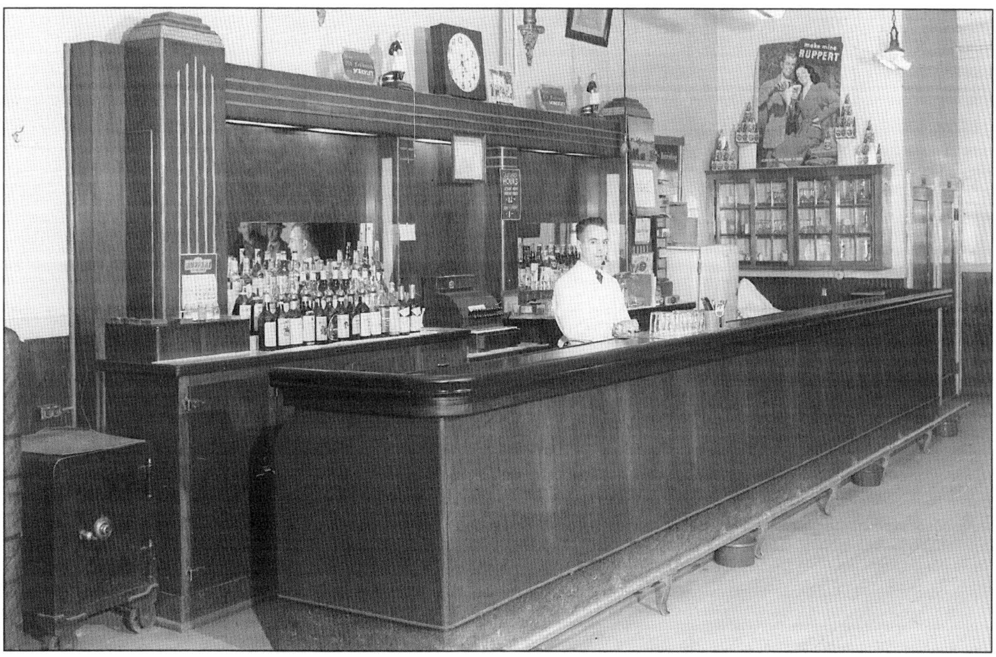

St. Stephen's Club. Located on Arch Street, this club attracted many of the city's Austrian residents. Between 1890 and 1920, immigrants from Austria arrived to work in the factories. Many of them gravitated to the German section in the south end of the city. (Fred Hedeler.)

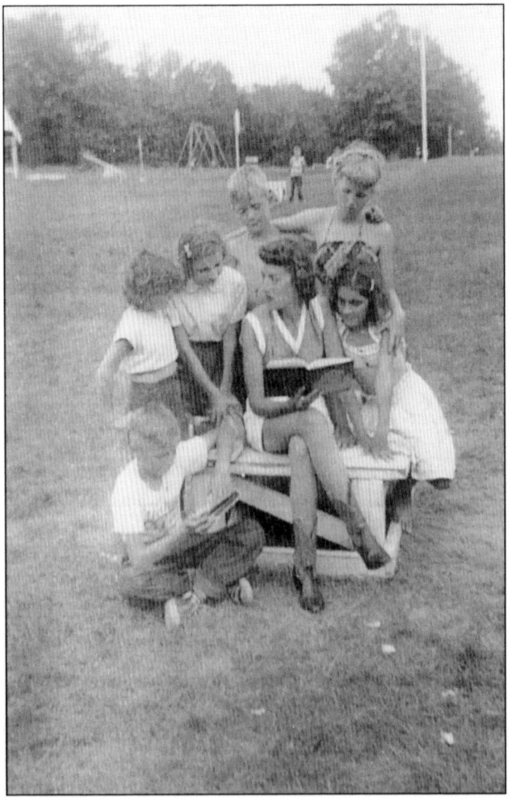

Nebraskan school teacher Louise Chandler with children of the Fresh Air Camp. With a desire to travel east, she wrote to the Chamber of Commerce inquiring about employment. Her letter was given to Frank Schade and soon Miss Chandler found a summer job as a camp counselor. (Ray Venberg.)

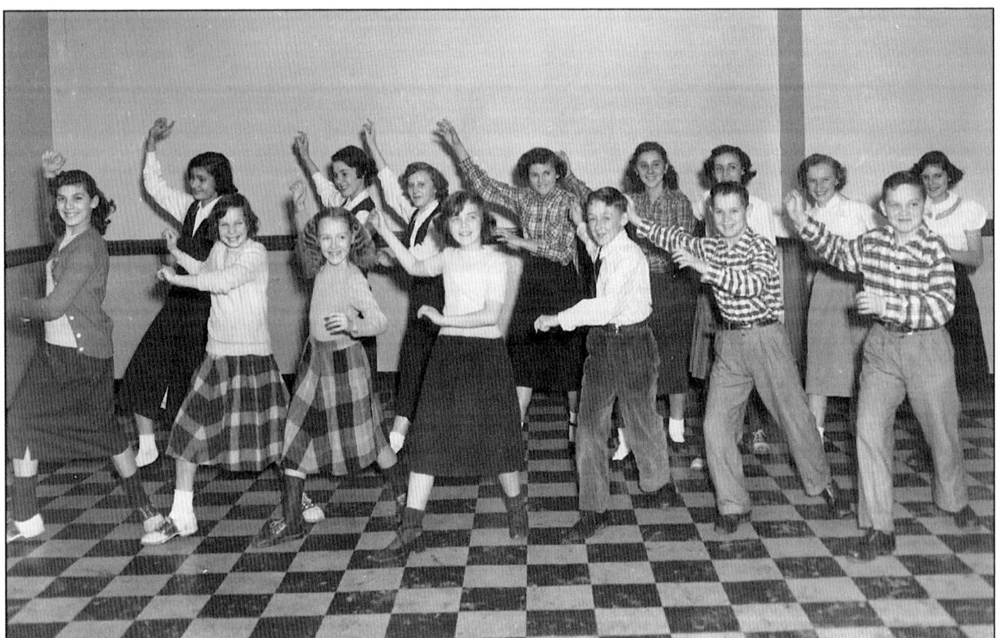

Many smiles from a tap-dancing class in 1951. Among the many accomplishments of Reverend Msgr. Lucyan Bojonowski was the founding of the Polish orphanage, where these children resided. (Local History Room/NBPL.)

Removing the chandelier from the Palace Theater in 1981. Originally known as Hanna's Opera House, it opened in May 1881 with a performance of *Faust*—the only time opera was presented here. Vaudeville and movies played at the theater, which was later named the Palace. Plans to refurbish the magnificent structure were thwarted when it was badly damaged by fire and water in 1980. (John D'Amato.)

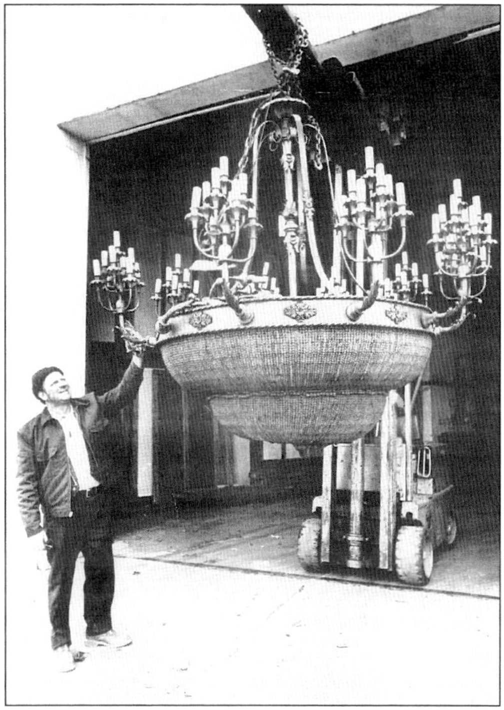

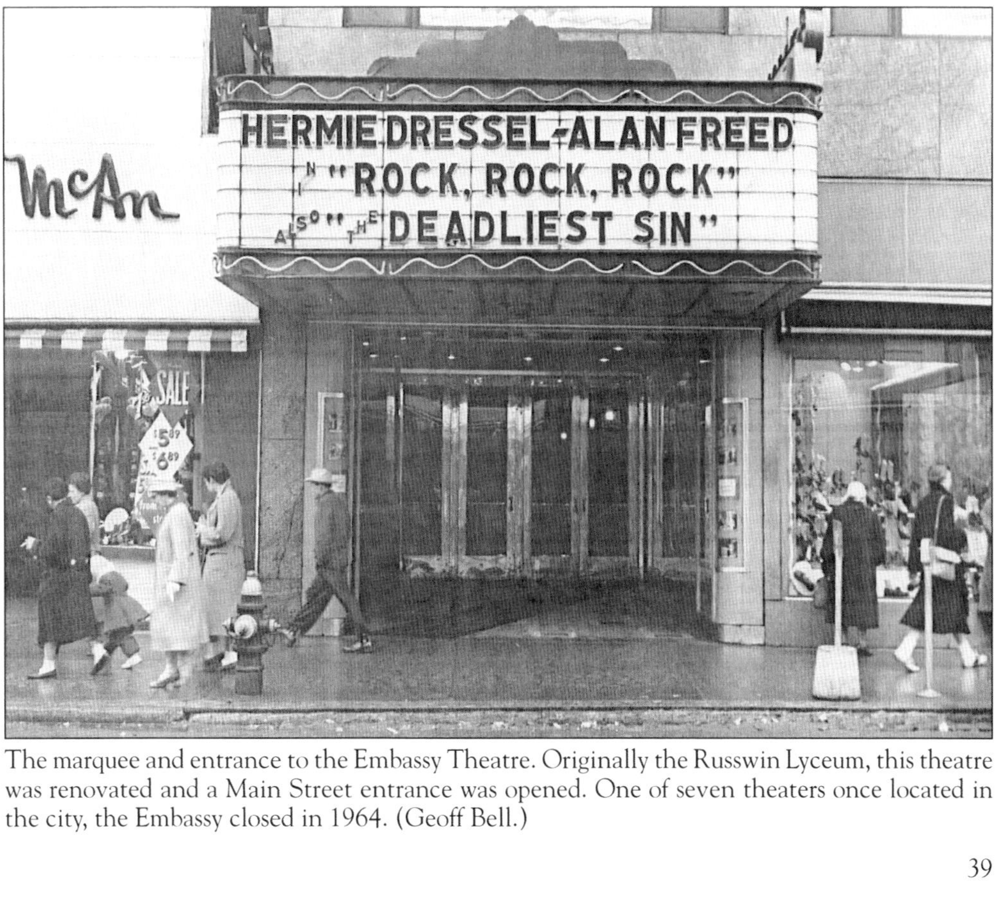

The marquee and entrance to the Embassy Theatre. Originally the Russwin Lyceum, this theatre was renovated and a Main Street entrance was opened. One of seven theaters once located in the city, the Embassy closed in 1964. (Geoff Bell.)

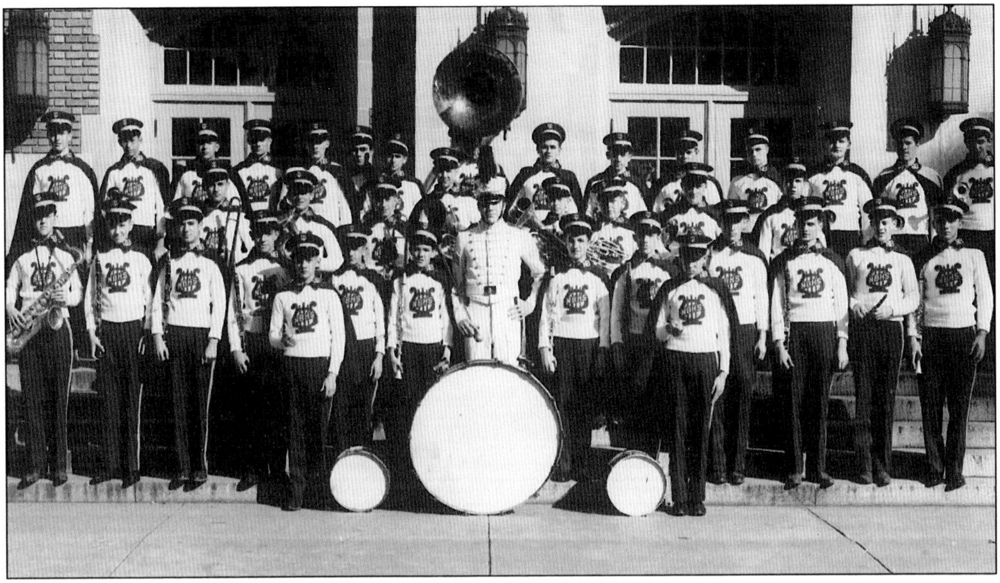

New Britain High School students. For years students have been entertaining citizens with their music. Today the upbeat tempo of the high school band impresses audiences as much as the above group, pictured in 1937, must have done. Below, a much more serious looking ensemble posed for the high school orchestra photograph in March 1917. (Local History Room, NBPL.)

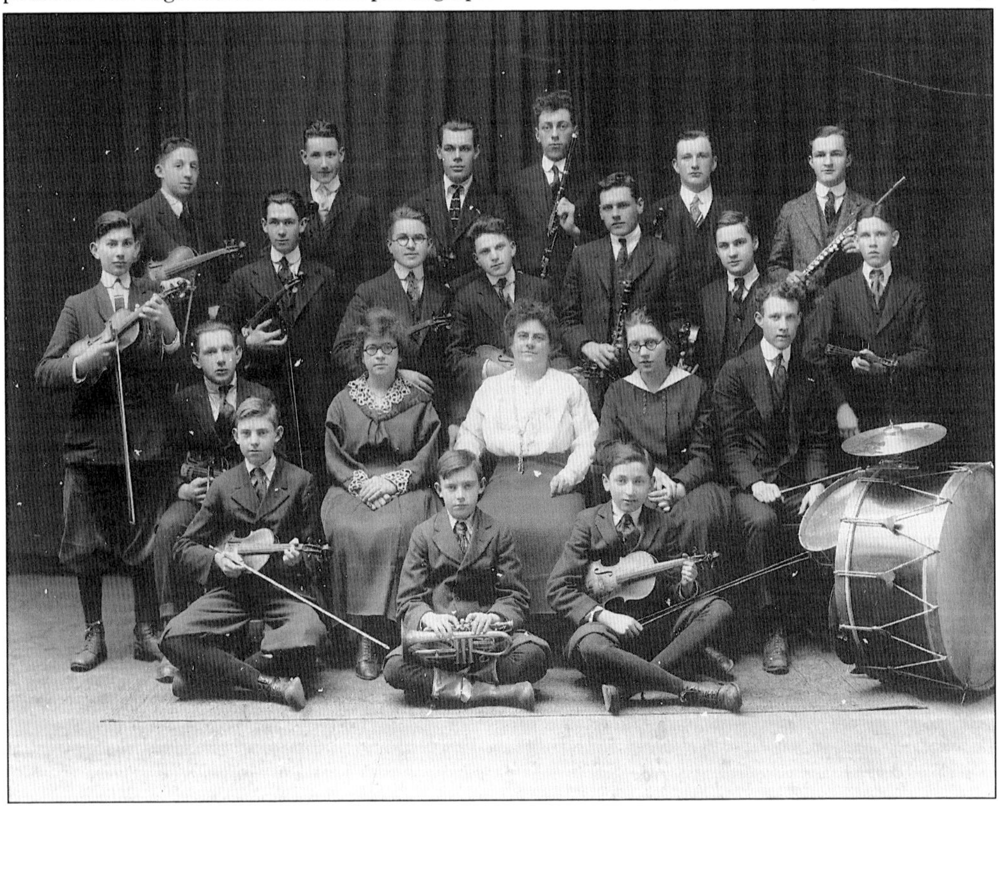

English-born Henry A. Littlehales, one of New Britain's best known musicians. A die maker at the Hart and Cooley Co., Mr. Littlehales was better known as a cornetist and the director of the Footguard Band of Hartford, the American Band in New Britain, and a Bristol band. He came to the city in 1897 and died in 1923. (Local History Room, NBPL.)

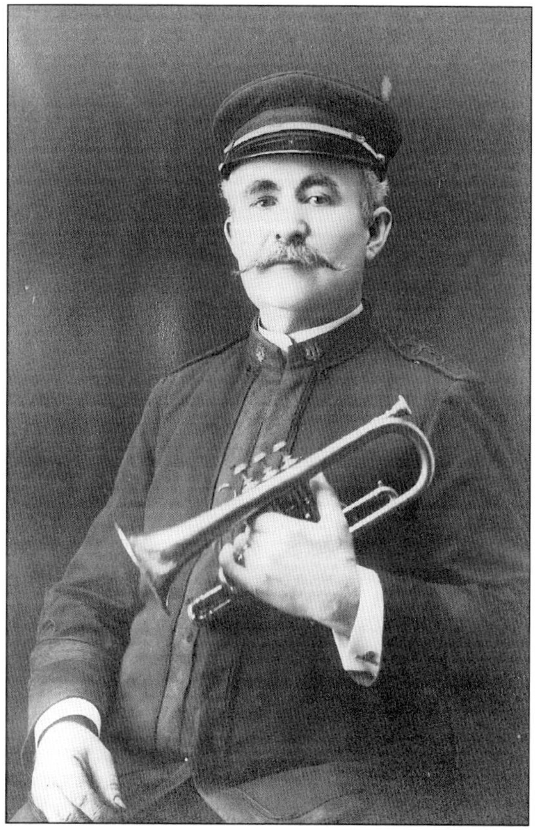

The Alpenland Dancers. The dancers perform at statewide affairs as well as at functions in Rhode Island, Massachusetts, and New York. From left to right are: (front row) J. Buthistome, B. Hurtig, E. Zoon, L. Riley, R. Kohlmann, M. Hernap, J. Wood, and U. Fransolino; (back row) M. Fainishe, C. Wolf, W. Kober, A. Herzog, B. Riley, B. Kohlmann, R. Weber, and J. Potitz. (Frances Bauer.)

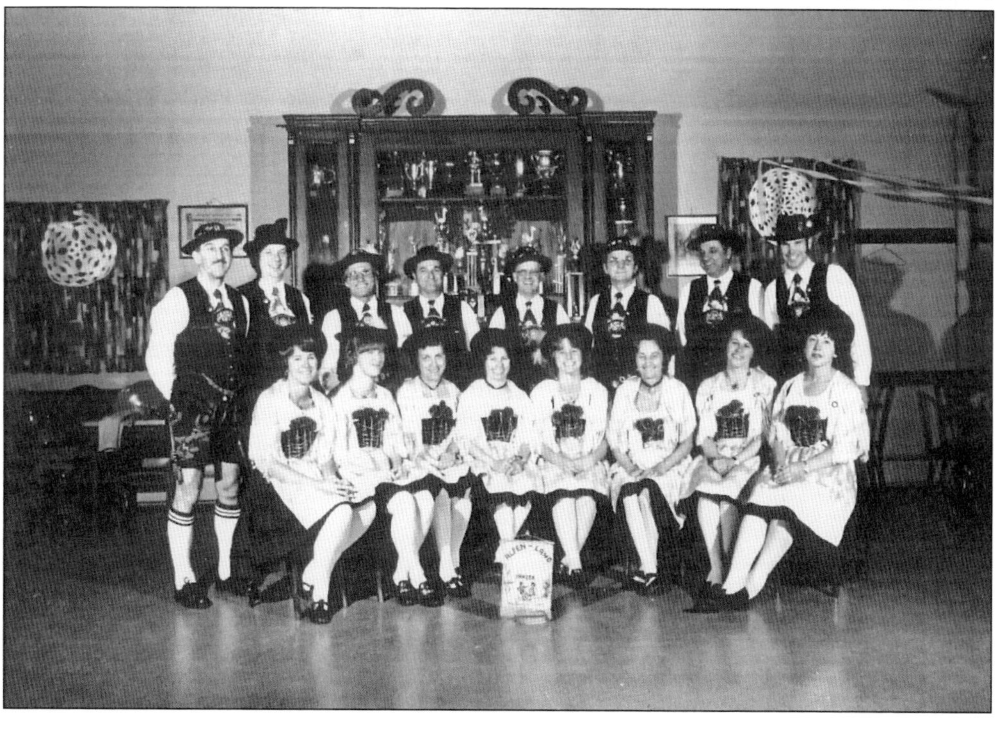

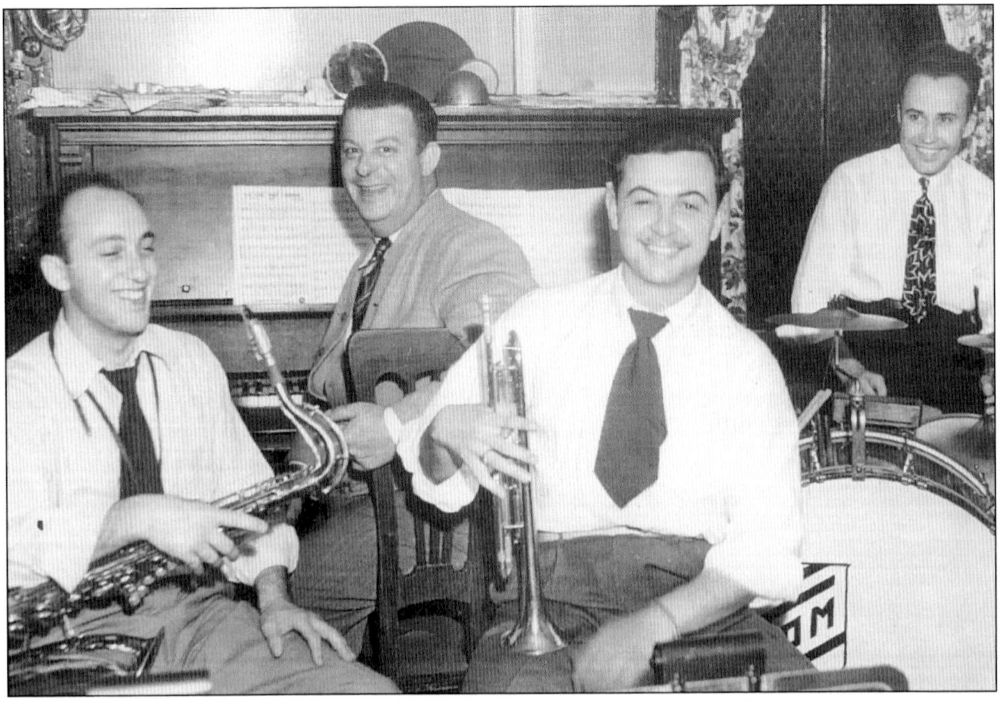

Bill Robinson's orchestra in the mid-1950s. The musicians entertained throughout the area as well as at Fafnir events, where half of the orchestra (Bill Robinson and Tony Spoasiano) was employed. (Russell Robinson.)

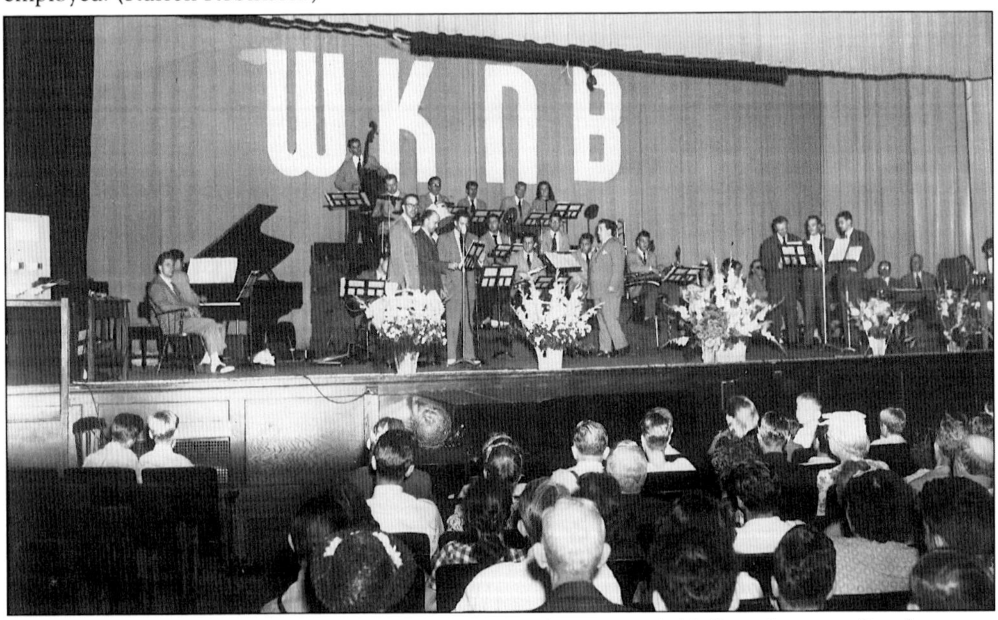

Al Gentile and his band. Mention a music man in the city and Al Gentile immediately comes to mind. Mr. Gentile's venues have ranged from New York's Empire Ballroom on Broadway to Old Orchard Beach, Maine. In the business for over sixty-five years, Mr. Gentile was awarded the Musician of the Year award by the American Federation of Musicians, Local 440, in 1993. (Local History Room, NBPL.)

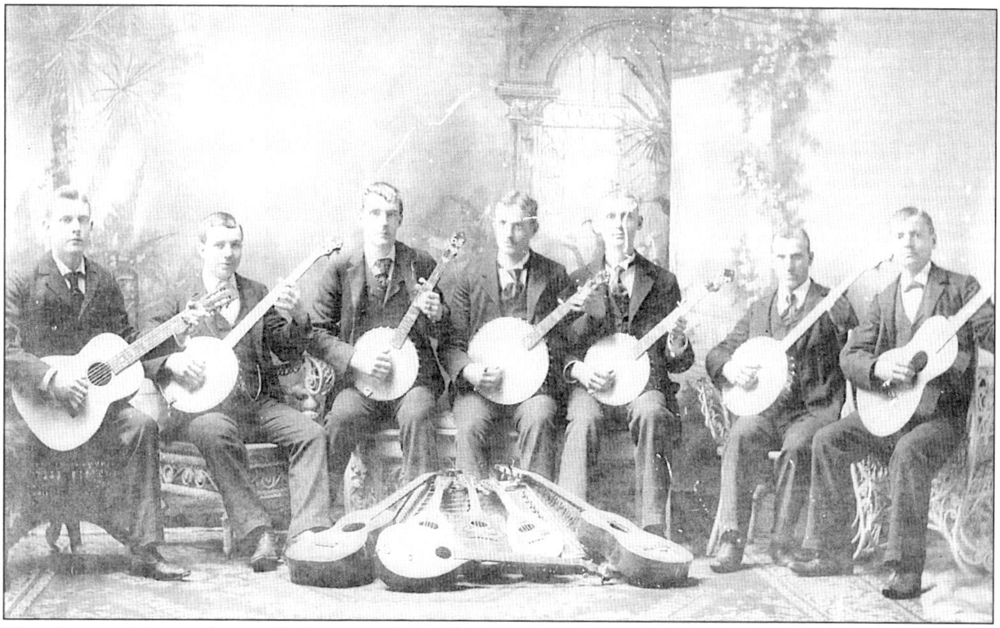

The Banjo, Mandolin and Guitar Club of New Britain. Although little is known about this club, we can only assume they brought a unique sound to audiences. The photograph was taken in 1896. (Mr. and Mrs. William Bonney.)

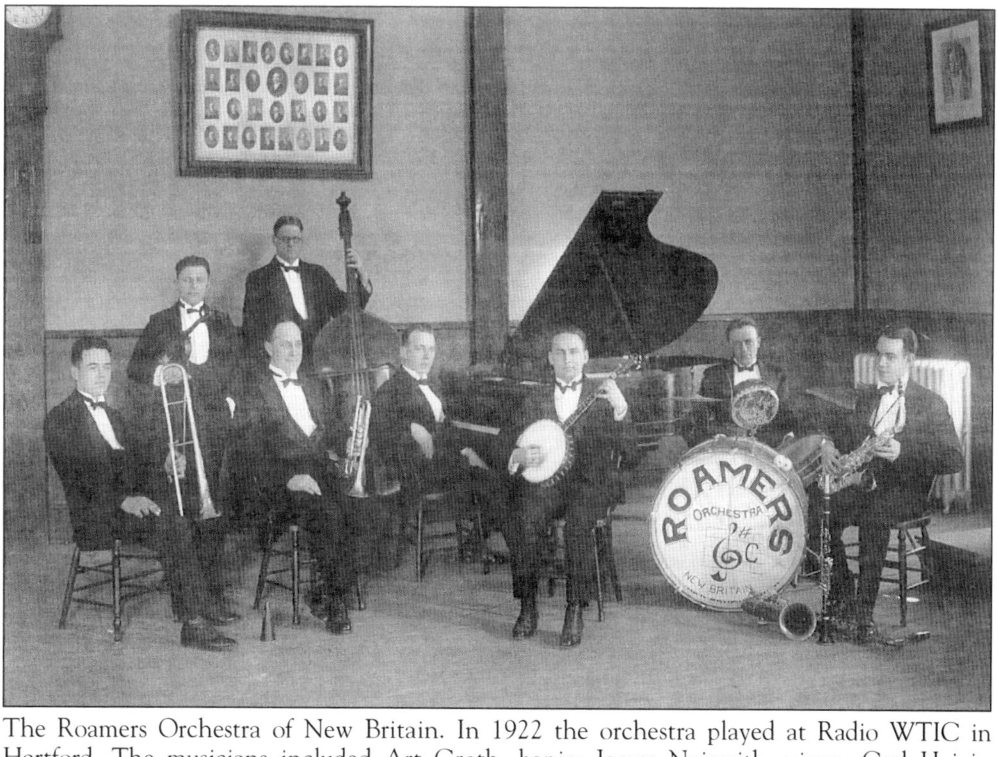

The Roamers Orchestra of New Britain. In 1922 the orchestra played at Radio WTIC in Hartford. The musicians included Art Groth, banjo; James Naismith, piano; Carl Haigis, trumpet; Mr. Nuss, bass viol; and Mr. Rysek, trumpet. The others are unidentified. (Mr. and Mrs. William Bonney.)

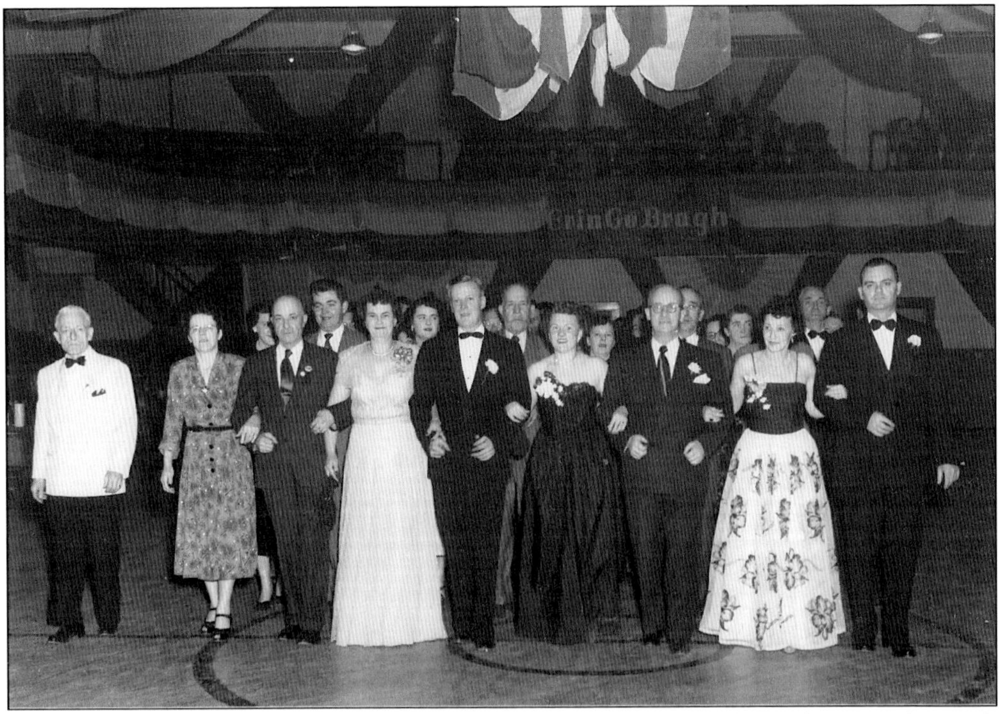

A St. Patrick's Day dance at the Stanley Arena. Whether it hosted wrestling matches with Gorgeous George, a boxing contest featuring Floyd Patterson, or a formal dance led by John L. Sullivan, the Stanley Arena on Church Street was a hub of activity. (Local History Room, NBPL.)

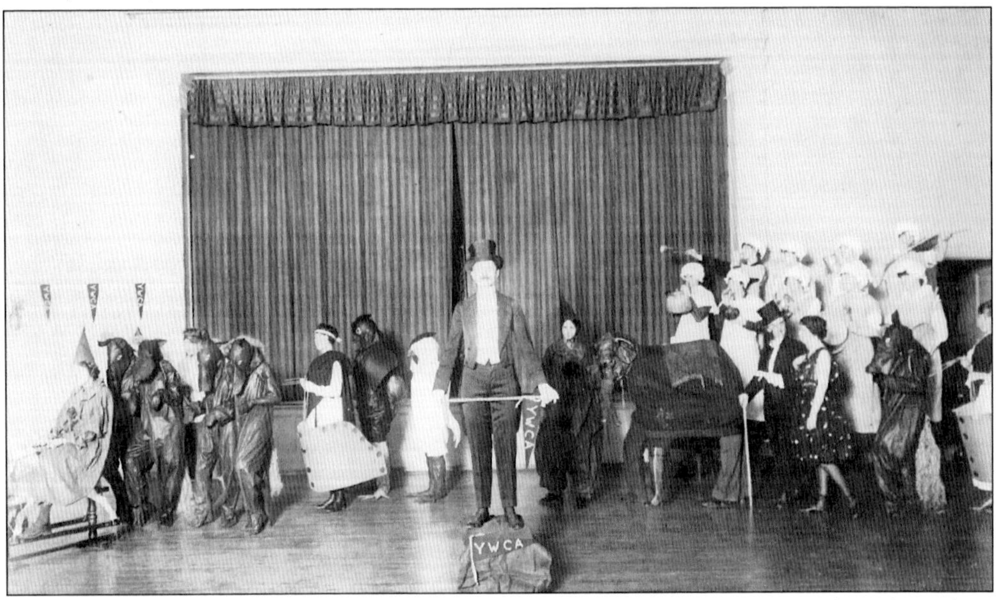

A "homemade" circus entourage parades at the YWCA. The 1918 event featured Gerda Carlson as ringmaster. Since its incorporation in 1910, the YWCA has provided an array of athletic programs for the city's women. Today the "Y" offers diverse programming that benefits women from their earliest years up through retirement. (YWCA.)

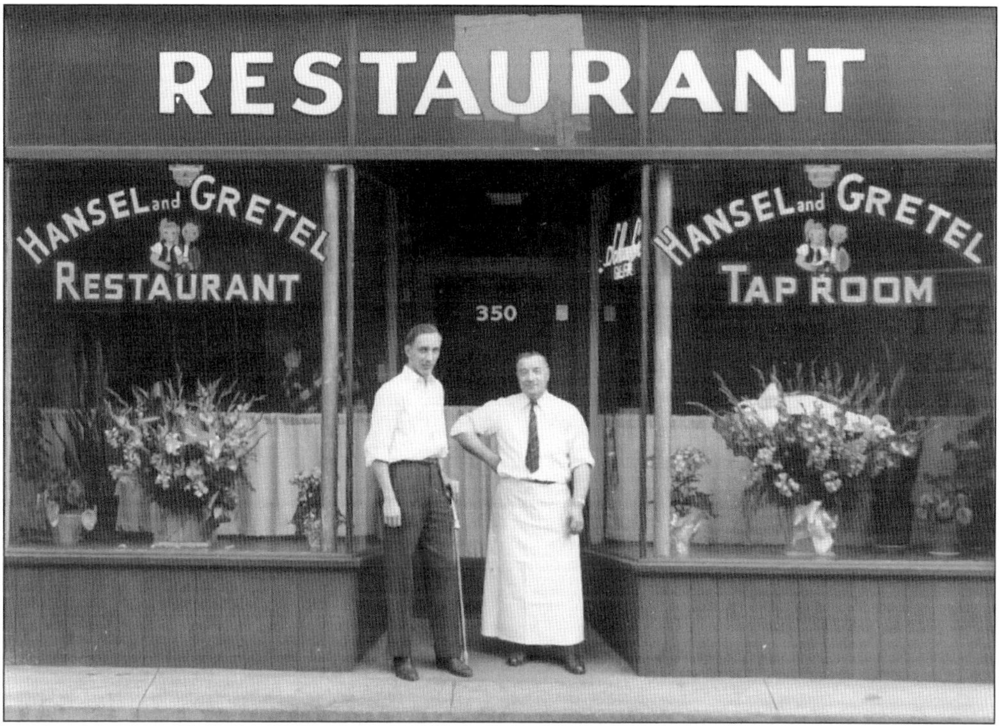

The opening of the Hansel and Gretel Restaurant. The front windows of the restaurant, located at 350 Arch Street, are filled with good wishes bouquets. In the late 1940s the city directory listed 110 lunchrooms and restaurants operating in the city. (Fred Hedeler.)

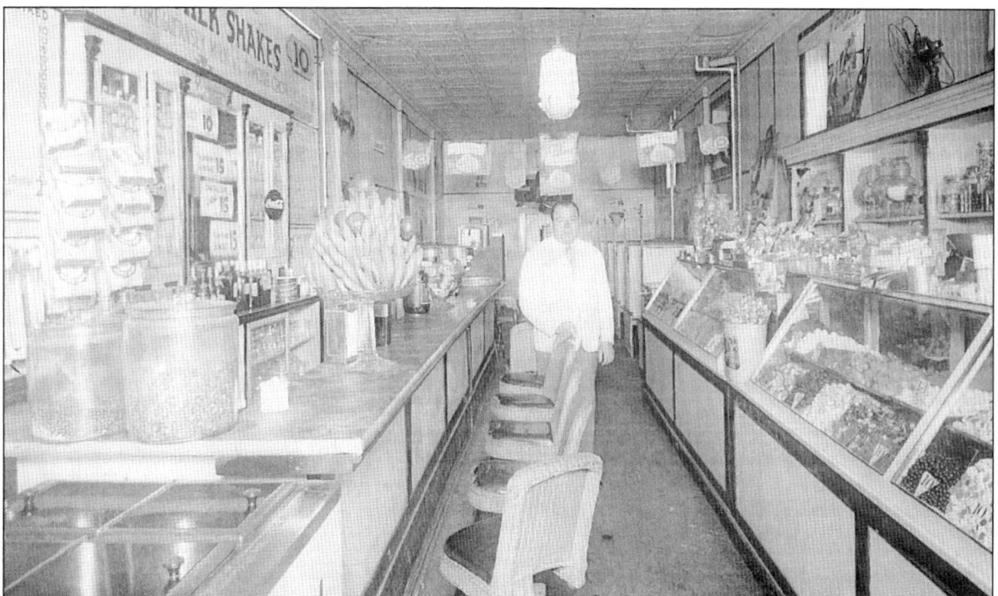

Michael Louis in his establishment, the Louis Luncheonette, *c.* 1937. Located at 503 Main Street, the luncheonette featured "Jumbo milkshakes, with Nichols pure Guernsey milk!" for 10¢. A stroll to the booths in the rear took customers past an incredible soda fountain and glass cases filled with tempting candy. (Jeff Louis.)

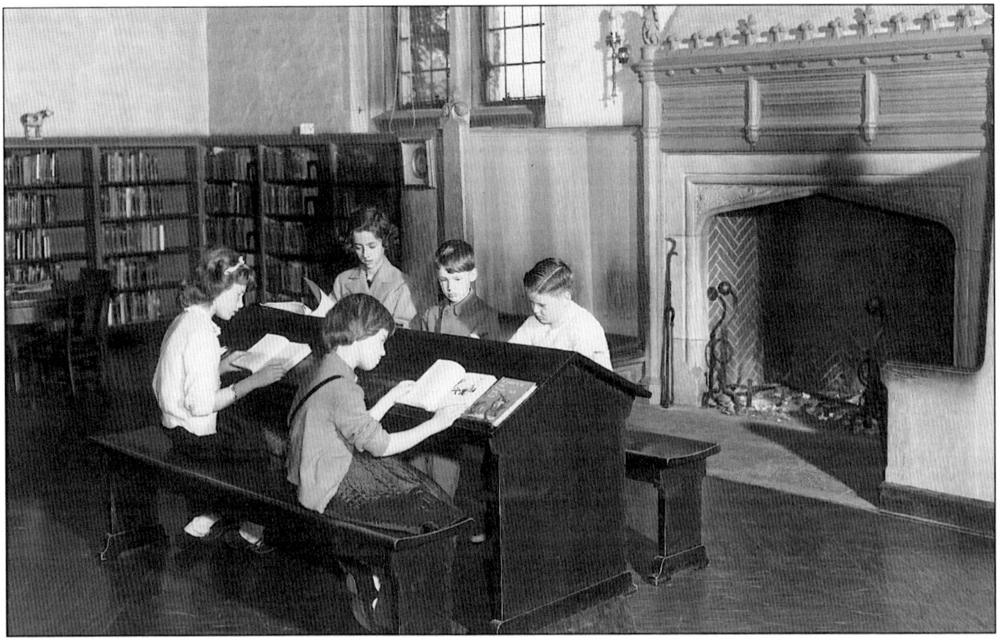

Avid readers perusing books in the Hawley Memorial Children's Library, October 1953. In 1976 this building and the Erwin building were joined by a modern addition. Family story hours are still held in front of this fireplace. (Irving Blomstrann.)

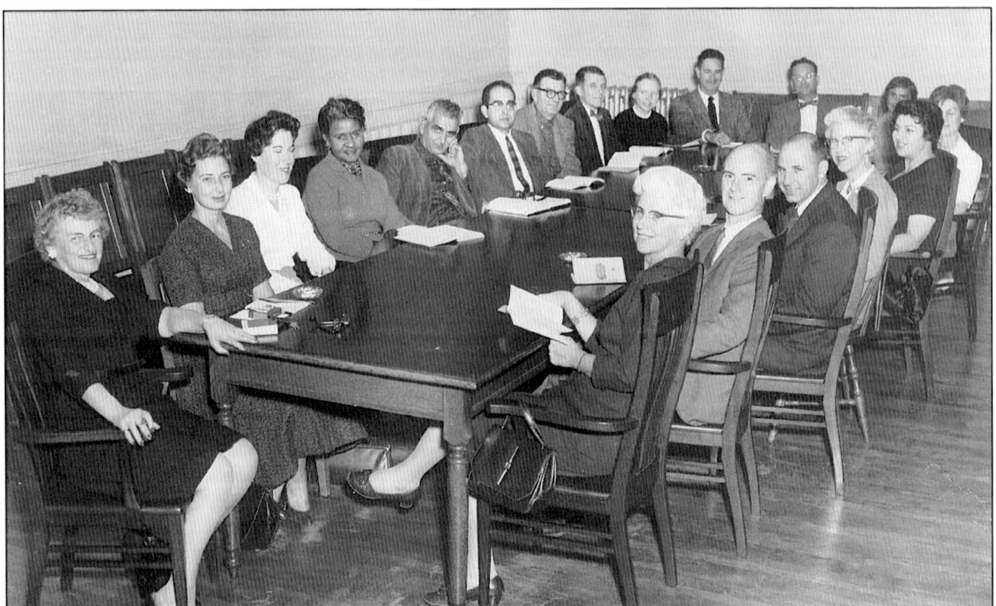

Author Ardis Whitman Rumsey (far left) and the Great Books Discussion Group at the public library in November 1960. Moving clockwise from the front are Mrs. George Richman, Kathryn Leaf, Mrs. Edgar Bellamy, Archie Hovanessian, Carlos Carreas, Ed Stankowicz, Mr. and Mrs. Paul Nuding, Joseph Massamino, Robert Eisner, Alice Berkowitz, Mrs. Sam Rubenstein, Mrs. A. Kotkin, Dortha White, Dr. George Richman, Spencer Reynolds, and Mrs. John White. (Local History Room, NBPL.)

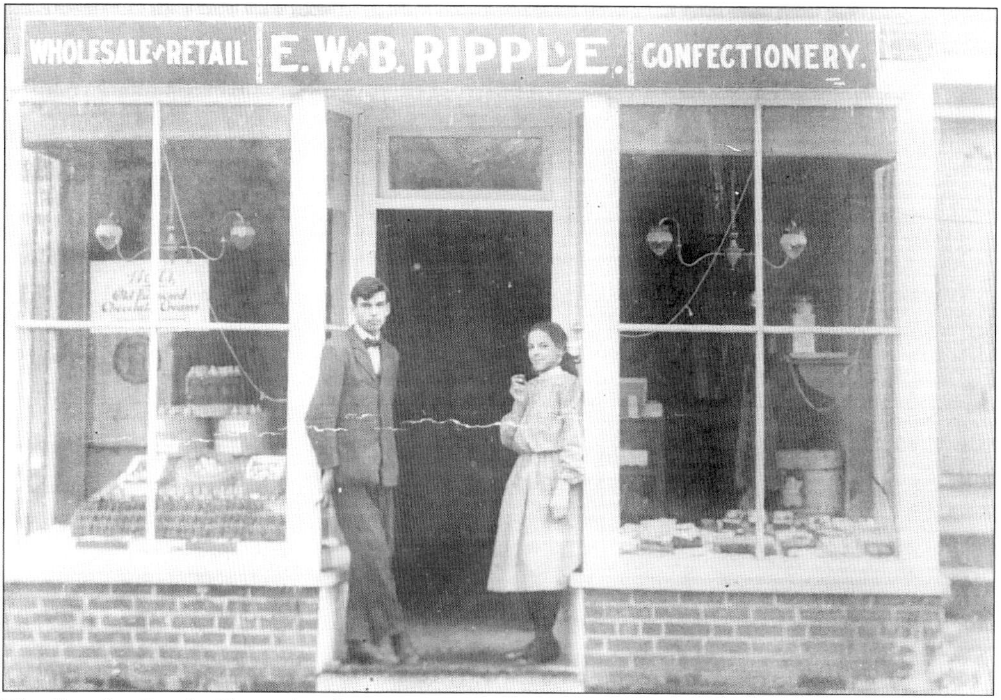

The Ripple Candy Shop. Confectioners were immensely popular, and this one, operated by Elmer W. Ripple at 463 Stanley Street, attracted the young couple pictured above. Below, the Star Confectionery at 329 Main Street offered old world charm. The giant urn on the counter dispensed water to make hot chocolate. Unusual by today's standards, cups of hot chocolate used to be served with saltine crackers! This photograph dates back to 1915. (*Herald* photograph file/Peter Veleas.)

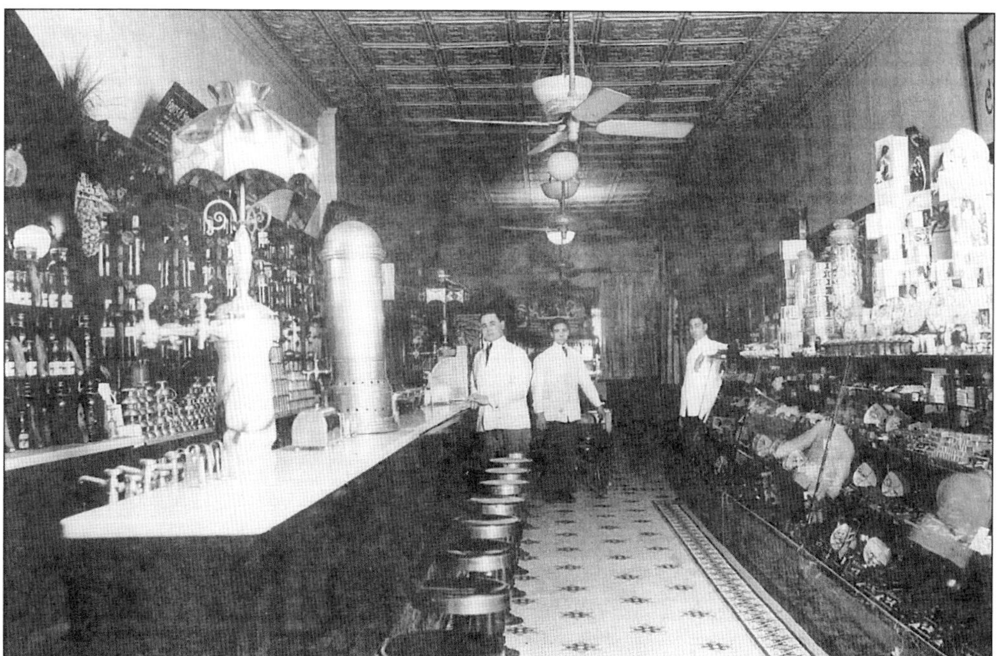

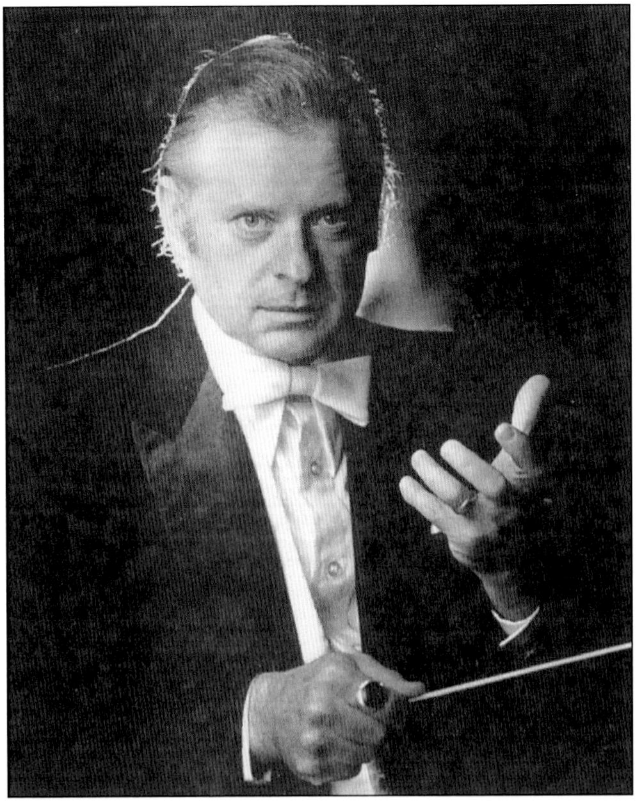

Dr. Jerome Laszloffy, conductor of the New Britain Symphony Orchestra. The current symphony dates back to 1950. Etzel Willhoit, the first conductor, and violinist Marcus Fleitzer formulated the idea of forming a symphony orchestra over a tennis match. Renowned artists have performed with the symphony, many of them brought here by coordinator Joseph Rubenstein, who is often called "Mr. Symphony." (New Britain Symphony.)

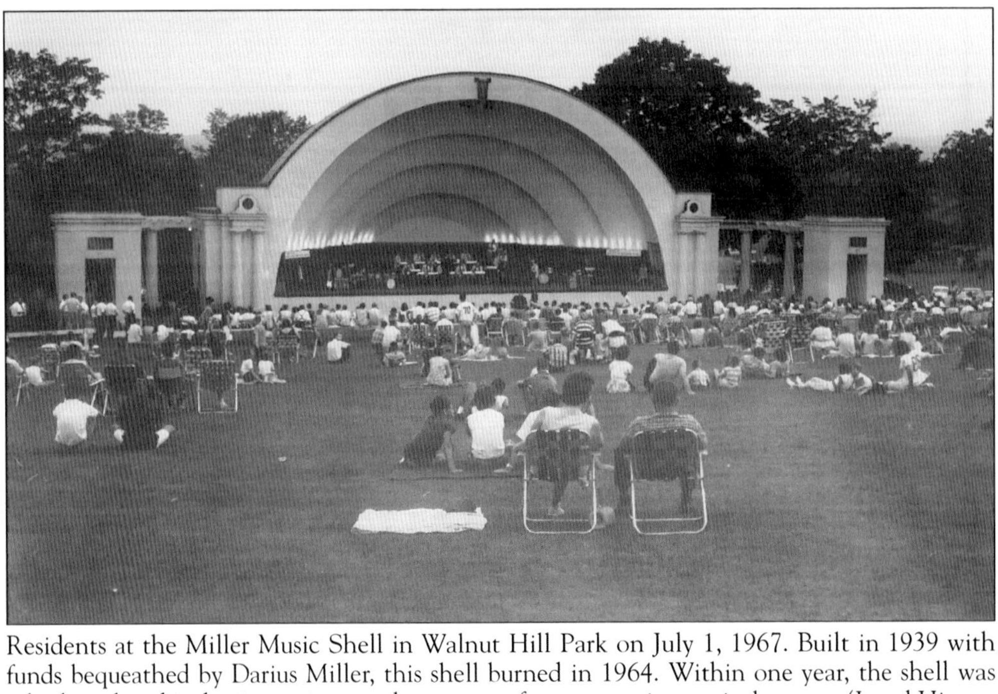

Residents at the Miller Music Shell in Walnut Hill Park on July 1, 1967. Built in 1939 with funds bequeathed by Darius Miller, this shell burned in 1964. Within one year, the shell was rebuilt and to this day it continues to be an arena for community musical events. (Local History Room, NBPL.)

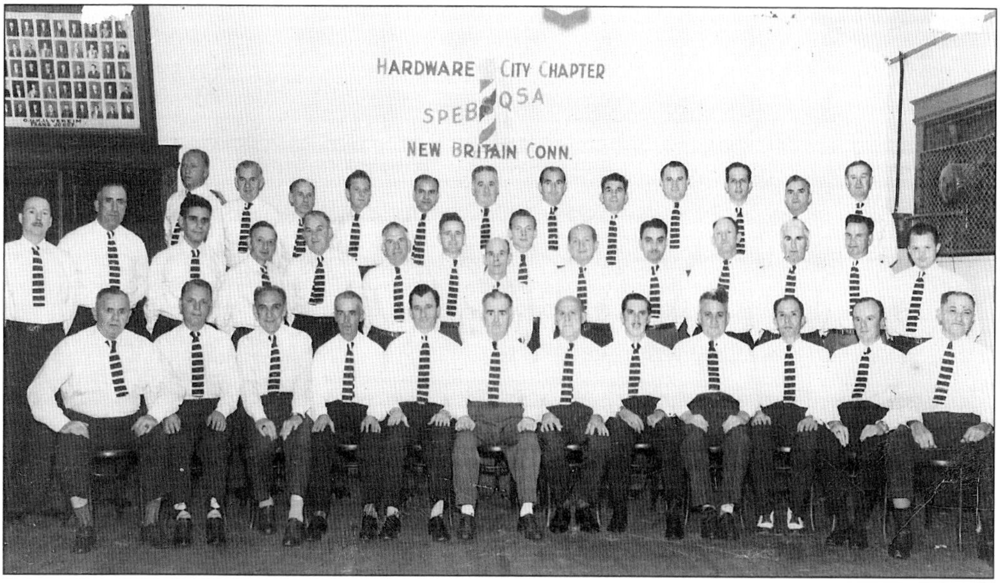

The Hardware City Chapter SPEBSQA (Society for Preservation & Encouragement of Barbershop Quartet Singing of America). At their second annual concert in October 1949 they raised $500 for the benefit of the Children's Home and the Polish Orphanage. The program included songs like "Dressed Up With Broken Heart" and "Seeing Nellie Home." (Robert Clinch.)

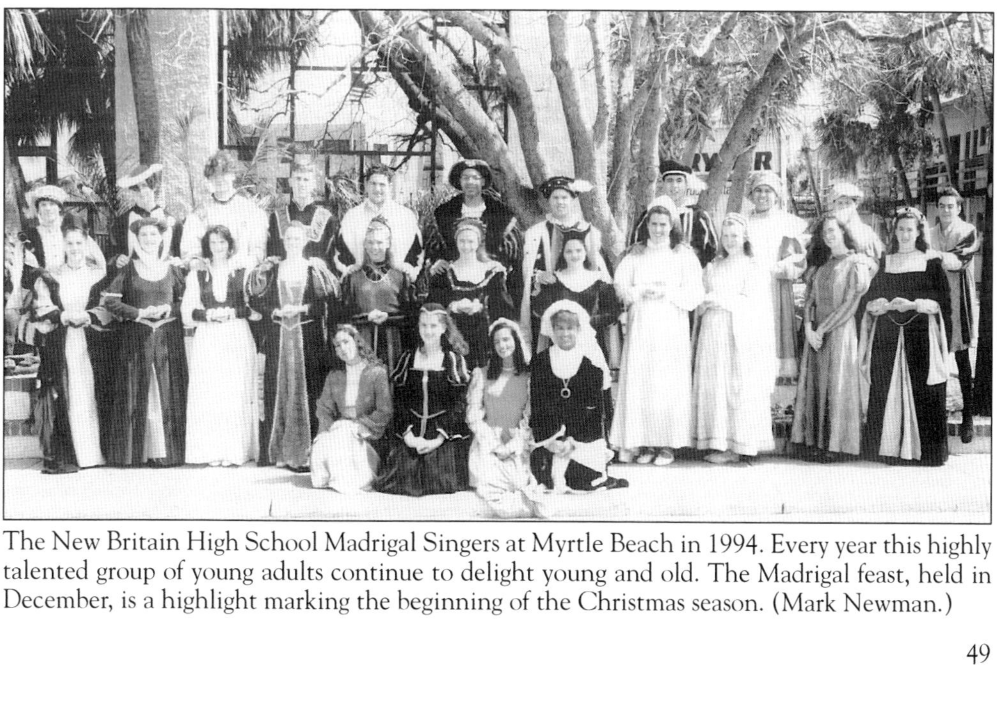

The New Britain High School Madrigal Singers at Myrtle Beach in 1994. Every year this highly talented group of young adults continue to delight young and old. The Madrigal feast, held in December, is a highlight marking the beginning of the Christmas season. (Mark Newman.)

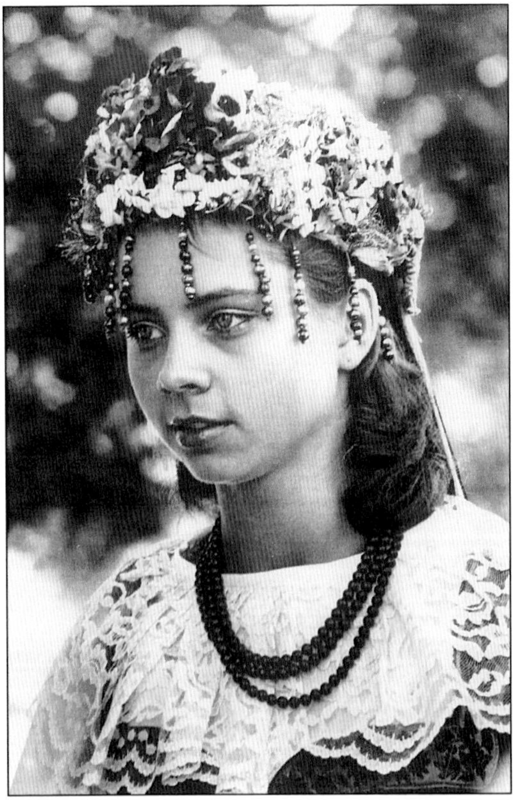

Grazyna Parejko dressed in a native Polish folk dance costume. The dancers participate in these beautiful costumes at the Dozynki (Harvest Festival). This event was traditionally held after the harvest had been gathered. New Britain's Dozynki has been an annual event since 1980. (Barbara Kirejczyk.)

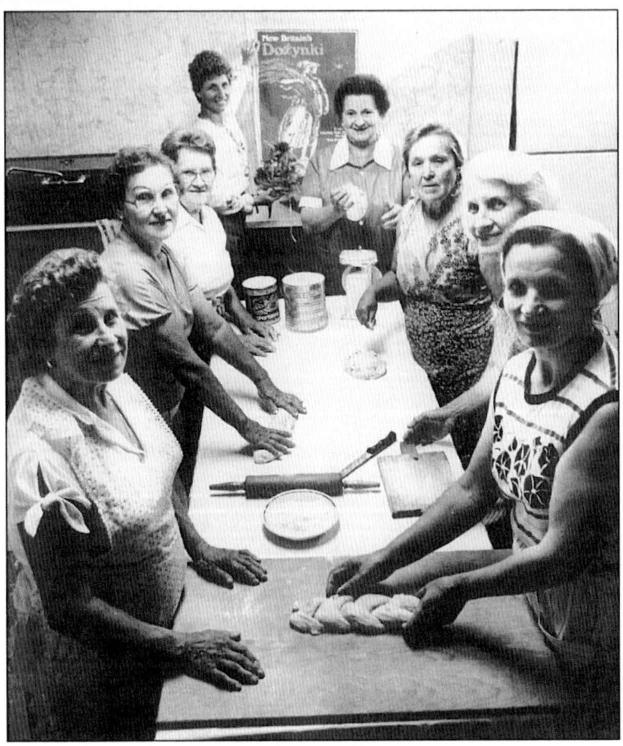

Women from the Haller Post Ladies Auxiliary at the Dozynki Festival in 1984. In addition to crafts, music, and dancing, the street festival offers a superb sampling of Polish fare. (Barbara Kirejczyk.)

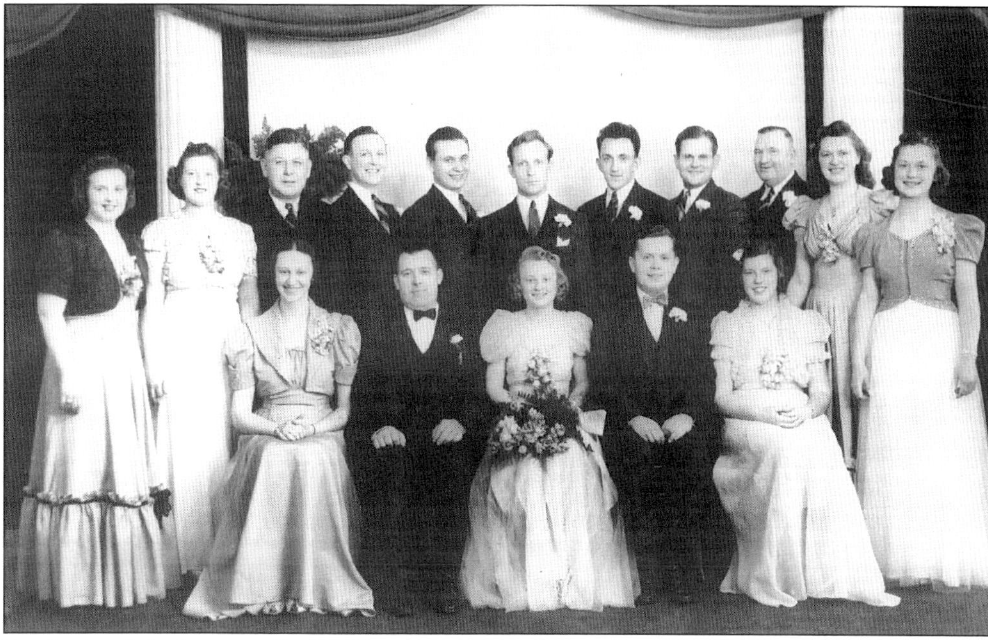

St. Andrew's Lithuanian Radio Chorus in 1940. Pictured are, from left to right: (front row) Mary Hicks, Mr. Rekus, Mary Chaponis, Eddie Ambrose, and Olga G. Nowak; (back row) Doris Mach, Bernice G. Usanis, Joe Satula, John Melinaushas, Joe Rusilowicz, Walter Pavasaris, Danny Usanis, Ed Pluhas, John Kuckailes, Helen M. Ausaska, and unknown. (St. Andrew's Church.)

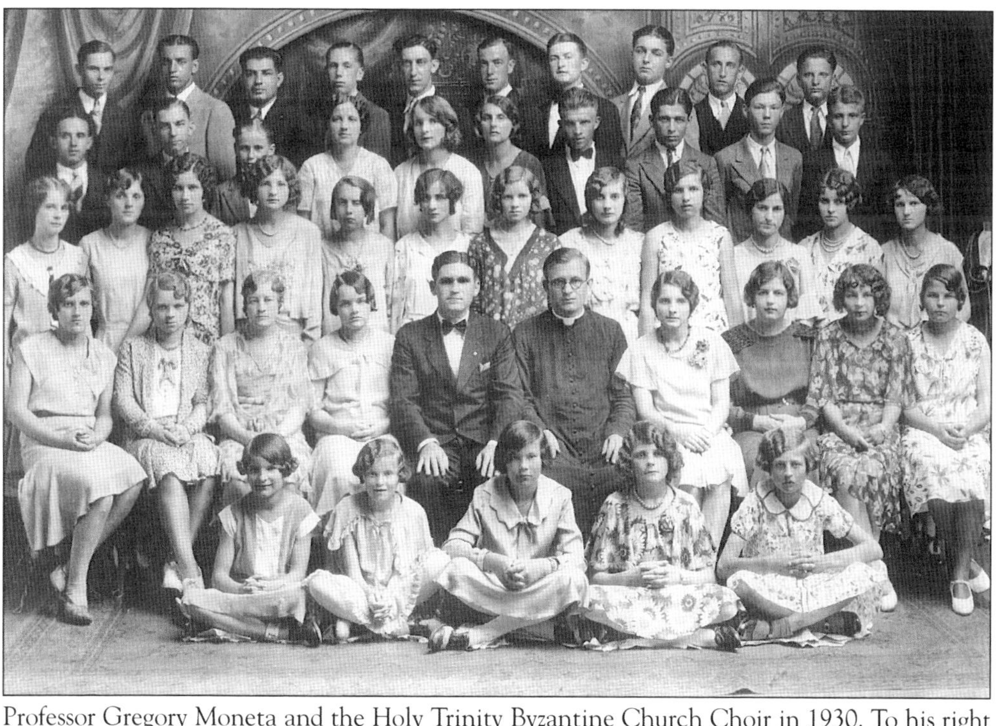

Professor Gregory Moneta and the Holy Trinity Byzantine Church Choir in 1930. To his right is the Reverend Ivan Romza. (Mary Grip.)

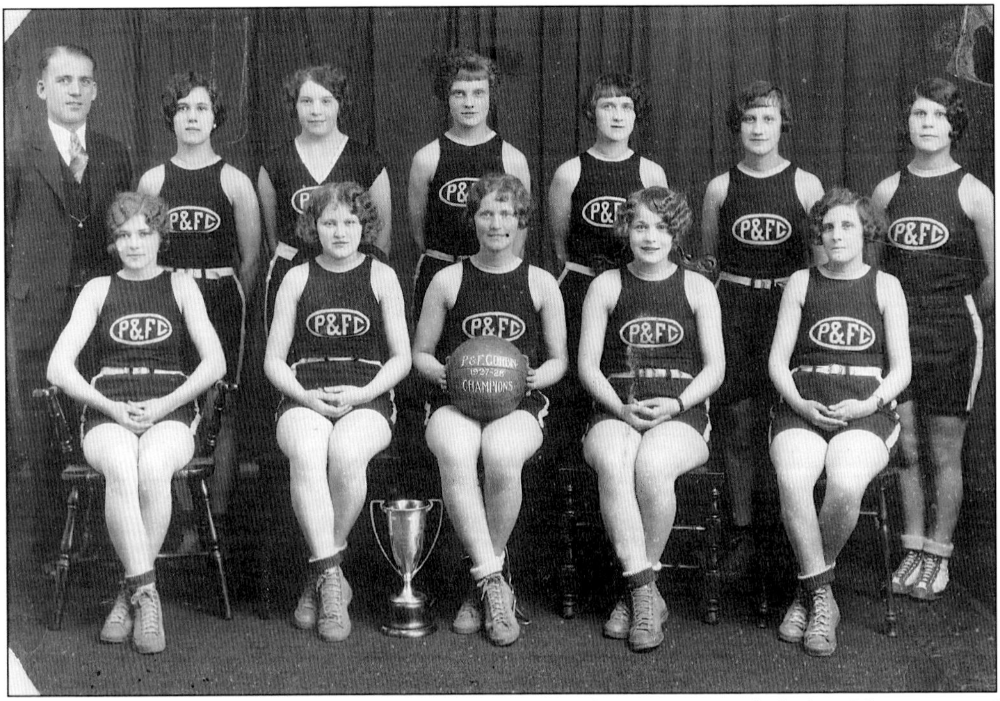

The P. and F. Corbin women's basketball team. This team equaled the University of Connecticut Lady Huskies feat of 1995. They won the championship in the 1927–28 season. (Robert Clinch.)

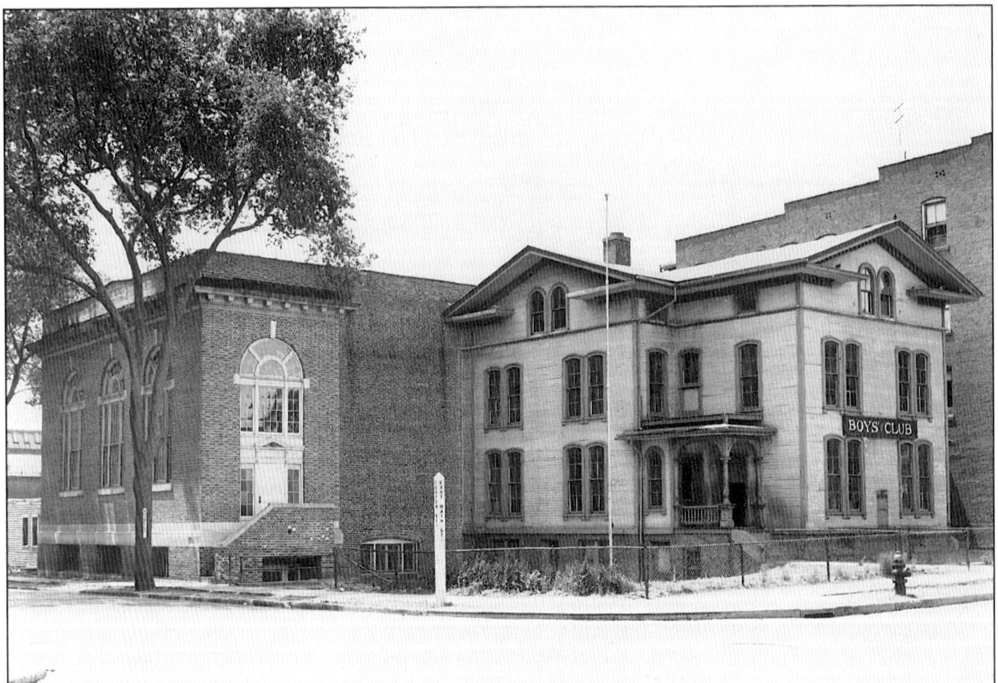

The corner of East Main and Center Streets. Before the current Boys' and Girls' Club was built on Washington Street, the building on the left was considered new. (Fred Hedeler.)

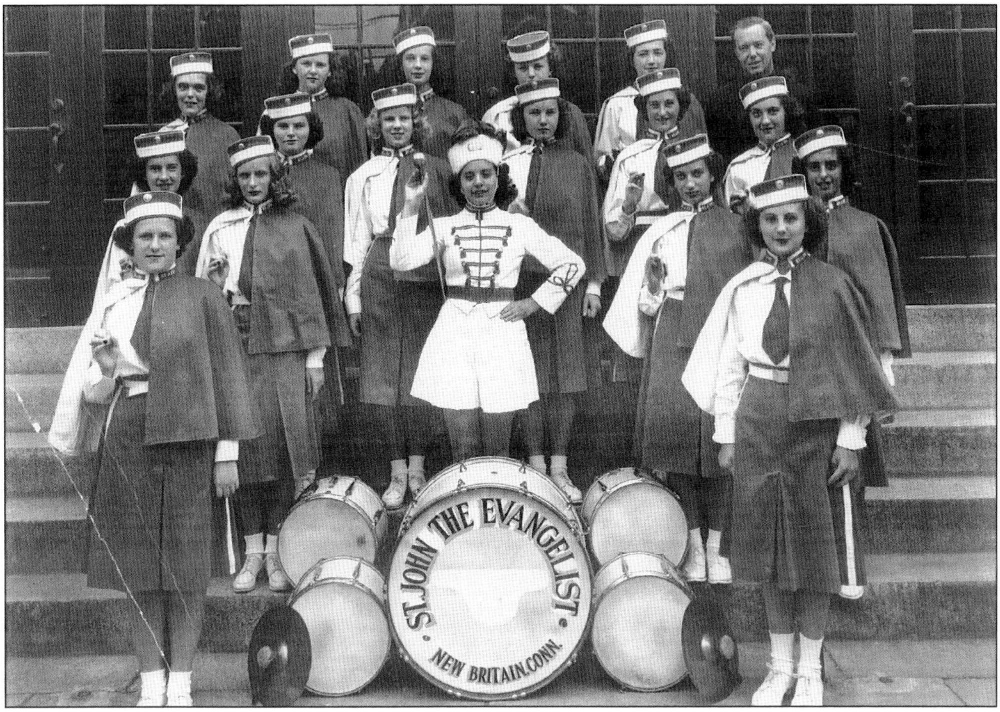

St. John the Evangelist corps, whose drum majorette would later become superintendent of schools (Dr. Marie Gustin). Fife and drum corps have been sources of entertainment for over fifty years. Below are the ladies of Holy Cross, winners of seven state championships. (Joan Eumendi Budnick/Louise Krawiec Saunders.)

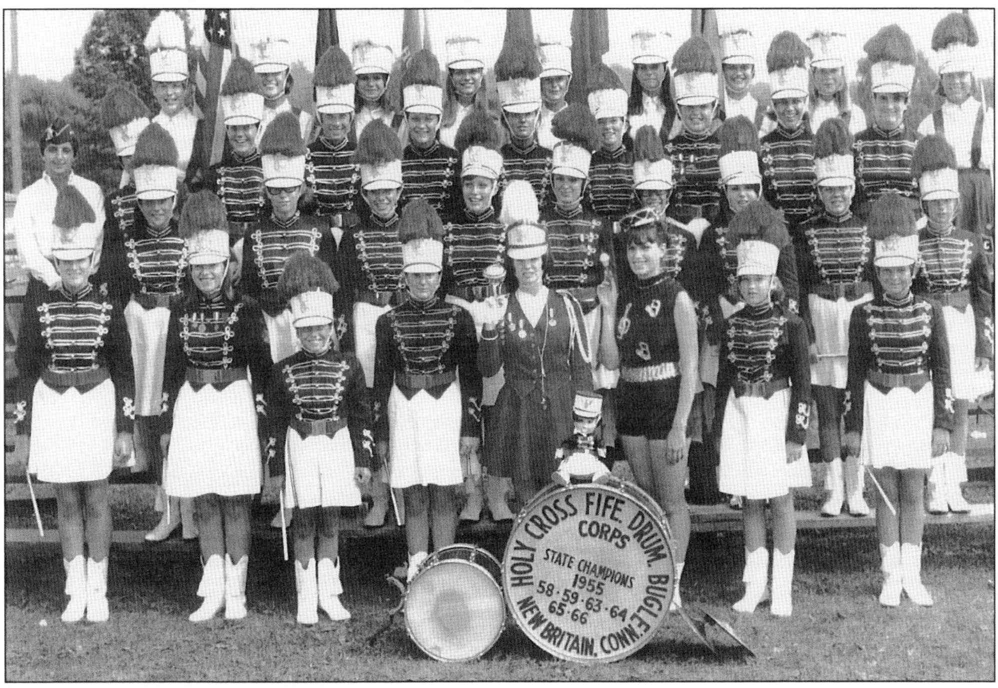

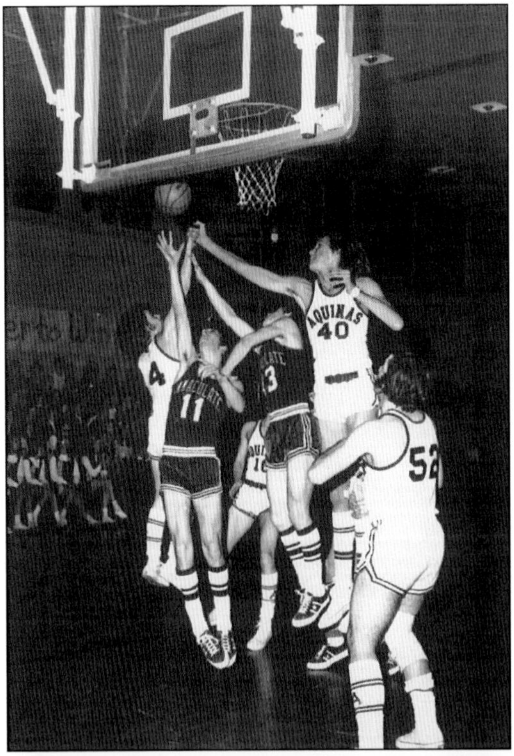

St. Thomas Aquinas High School student/athletes in 1973. Chuck McKeon (#40) displays his skill along with teammates Bill Gertz (#4), Jay McLaughlin (#52), and Tom Farrell (#10). (Charles McKeon.)

The Stanley Bobcats, runners up in the 1950 Junior City Recreation Tournament. Pictured are: (front row) J. Stuart, W. Soares, E. Aparo, R. Siderowf, J. Stuart; (back row) P. Cenate, E. Mercier, R. Lindgren, N. Koppel, and D. Depianta. (Local History Room, NBPL.)

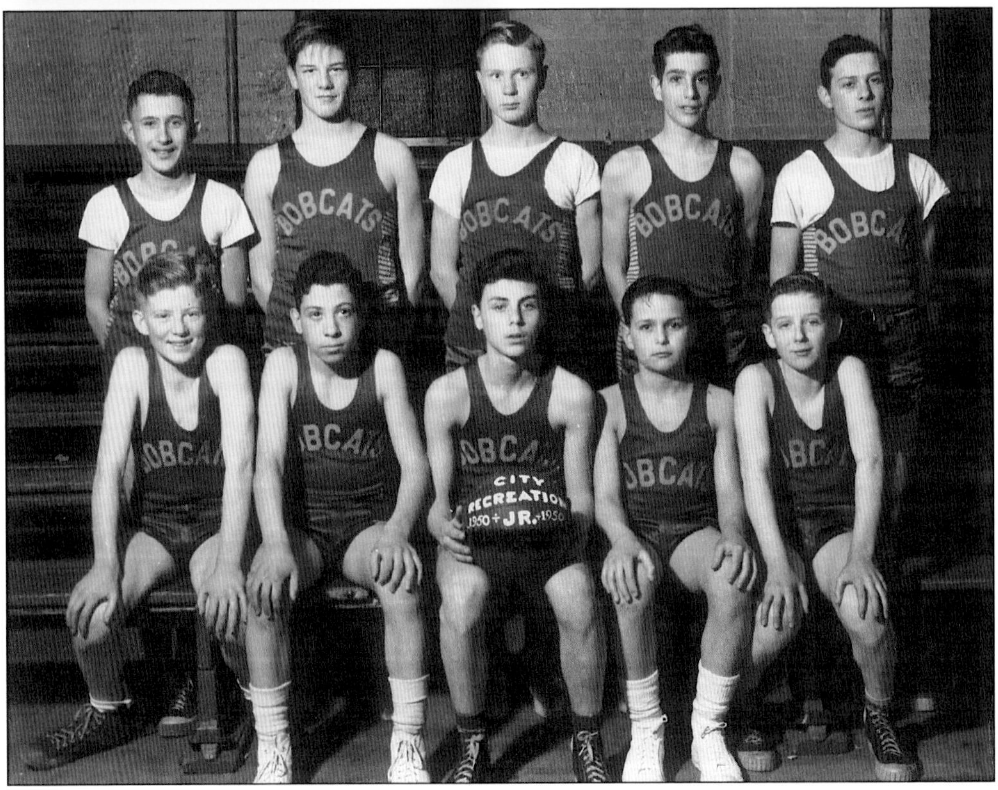

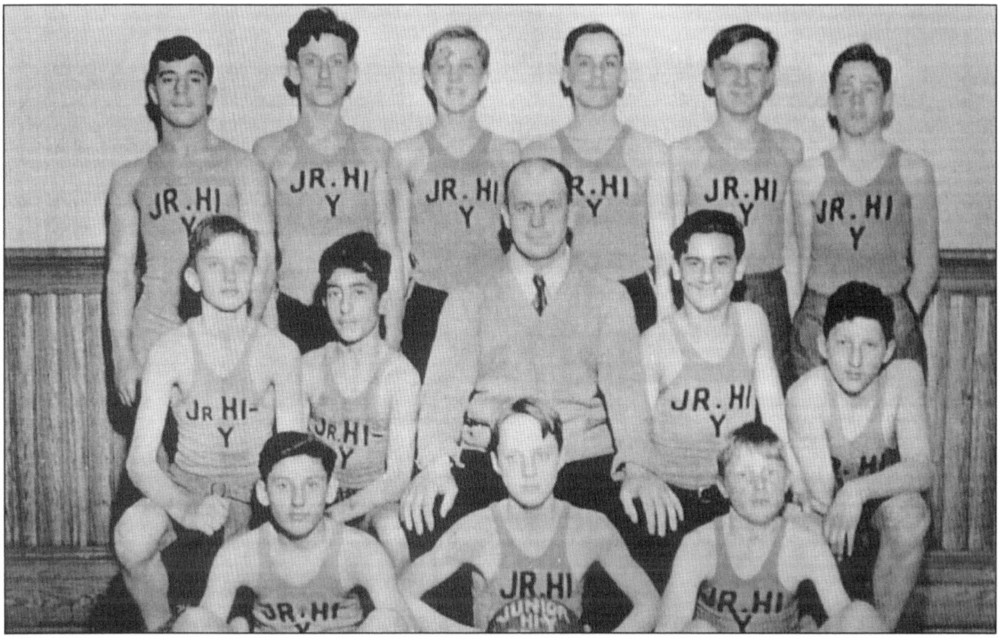

The 1935–36 Junior High "Y" team, made up of boys from the city's junior high schools who belonged to the YMCA. Team members shown are: (front row) Frank Casa, Bob Smith, and Carl Cellezz; (middle row) George Colwick, George Lazar, Coach Charley Miller, Mike Borselle, and Francis Joyce; (back row) Jimmy Dooman, Mike Colwick, Don Colwick, Paul Basile, unknown, and ? Callahan. (Mike Borselle.)

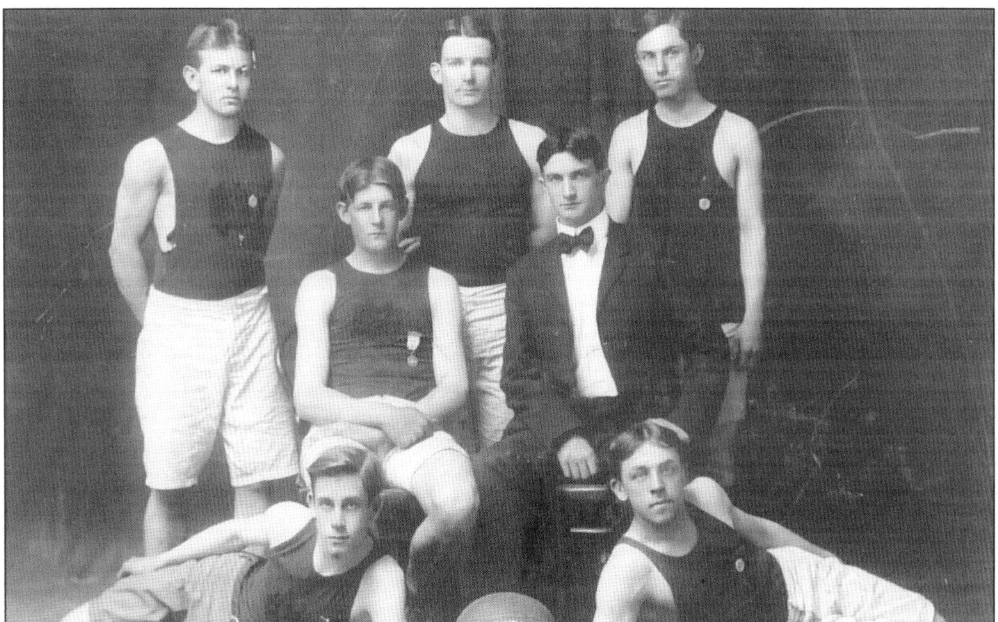

Members of the 1906 YMCA championship basketball team sporting their medals. It is possible that the art of dribbling was developed in New Britain by "Bert" Loomis, who took basketball founder James Naismith's rules one step further—if a player dribbled, he was not running with the ball and could not be penalized. (Local History Room, NBPL.)

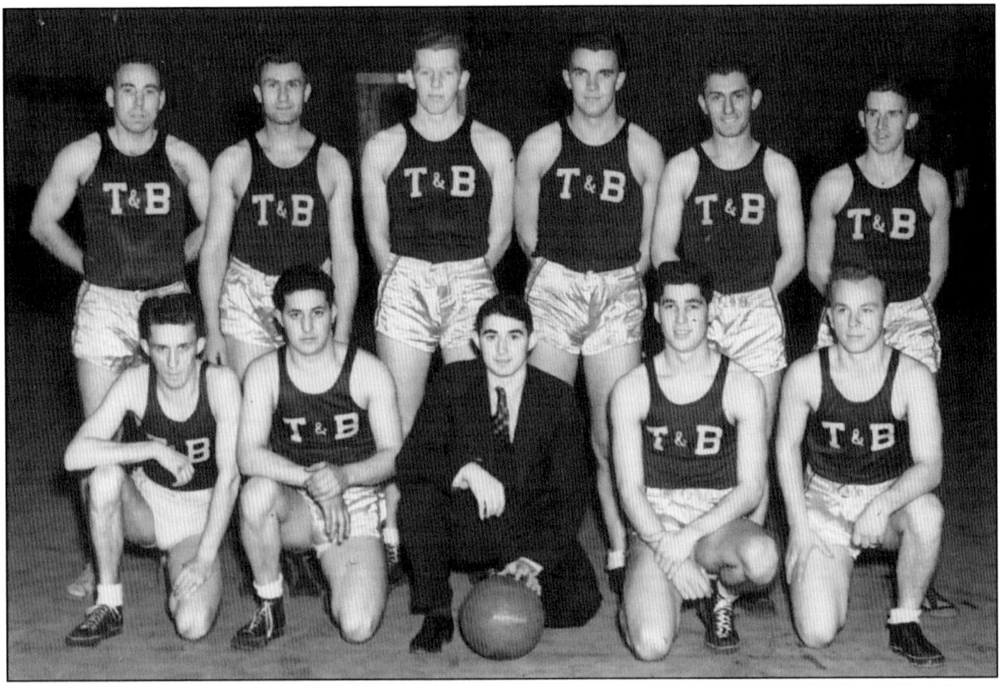

"Dusty" Tuttle and the Bailey squad on March 26, 1938. The popularity of basketball did not exist solely in the city's athletic clubs. Industrial leagues were popular for years. Below is the Landers, Frary and Clark team on March 31, 1938. (Local History Room, NBPL.)

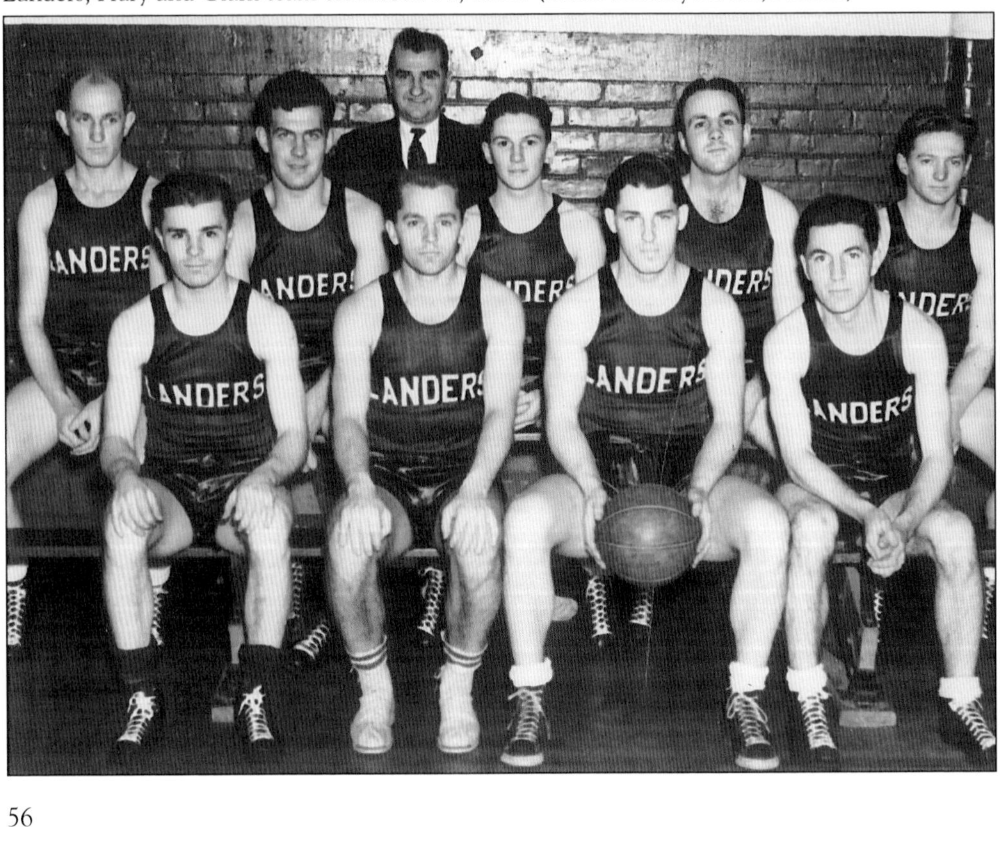

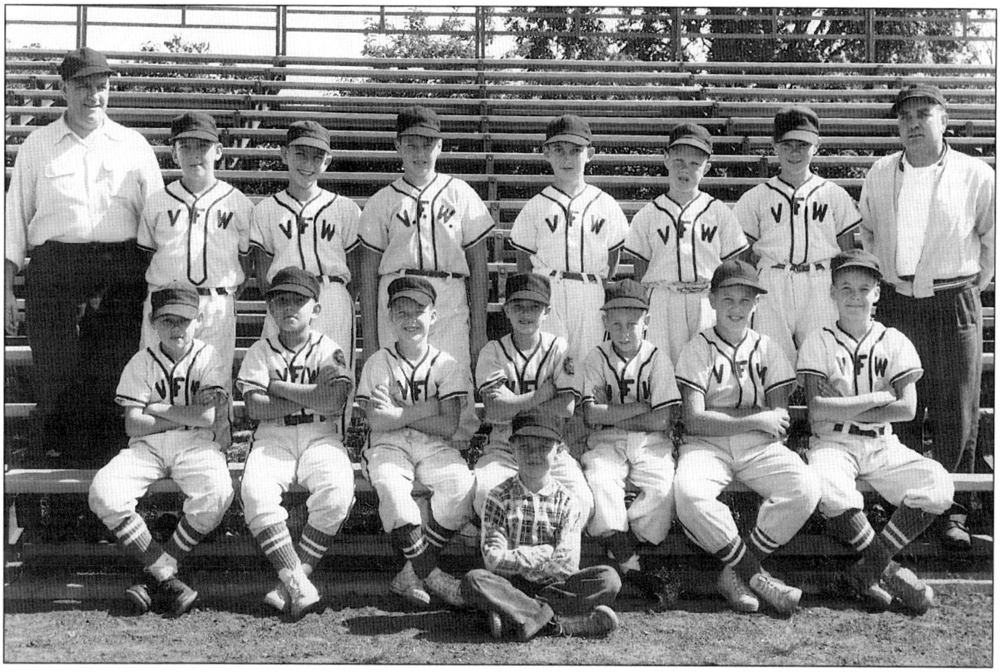

The V.F.W. Tigers. Clubs and organizations also sponsored sports teams. The earliest recorded baseball team in the city was the Phoenix Baseball Club of New Britain, organized on May 8, 1866. (Christine Cocores Balint.)

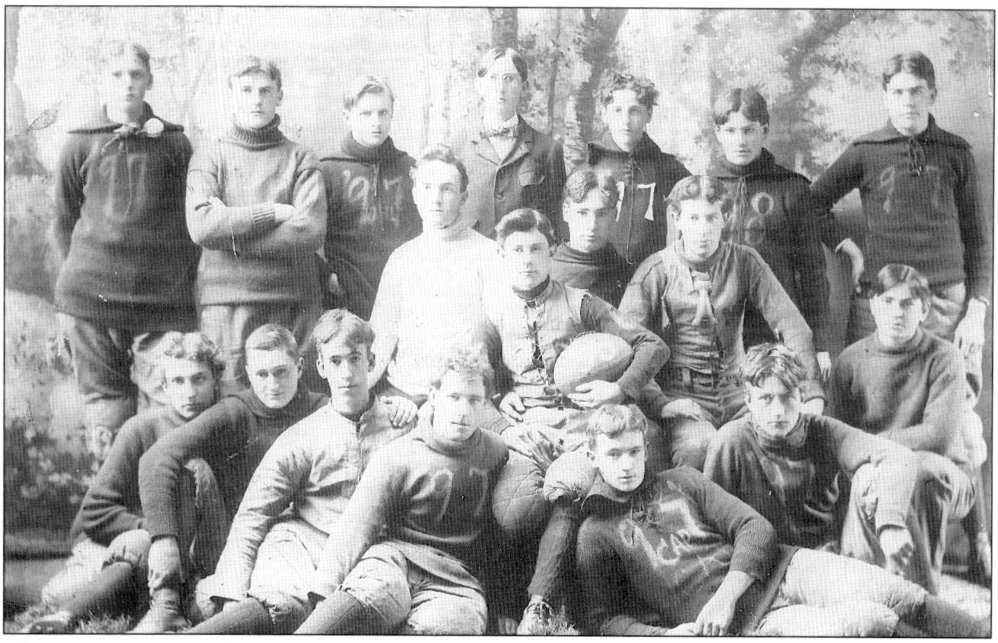

The New Britain High School football team of 1897. These athletes relied on padded knickers and thick jerseys—a far cry from the elaborate equipment used to protect players today. Prominent citizens William H. Hart, president of Stanley Works, and A. J. Sloper, president of New Britain National Bank, absorbed the costs of purchasing equipment in the 1890s. (Local History Room, NBPL.)

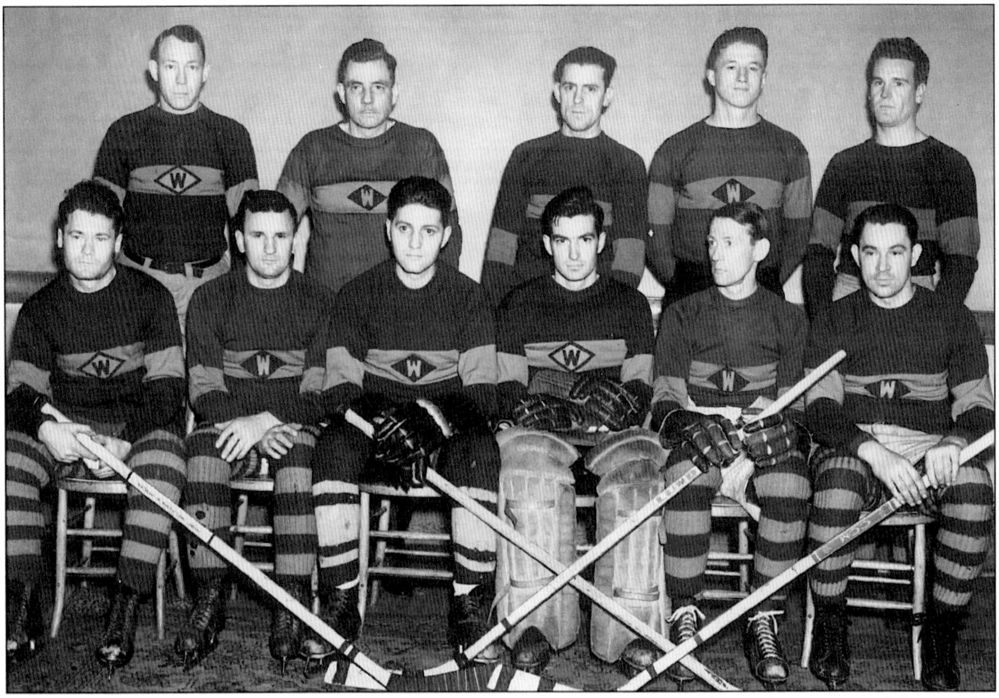

The Wanderers Hockey Club. This was among the incredible number of sporting clubs in the city in 1938. Ice hockey does not enjoy the same popularity here today, as the city lacks a public rink. (*Herald* photograph file.)

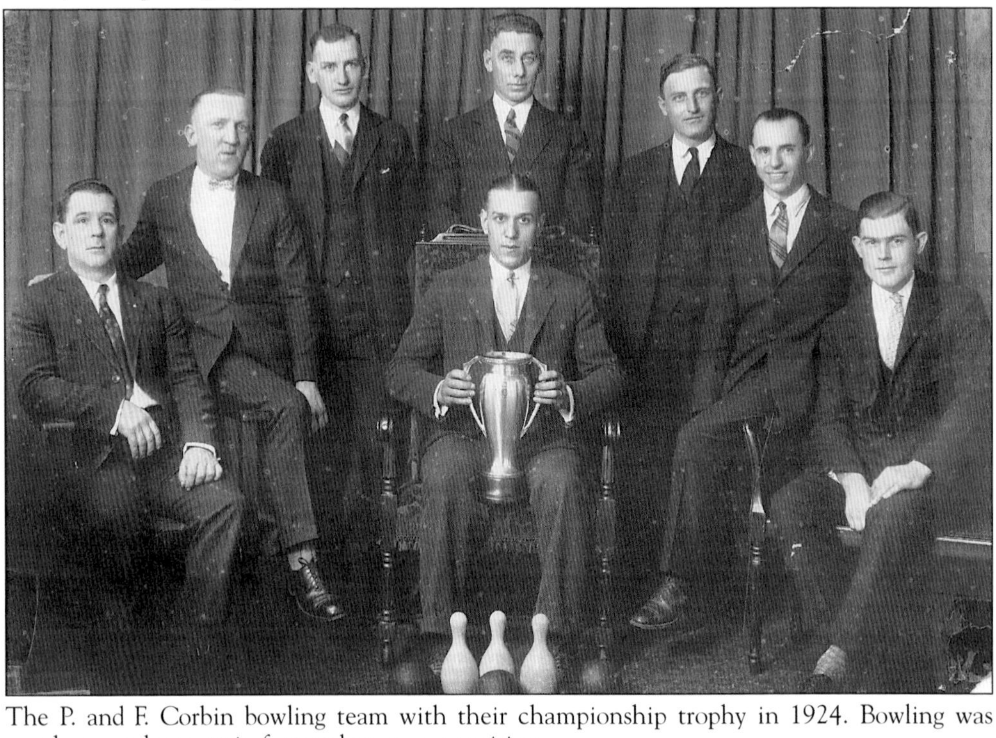

The P. and F. Corbin bowling team with their championship trophy in 1924. Bowling was another popular sport in factory league competition.

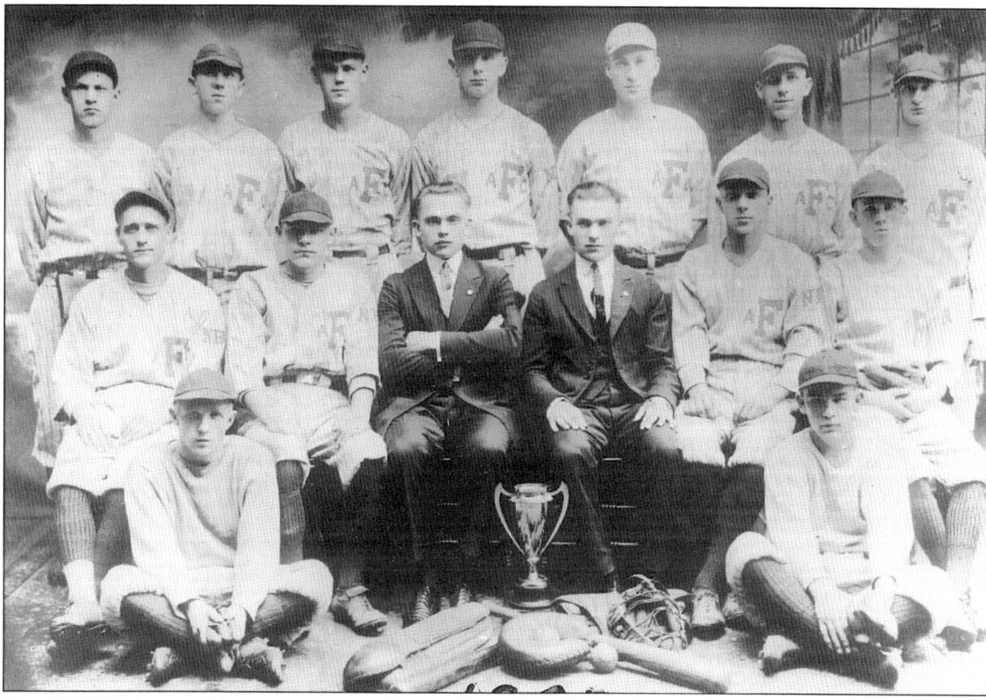

The 1923 Falcons. This was among the city's many ethnic teams. Shown are, from left to right: (front row) Mssrs. Nurczyk, Pytel, Mikolajczyk, Januszewski, Coach Cabay, Sidlik, Raczkowski, Dzwonkowski, Matusiak, and Raczek; (back row) Dr. Lekston, Marut, Cichowski, Radziewicz, Koboski, Chudecki, Buslewicz, Sytulek, Baczewski, Milewski, Kowalczyk, Kowalewski, and Niklinski. (*Herald* photograph file.)

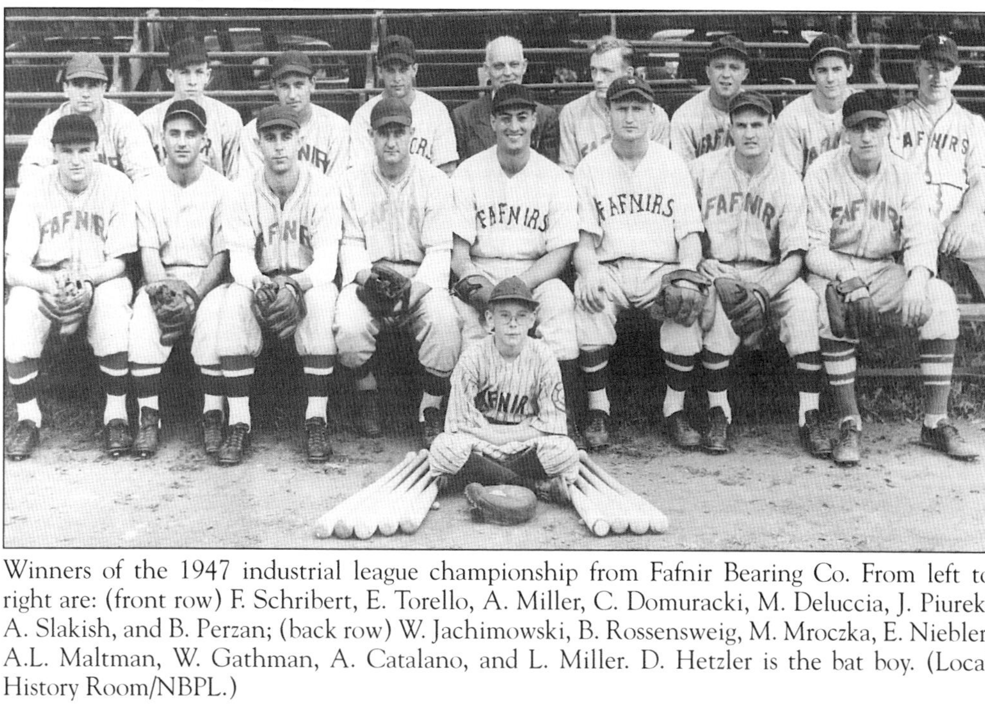

Winners of the 1947 industrial league championship from Fafnir Bearing Co. From left to right are: (front row) F. Schribert, E. Torello, A. Miller, C. Domuracki, M. Deluccia, J. Piurek, A. Slakish, and B. Perzan; (back row) W. Jachimowski, B. Rossensweig, M. Mroczka, E. Niebler, A.L. Maltman, W. Gathman, A. Catalano, and L. Miller. D. Hetzler is the bat boy. (Local History Room/NBPL.)

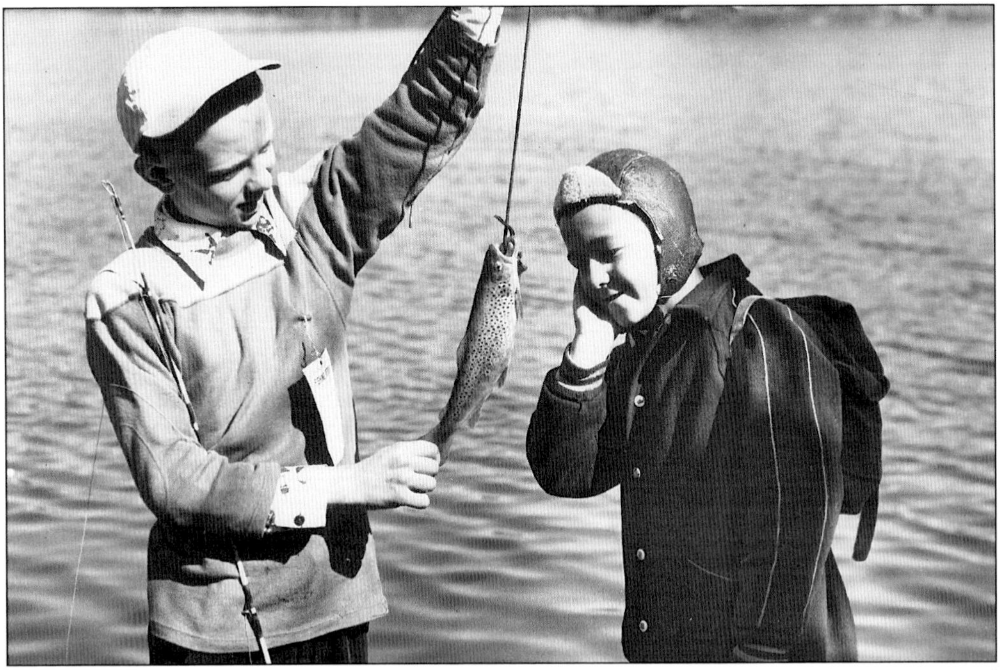

"That's the one I almost caught!" A local youth displays his catch during the 1952 annual fishing derby. Once known as the Fishing Rodeo, based on the National Fishing Rodeo, this event was sponsored by the Municipal Recreation Department. (Local History Room, NBPL.)

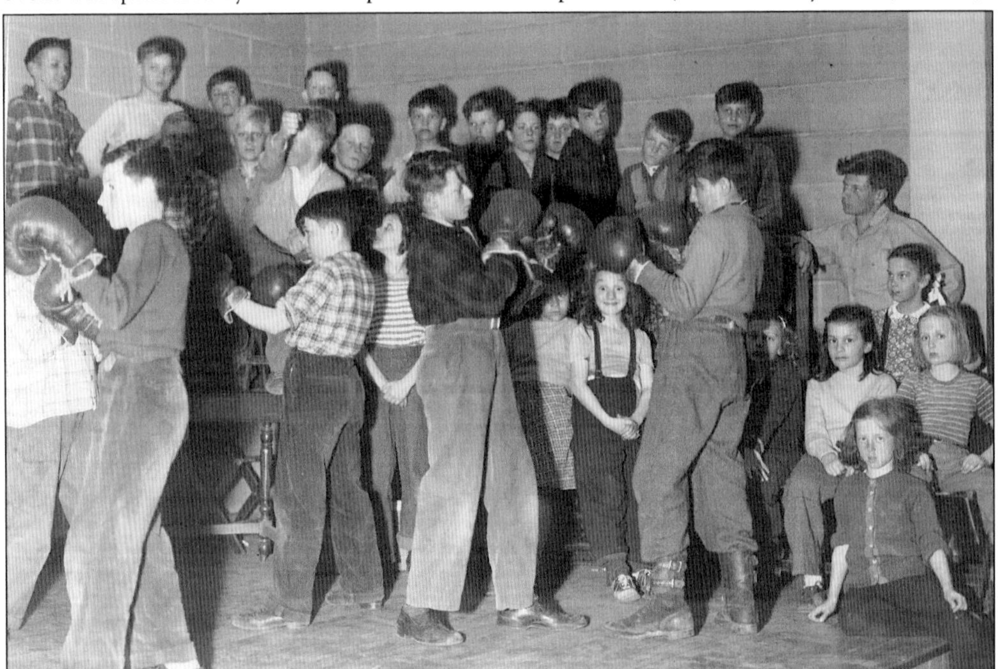

Municipal recreational boxing. With dreams of Jack Dempsey and Joe Lewis, these young boxers spar during a municipal recreation program. The program was discontinued in 1948 due to apprehension of possible injury. (Local History Room, NBPL.)

Three

Where We Worked

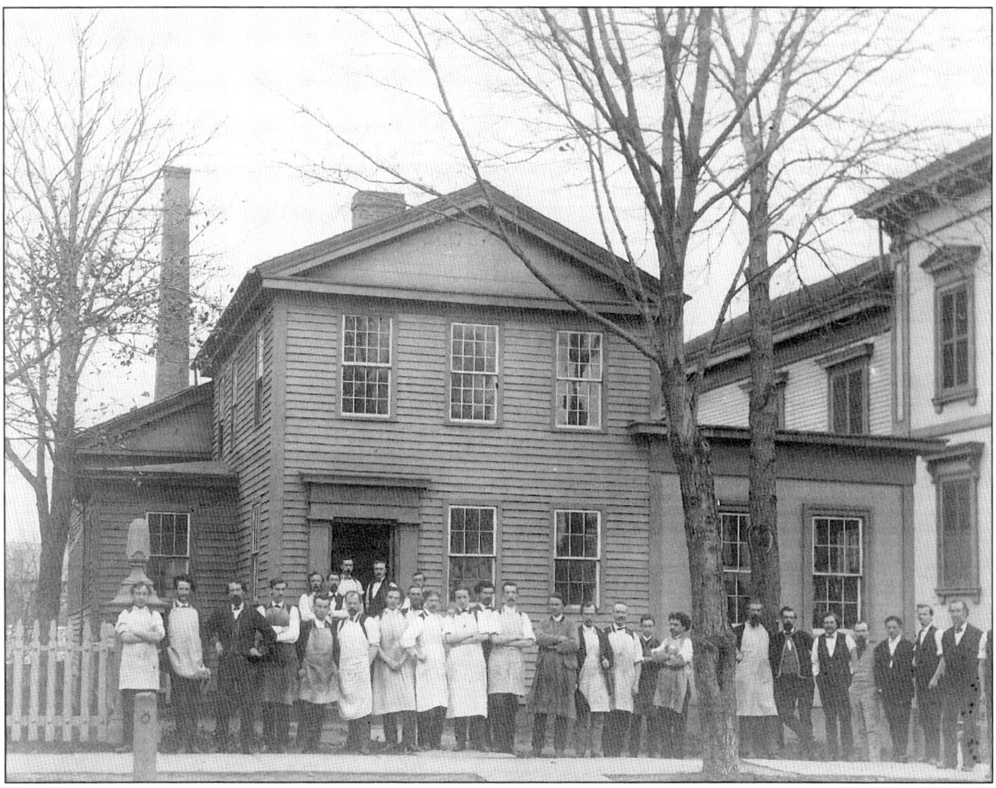

Employees of the Churchill and Dana Jewelry factory in November 1871. New Britain native William Burnham North, born in 1797, started this business, which changed names several times before becoming Porter and Dyson in 1893. The building was located on Main Street, south of the South Congregational Church. The firm, which made jewelry for the likes of Tiffany and Co. of New York, closed in the early 1970s. (Local History Room, NBPL.)

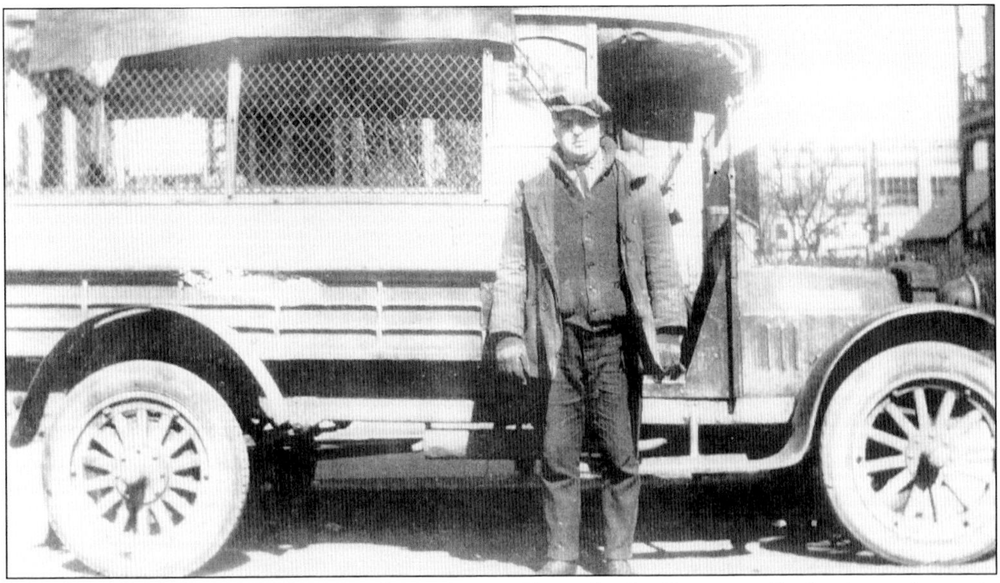

Postal service worker Joseph J. Lynch, in front of his vehicle. Occasionally, business does mix with pleasure—part of Mr. Lynch's route included the American Hosiery Co., where he met his future wife, Olga Sabottke. They were married in 1923. (Lois Lynch Blomstrann.)

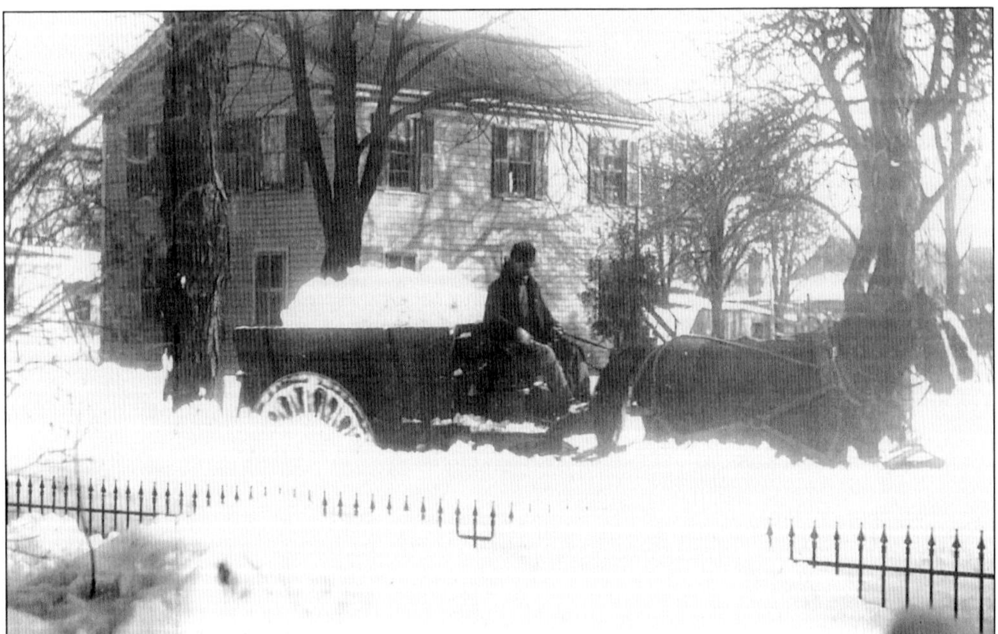

Old fashioned two-horse-powered snow removal on Chestnut Street. On March 12, 1888, a blizzard struck the area. Factories closed, telephone and telegraph wires were downed, and even mail came to a halt. (Marie Ruschkowsky Venberg.)

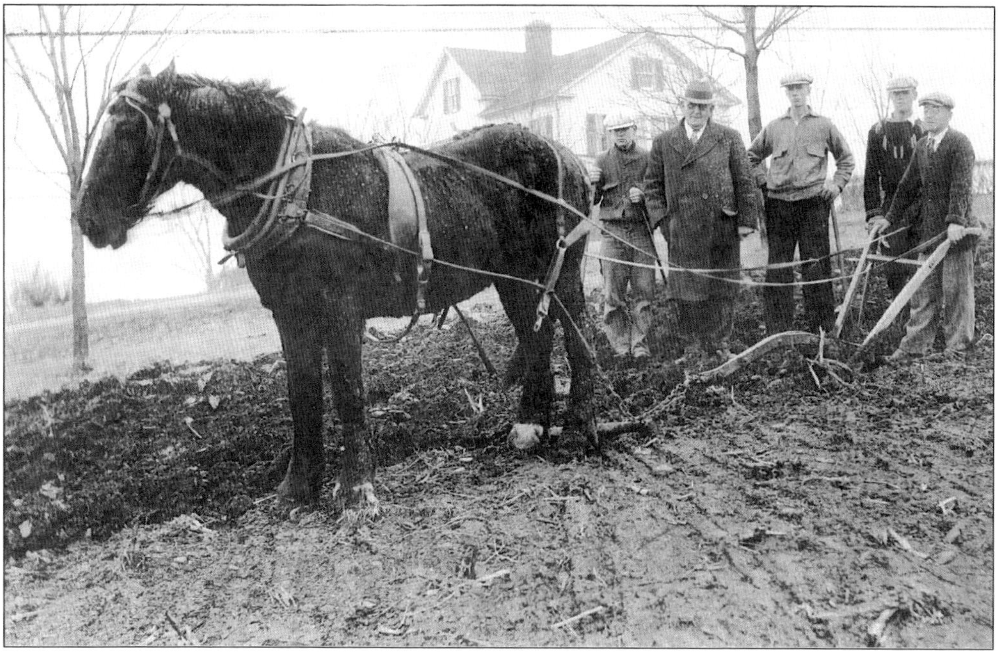

Clearing a field at the Klingberg Children's Home. The scene reminds us that agriculture once played a more important part in New Britain's history. (Klingberg Family Center.)

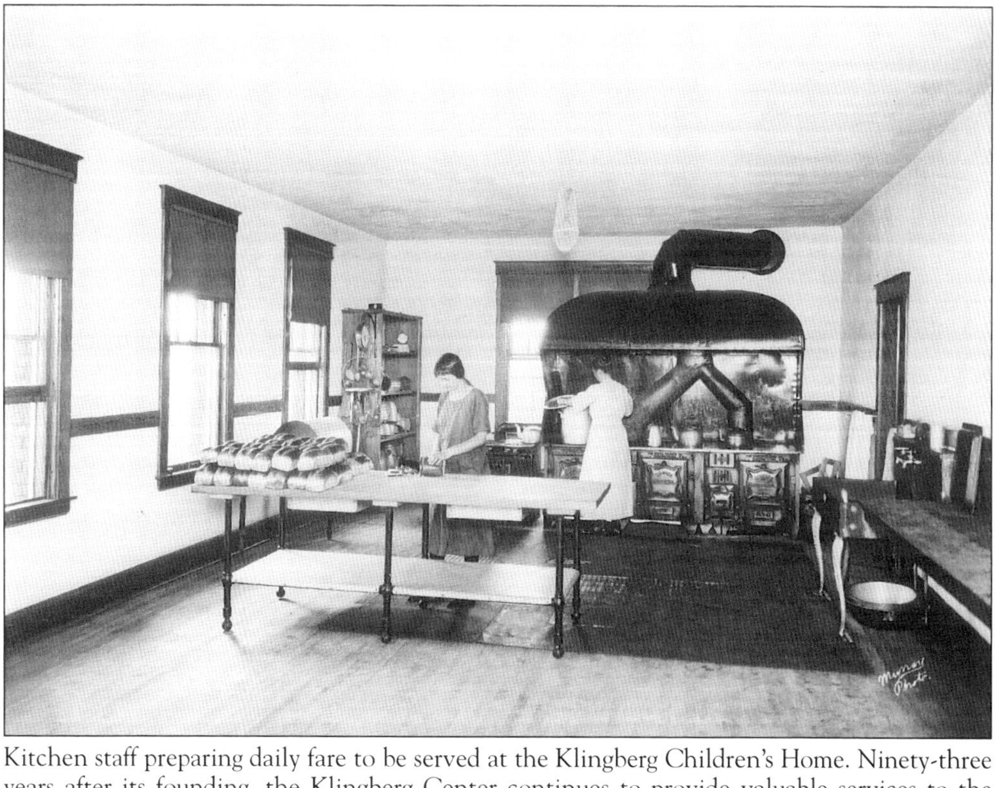

Kitchen staff preparing daily fare to be served at the Klingberg Children's Home. Ninety-three years after its founding, the Klingberg Center continues to provide valuable services to the community. (Klingberg Family Center)

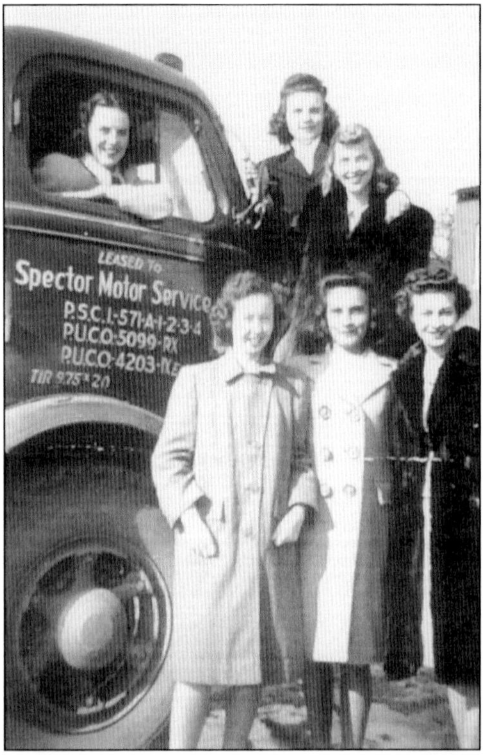

Employees of Spector Motor Services. Proving a woman's work is not always in the home, this 1942 photograph shows Artemese Blanchette (in the cab) and co-workers Lorraine Rouskie, Pat Anderson, Mary Pampuro, Mary Grazlavich, and Rosalie Albanese. (Artemese Blanchette McKeon.)

Fafnir Bearing Co. employees receiving checks during a strike. Donald Hamm, guard, and Art Glaeser, payroll supervisor, look on as Mage Jurewicz, Nancy Clark, and Terry Podogorski distribute checks from the John Street plant. (Nancy Clark.)

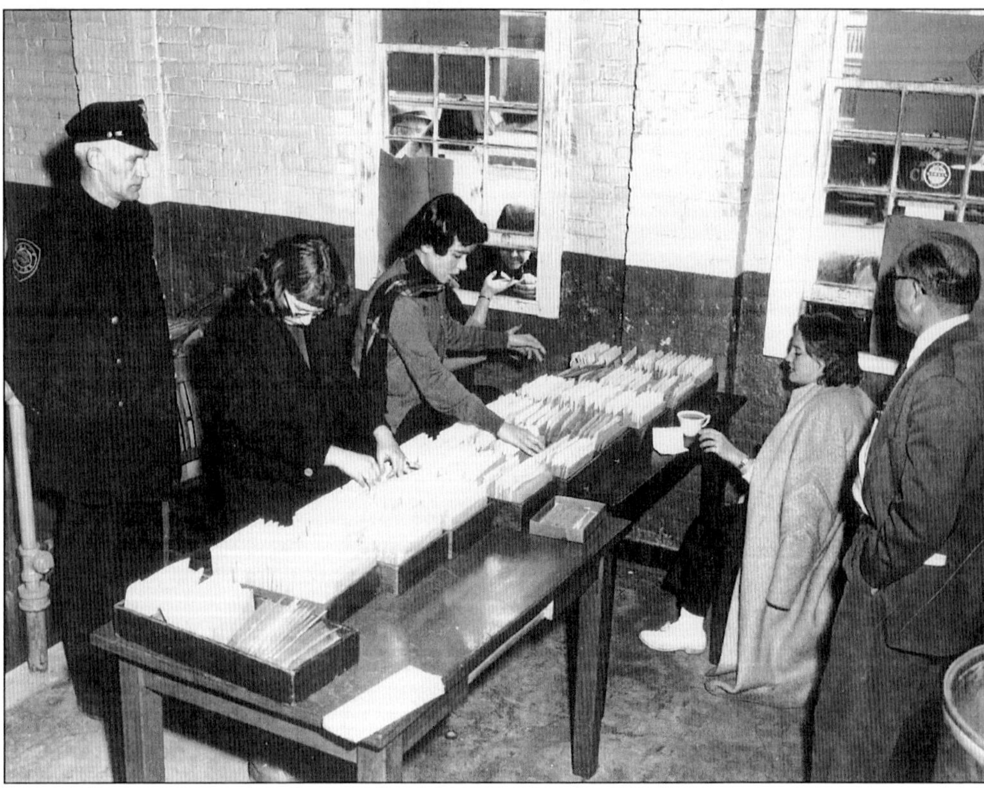

Best friends. Samuel M. Davidson (left) and Alexander Leventhal met as teenagers. In 1911, they formed what would become one of the city's most successful businesses. Today, the D. and L. Venture Corporation, located on John Downey Drive, remains family owned and operated. (Philip Davidson.)

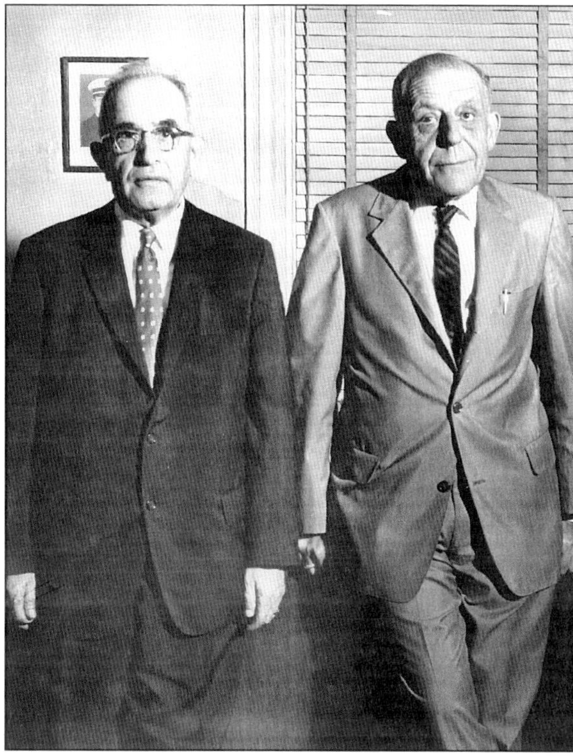

The Fair, Davidson and Leventhal's first store. Mary Reardon, head of the drug department, is shown in 1947 with two employees. The store contained a marvelous array of goods—from thimbles to shoe polish. As the business expanded, concentration was placed on clothing. By the 1980s, the corporation consisted of D & L, J. Putnam, and Weathervane stores from Maine to Georgia. (Philip Davidson.)

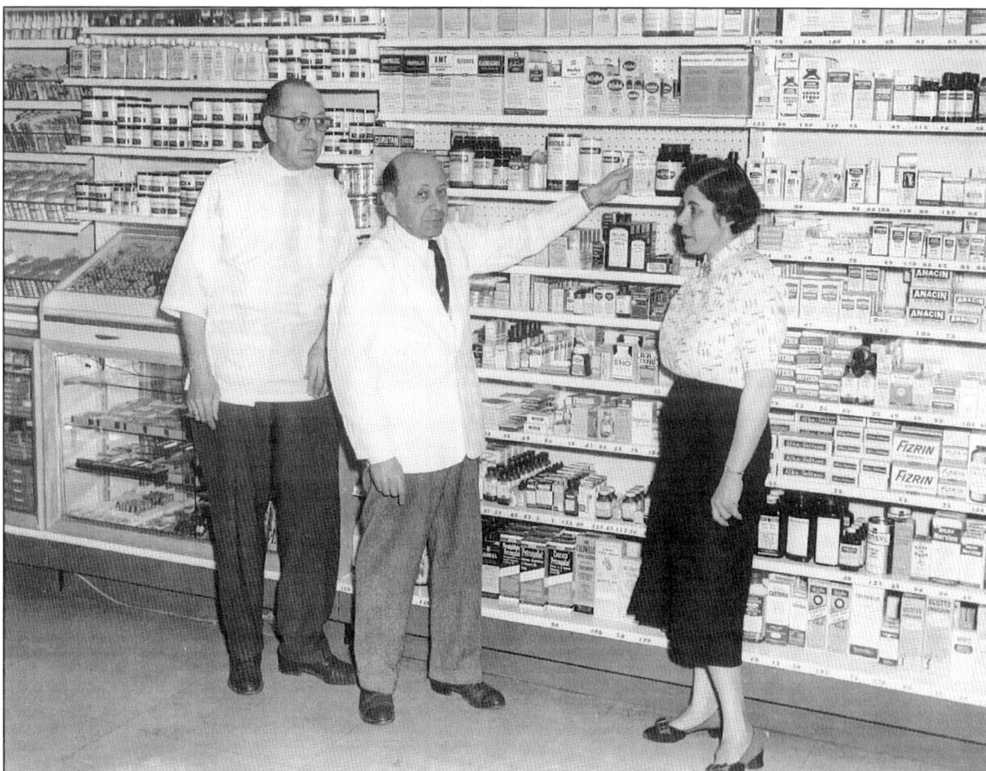

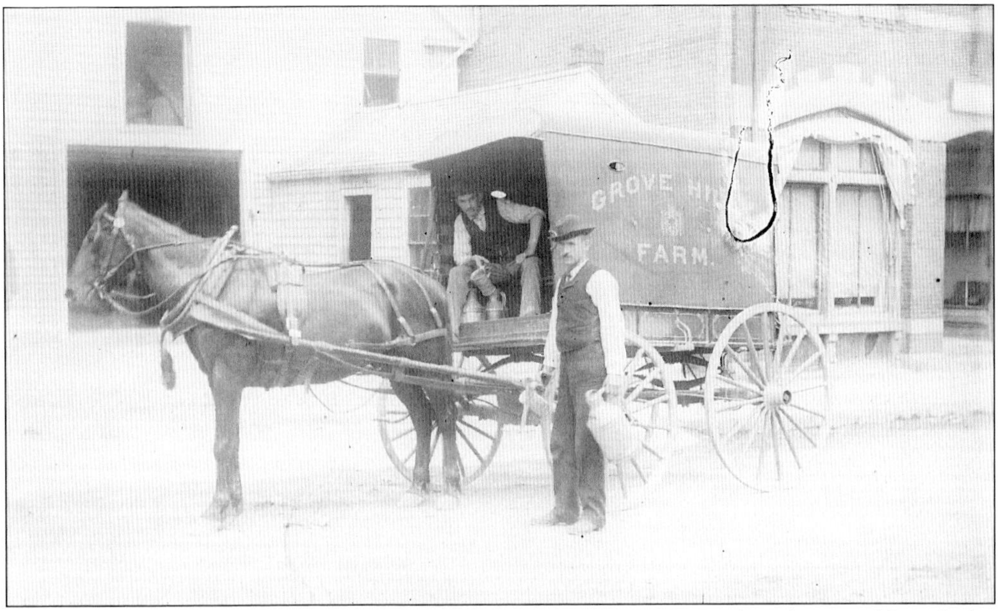

The Grove Hill farm vehicle, another reminder of New Britain's agricultural past. Although the city gained its reputation as a hardware giant, it was once the site of numerous farms, sawmills, and quarries. (Local History Room, NBPL.)

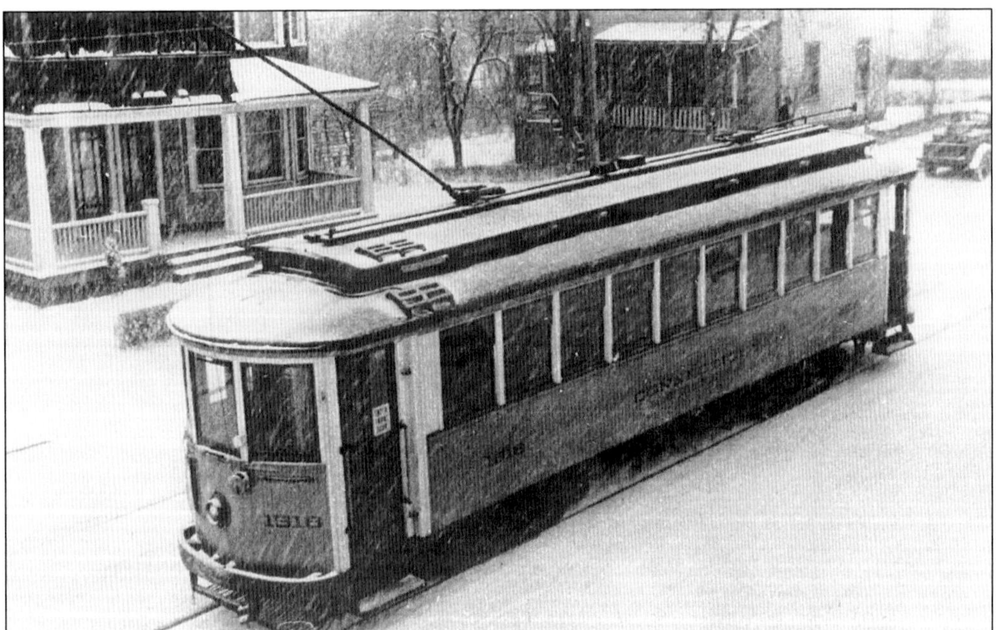

Jubilee Street, c. 1930. By the late 1930s, buses and automobiles would lead to the demise of trolleys. The last local run departed for Hartford at 11:35 pm on April 26, 1937. (Gordon Alling.)

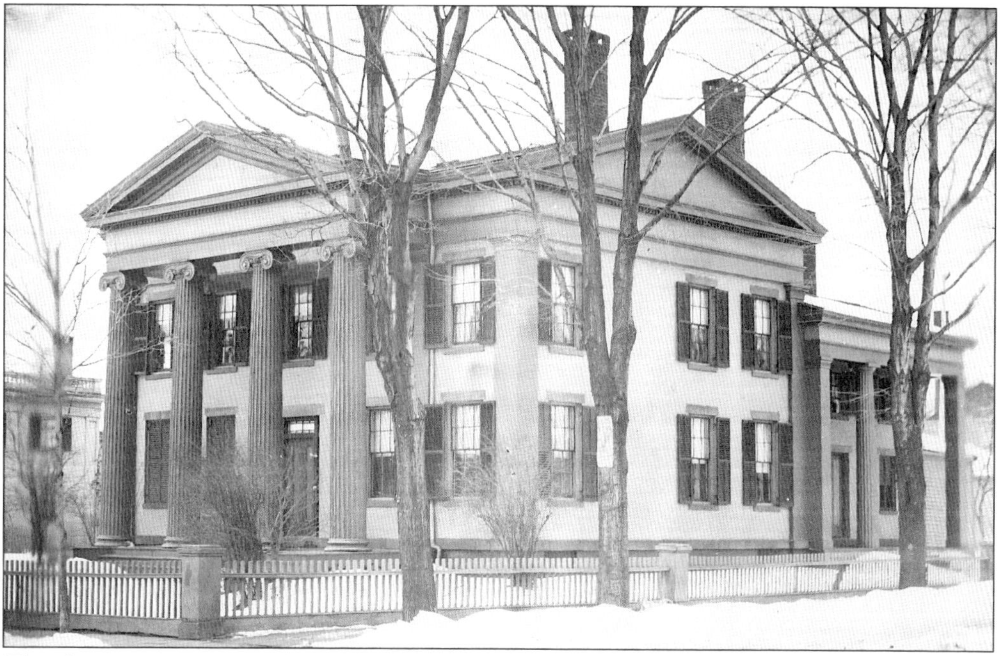

The elegant mansion on the corner of Main and Myrtle Streets. Built by Curtis Whaples in 1837, this mansion, unlike other large homes of the era, escaped the wrecking ball and became the Bassett Hotel. By the 1960s, the structure (shown in the foreground of the photograph below) was almost swallowed by the buildings that wrapped around it. Redevelopment brought about the demolition of this entire area. (Local History Room, NBPL.)

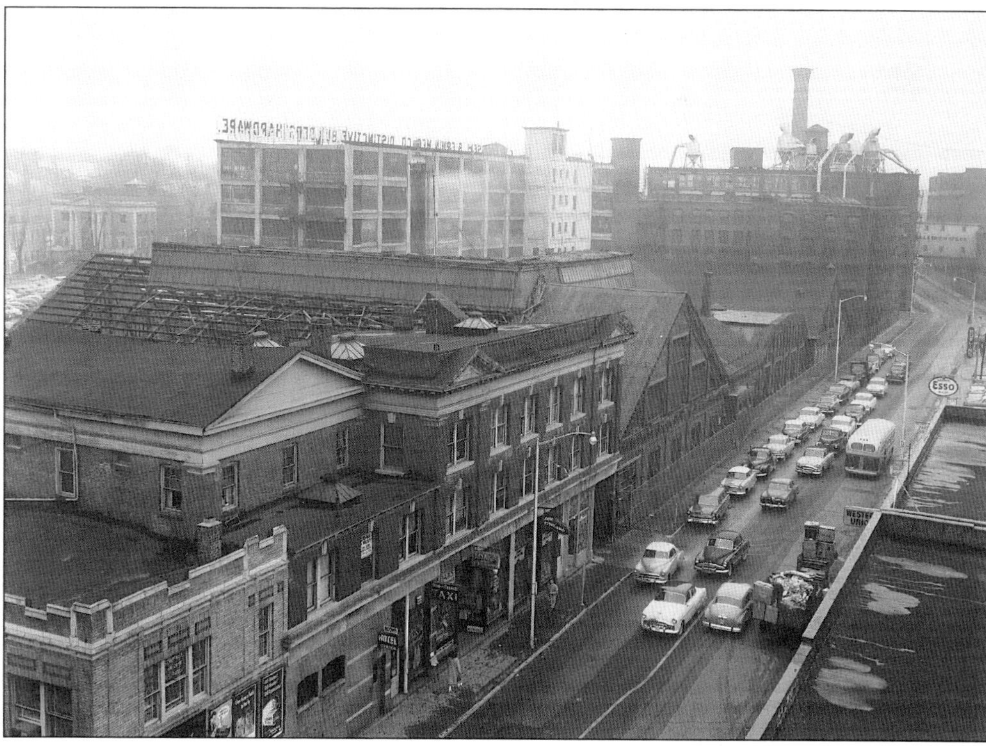

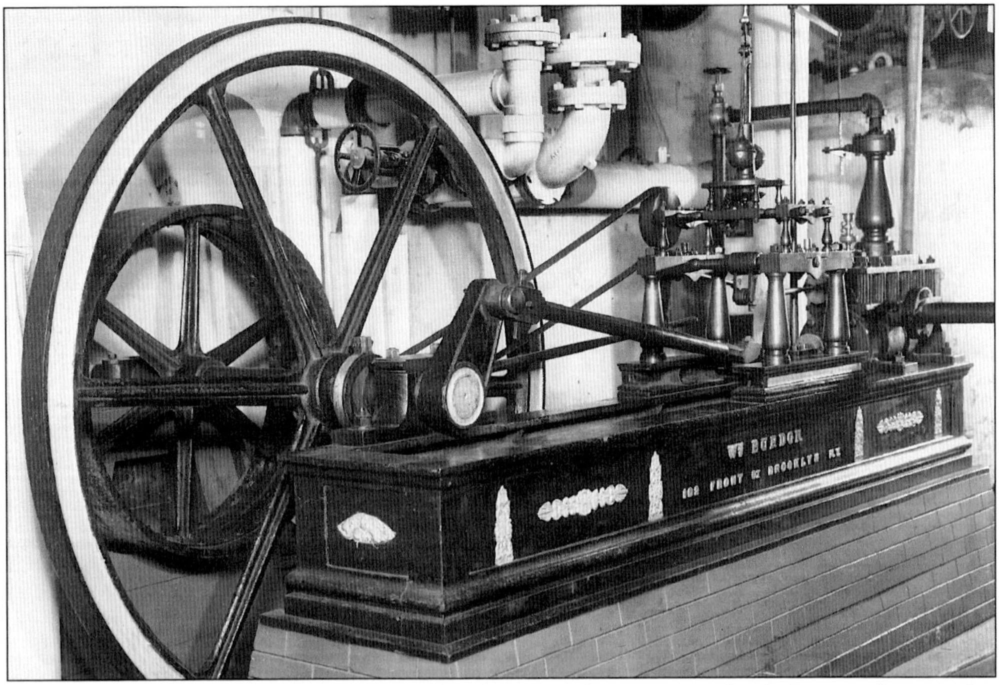

The Stanley Steam Engine. Used by Frederick T. Stanley to power his bolt manufactory, this engine was the first of its kind in New Britain and possibly all of Connecticut. From Stanley's one-shop operation rose the internationally known Stanley Works of today. (Local History Room, NBPL.)

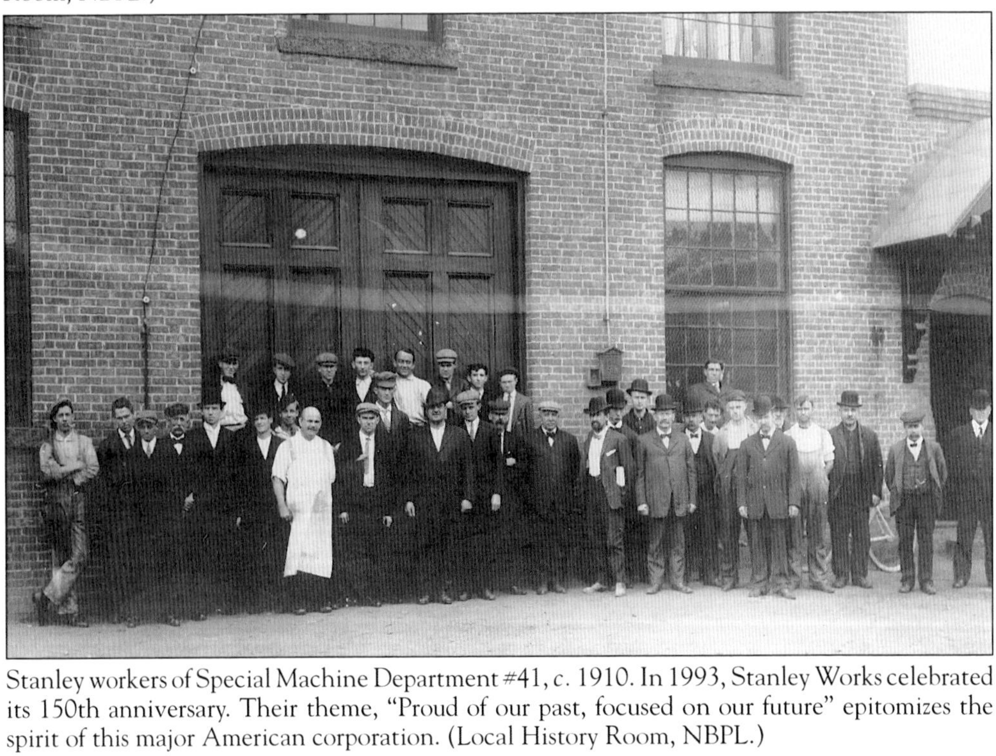

Stanley workers of Special Machine Department #41, *c.* 1910. In 1993, Stanley Works celebrated its 150th anniversary. Their theme, "Proud of our past, focused on our future" epitomizes the spirit of this major American corporation. (Local History Room, NBPL.)

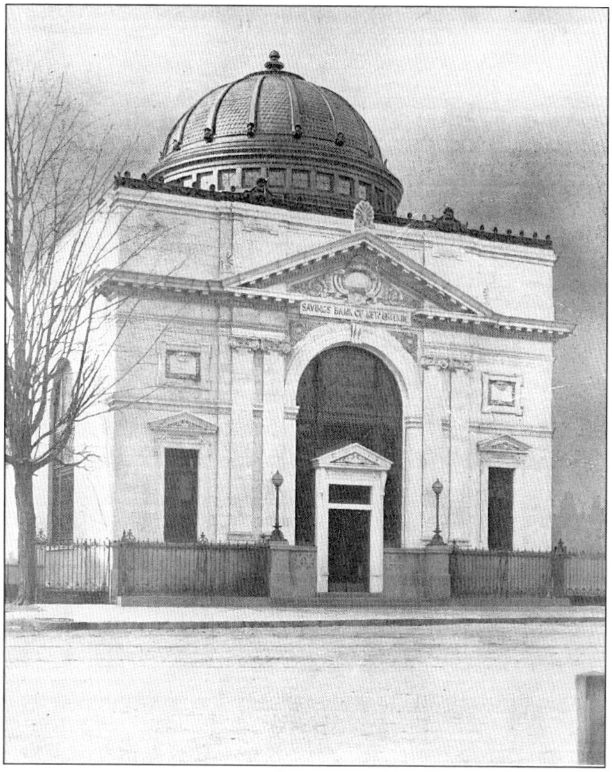

The Savings Bank of New Britain. The bank, organized in July 1862, opened this ornate, domed building in 1902. It was previously located in a narrow brick building, later the site of the John A. Andrews Co. on Main Street. (Local History Room, NBPL.)

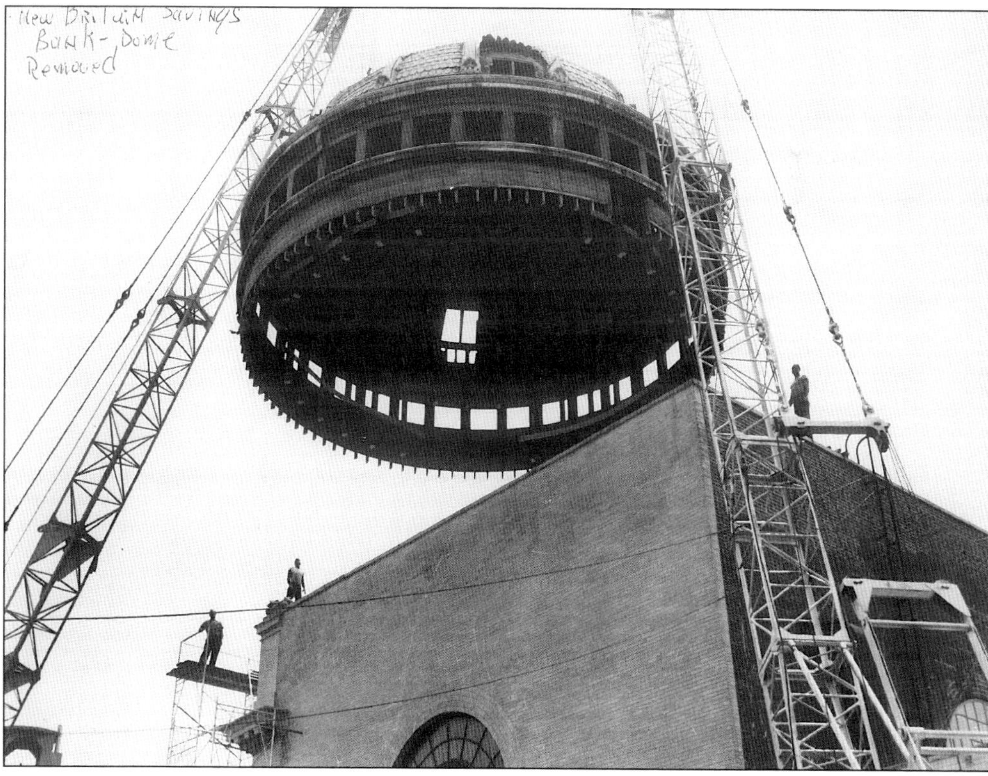

The dome of the Savings Bank being removed. By the 1960s, plans were made to modernize the bank, which included removing much of the ornamentation and the dome. Now called the American Saving Bank, the corporation's deposits passed the one billion mark in 1995. (*Herald* photograph file.)

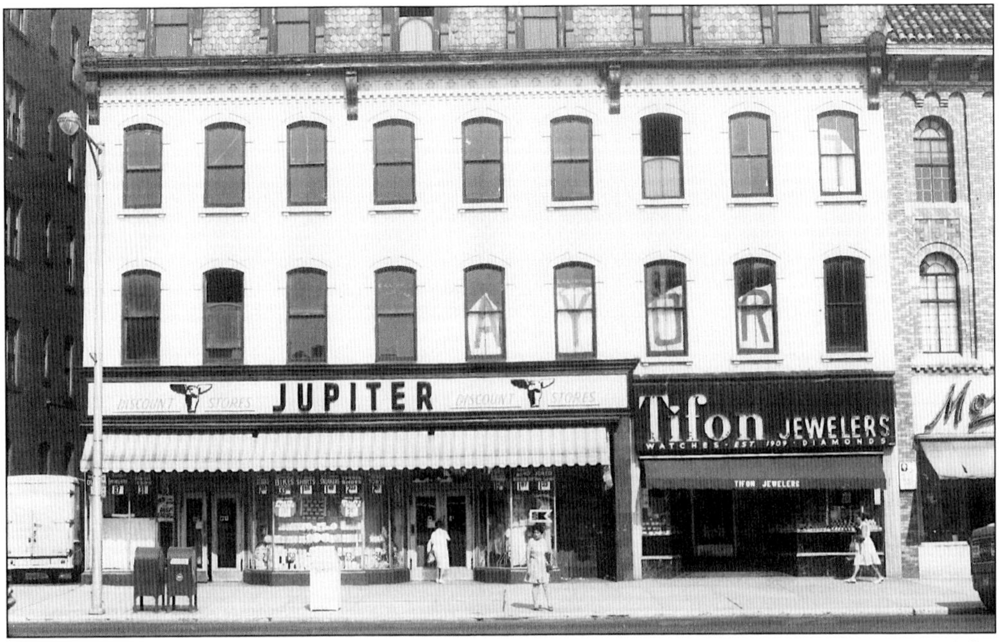

Jupiter Discount Store and Tifon Jewelers, located on the east side of Main Street. Some of the oldest buildings in the downtown area were recycled for retail use. Often beautiful architectural details were hidden behind promotional signage. (Local History Room, NBPL.)

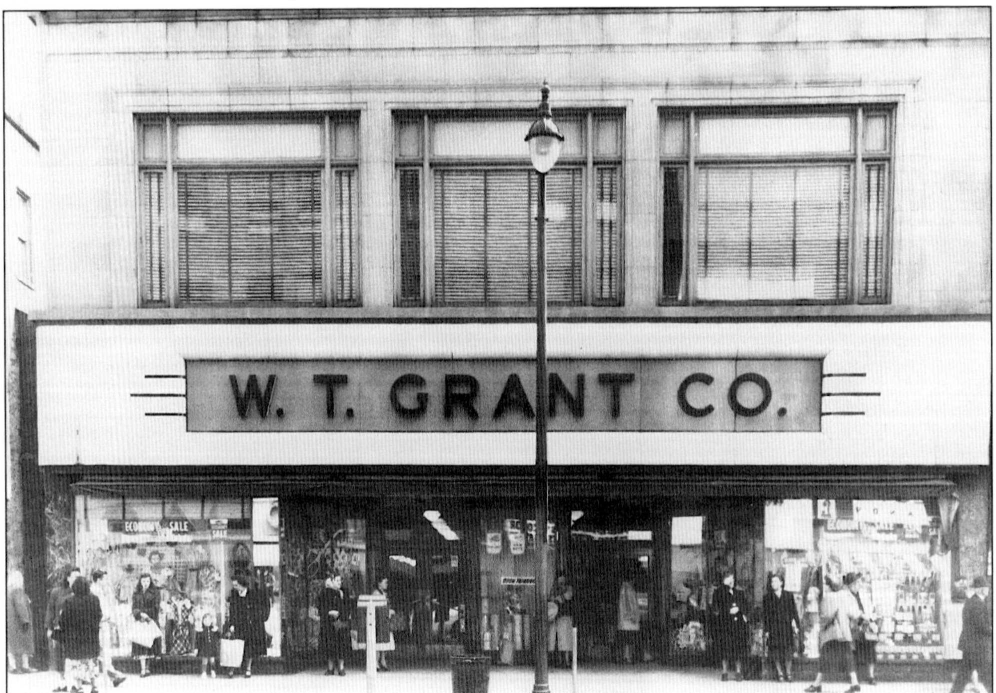

The W.T. Grant Co., in operation since 1925. A familiar name to all, the company was located at 283 Main Street. It closed in the summer of 1973 with the owners citing its small size and outdated goods as justification. (Local History Room, NBPL.)

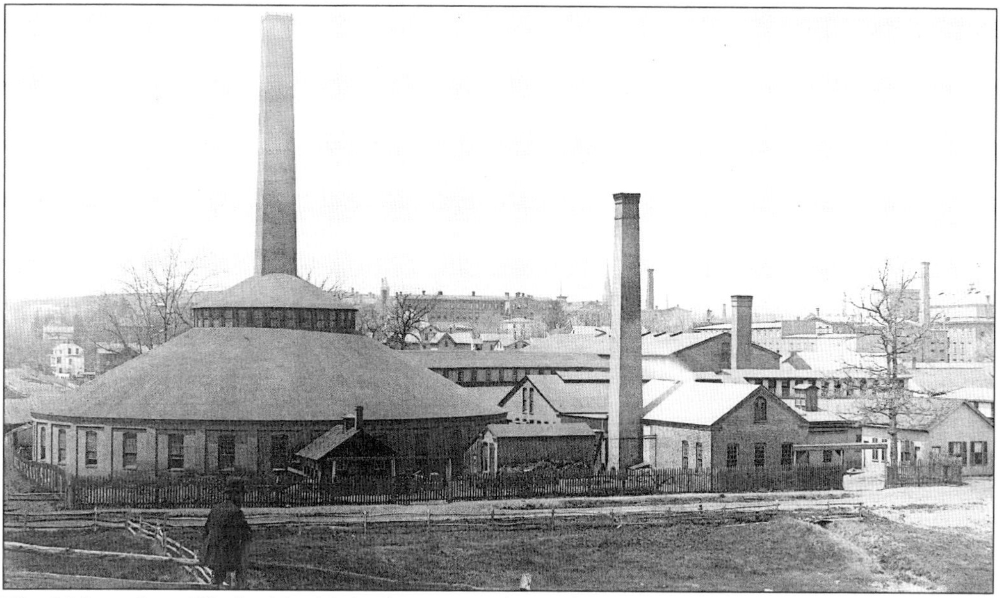

The Vulcan Iron Works. Established in 1878, the Vulcan Iron Works grew from one foundry to three within a forty-year span. Vulcan and Malleable, New Britain's second iron works, merged with the Eastern Malleable Iron Company and relocated to another city. (Local History Room, NBPL.)

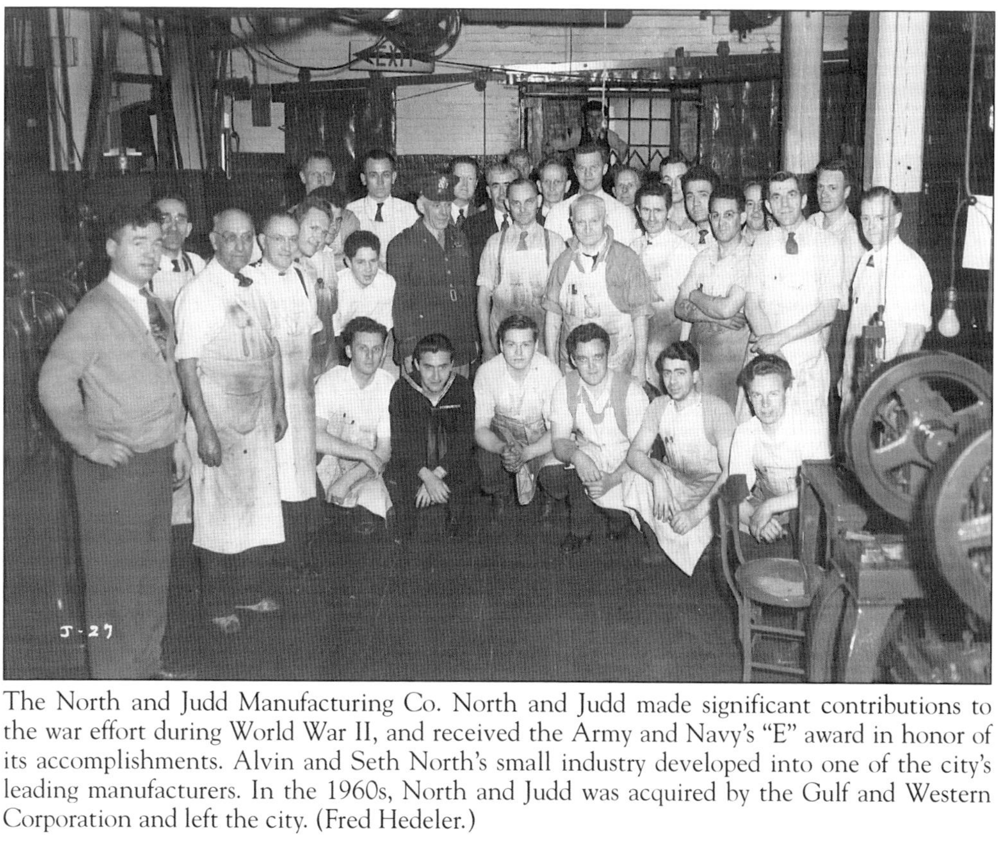

The North and Judd Manufacturing Co. North and Judd made significant contributions to the war effort during World War II, and received the Army and Navy's "E" award in honor of its accomplishments. Alvin and Seth North's small industry developed into one of the city's leading manufacturers. In the 1960s, North and Judd was acquired by the Gulf and Western Corporation and left the city. (Fred Hedeler.)

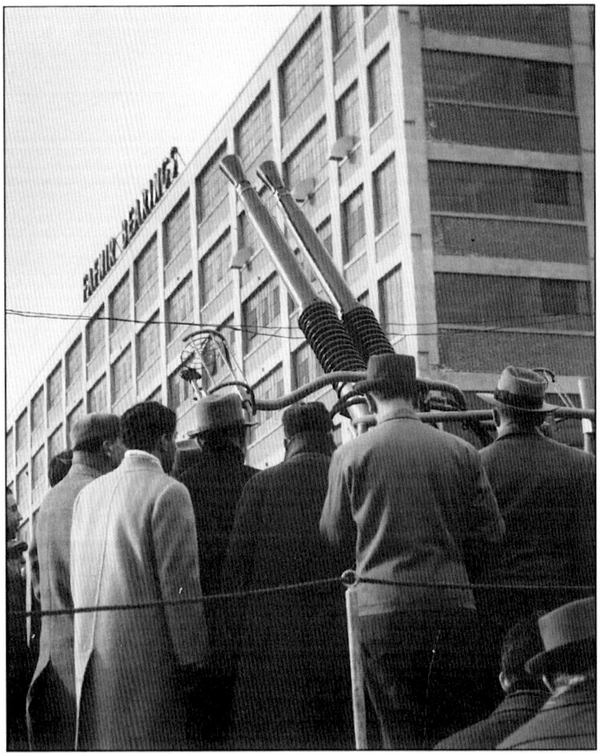

An anti-aircraft gun outside the Fafnir Bearing Co. plant during World War II. Founded in 1911 with a staff of seven, and led by general manager Elisha H. Cooper, who retired in 1947 as chairman of the board, the company grew to employ over 7,500 employees, some of whom are pictured below. Although Fafnir is no longer located in the city, its Grove Street plant site is being considered for possible new uses. (Fred Hedeler/Fafnir.)

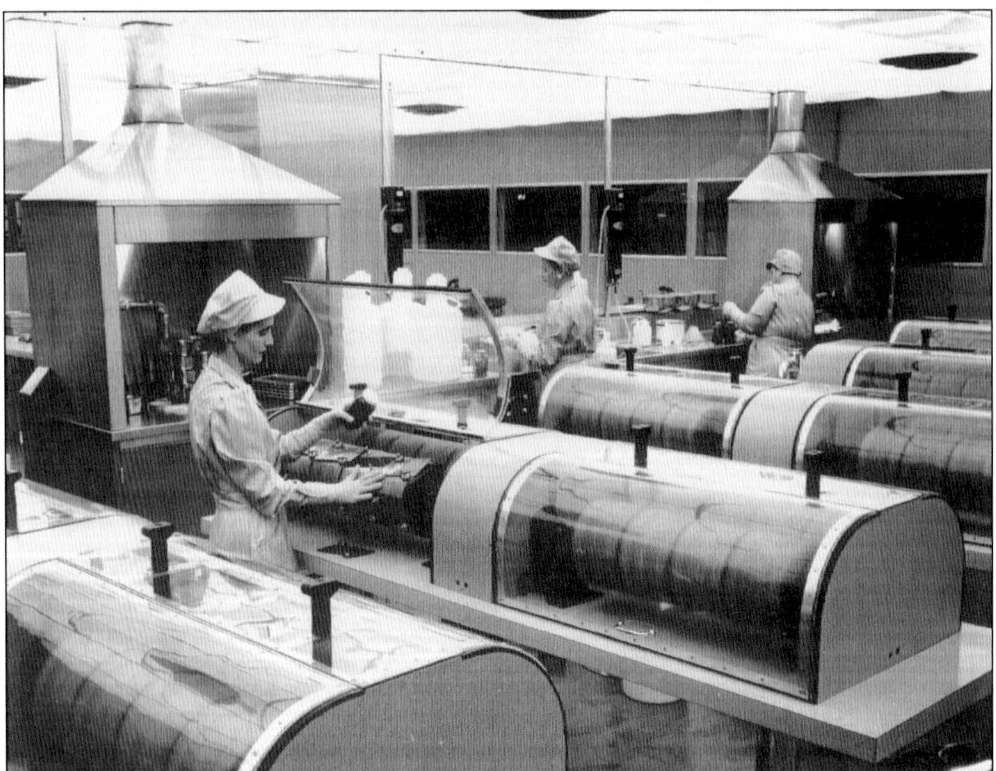

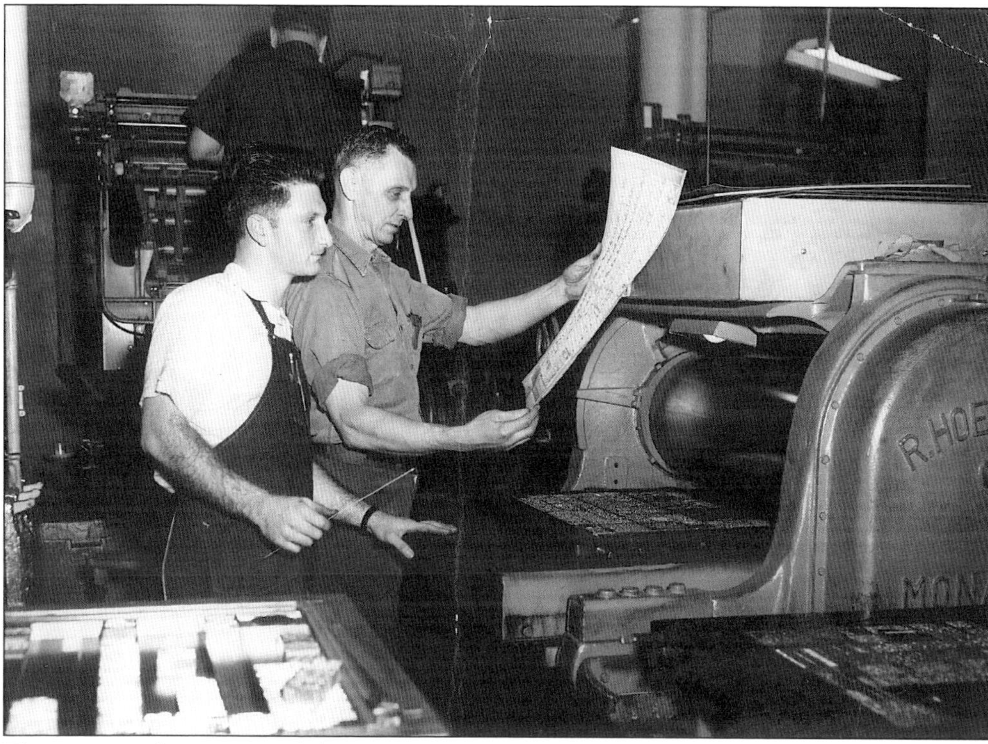

The printing department of the *New Britain Herald*. Now part of the Journal Register chain of papers, the name *Herald* remains intact on the local paper. Founded in 1880, the *Herald* absorbed the old *New Britain Record* in 1932. For well over one hundred years, the paper was owned and run by the same family. Judith Weld Brown, the founder's granddaughter, continues to serve as editor. (*Herald* photograph file.)

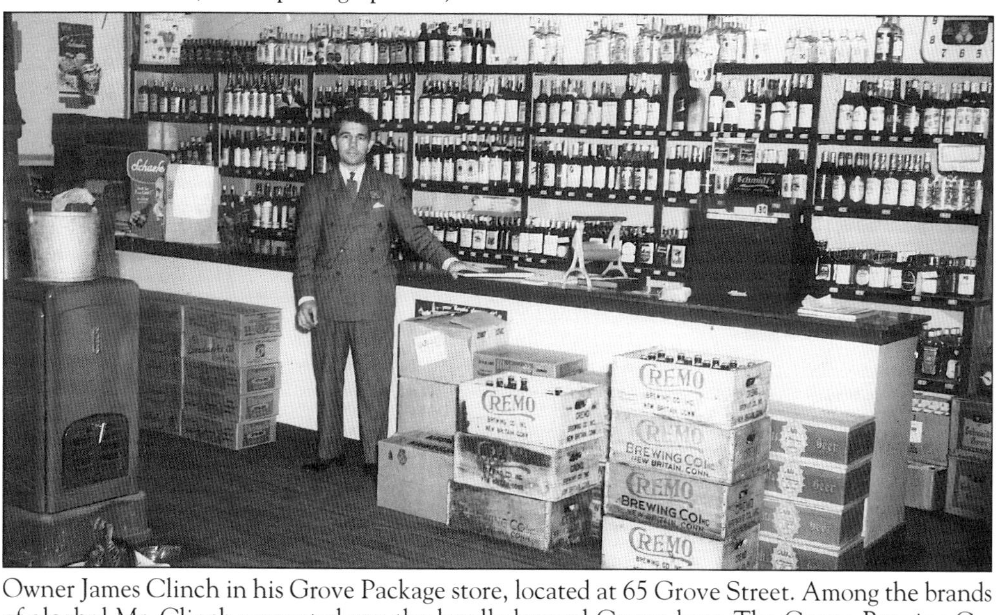

Owner James Clinch in his Grove Package store, located at 65 Grove Street. Among the brands of alcohol Mr. Clinch promoted was the locally brewed Cremo beer. The Cremo Brewing Co. closed in 1955. (Robert Clinch.)

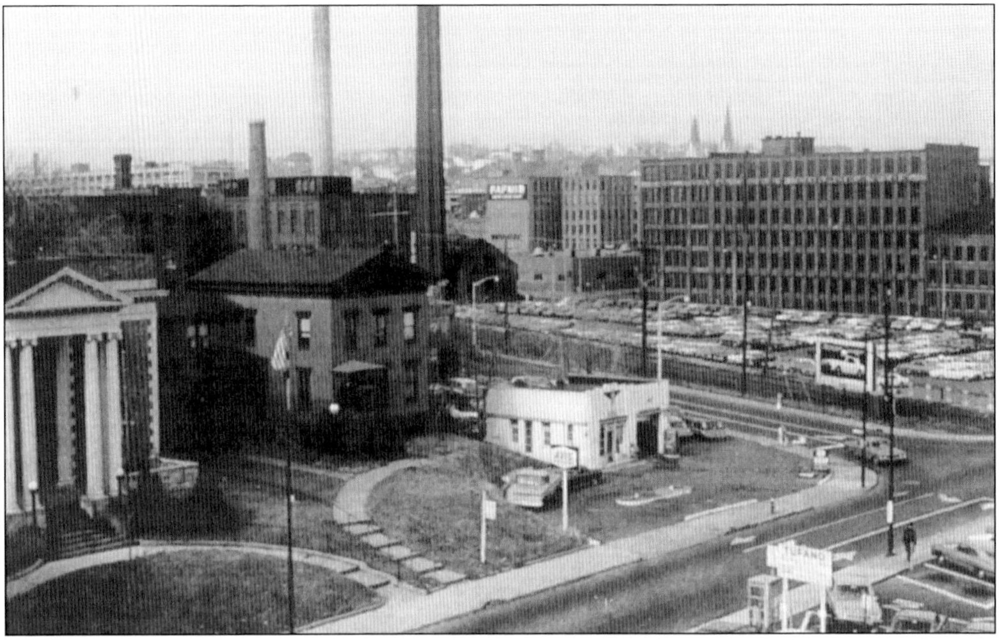

An aerial view of Washington Street. This view lends credence to New Britain's old nickname, "Hardware City." The Elks Club, American Legion hall, and gas station are dwarfed by the towering smokestacks of Russell and Erwin, Stanley Works, and the Fafnir Bearing Co. (Local History Room, NBPL.)

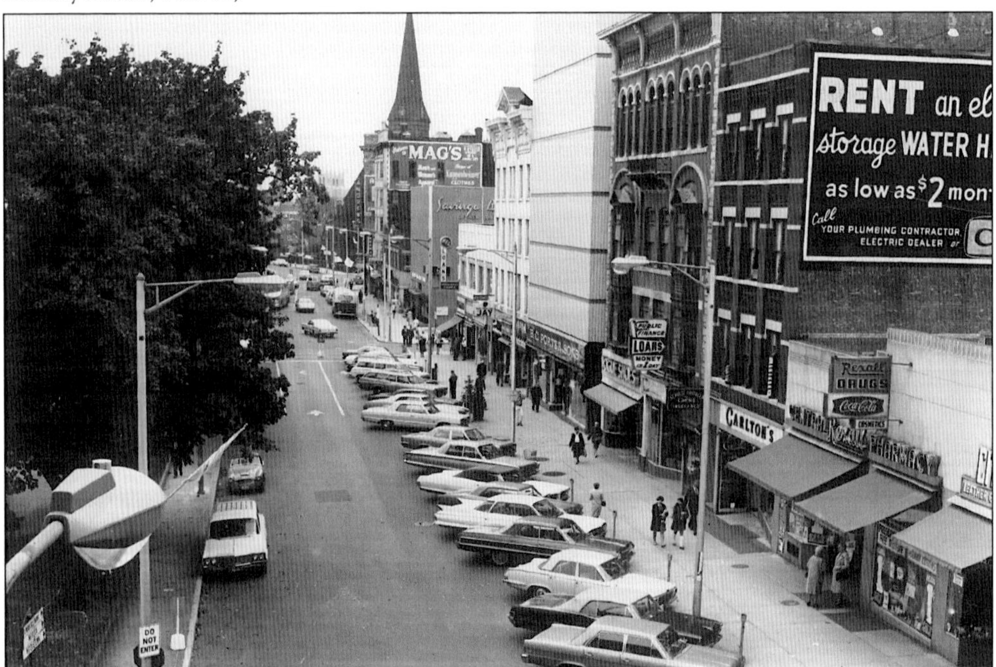

The west side of Main Street as seen from an office in City Hall in 1967. Central Park (to the left) borders the busy street, which once housed Mag's, B.C. Porter's, Vogue Shoes, Carlton's, and Central Pharmacy. (Local History Room, NBPL.)

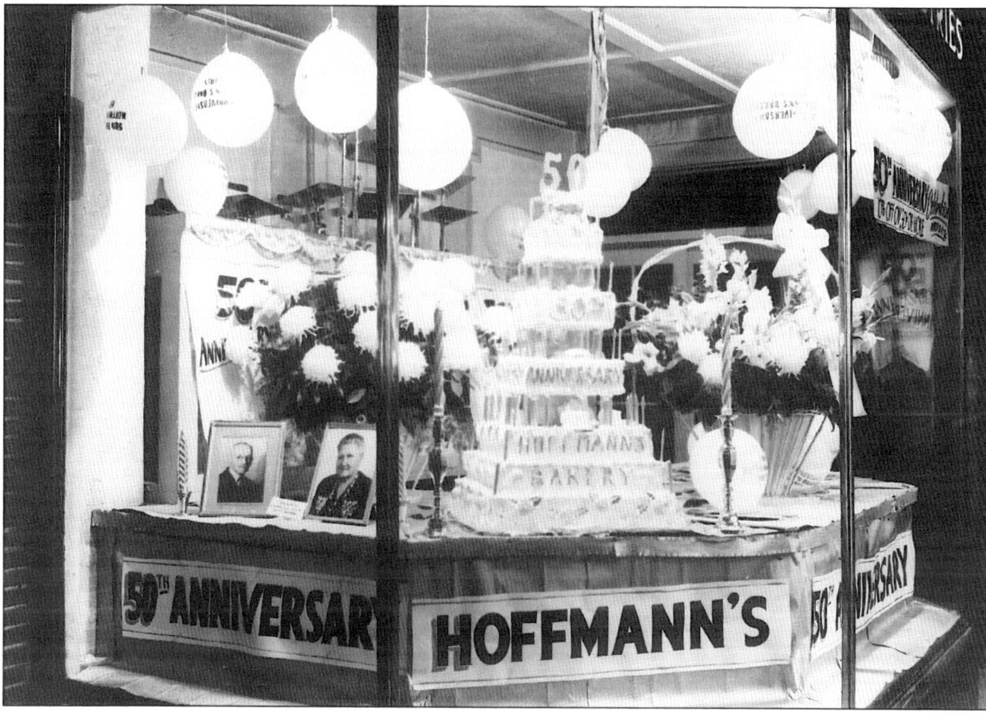

Hoffman's Bakery. This bakery lasted long enough to celebrate its 50th anniversary—a feat most small businesses will never experience today. Long before there were "superstores," individual establishments such as bakeries, green grocers, butchers, and confectioners were the norm. (Fred Hedeler.)

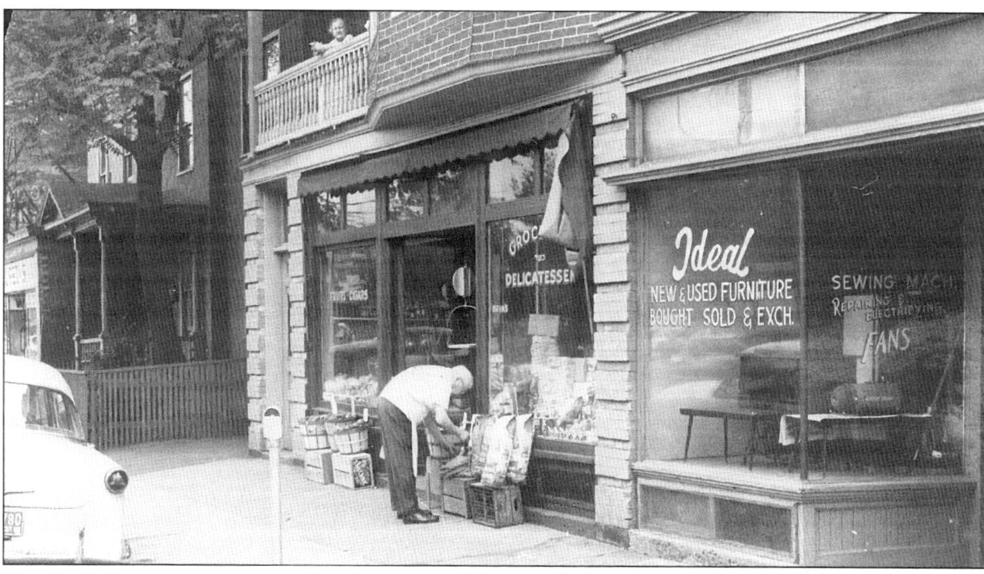

Hartford Avenue prior to redevelopment. Often called "The Avenue," this street was like a mini-city. The upper portions of buildings were tenements, while the ground-floor storefronts offered wares such as fresh meats, fish, baked goods, plants, second-hand furniture, hardware, liquor, and locks. Seven grills and taverns kept the Avenue humming well past midnight. (Local History Room, NBPL.)

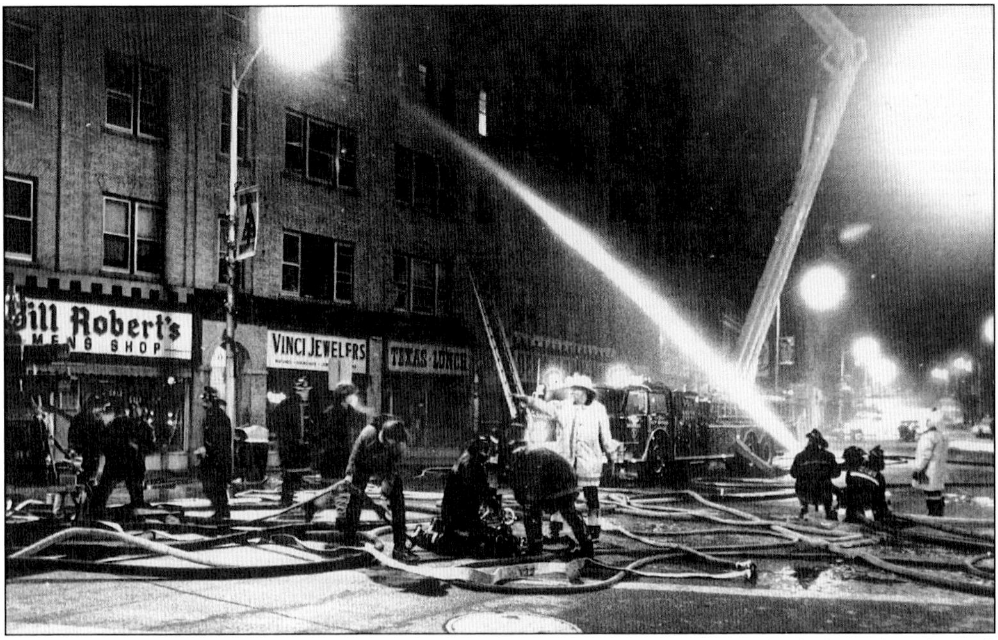

A fire on Main Street in the late 1970s. Fire Chief Edward McKeon (in the light-colored coat) directs his men as they battle the fire. Chief McKeon dedicated forty-five years of his life to his profession. When he entered the military during World War II, he trained servicemen in fire-fighting. Upon discharge he resumed his work with the New Britain Fire Department, retiring in 1983. (Deborah McKeon Nelson.)

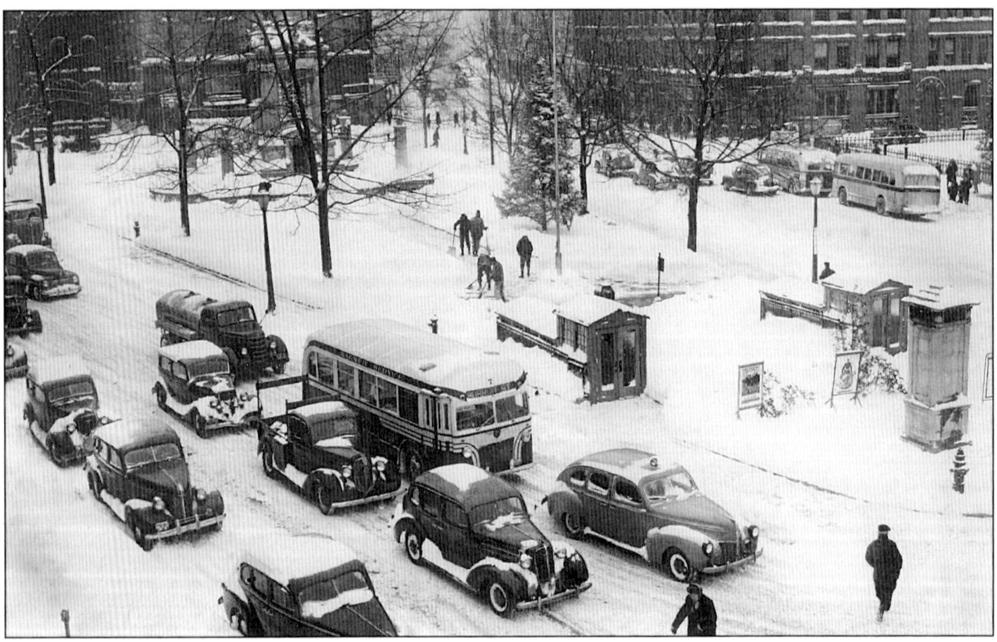

Central Park at Main and West Main Streets. Working did not always mean employment in a factory, office, or store. New England winters found city workers devoting hours to clearing roads and sidewalks. The comfort stations, located in the foreground, illustrate the length the park once enjoyed. (*Herald* photograph file.)

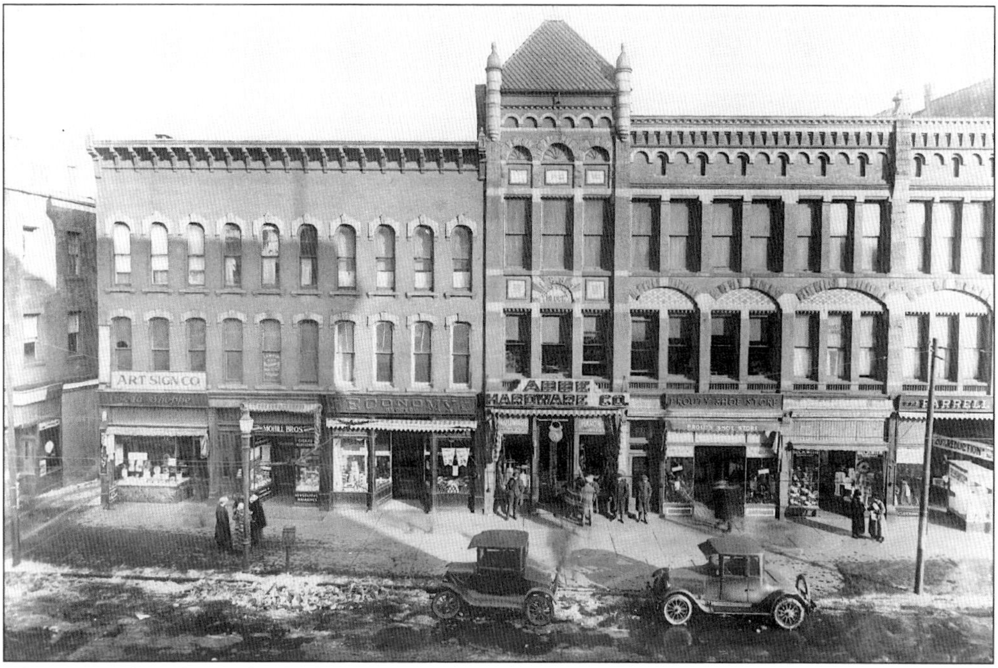

The Central and Ward Blocks. Highly decorative buildings such as the ones pictured here adorned both sides of the city's main thoroughfare. Note the sign for the Abbe Hardware Co. on Main Street resembling a movie marquee. (*Herald* photograph file.)

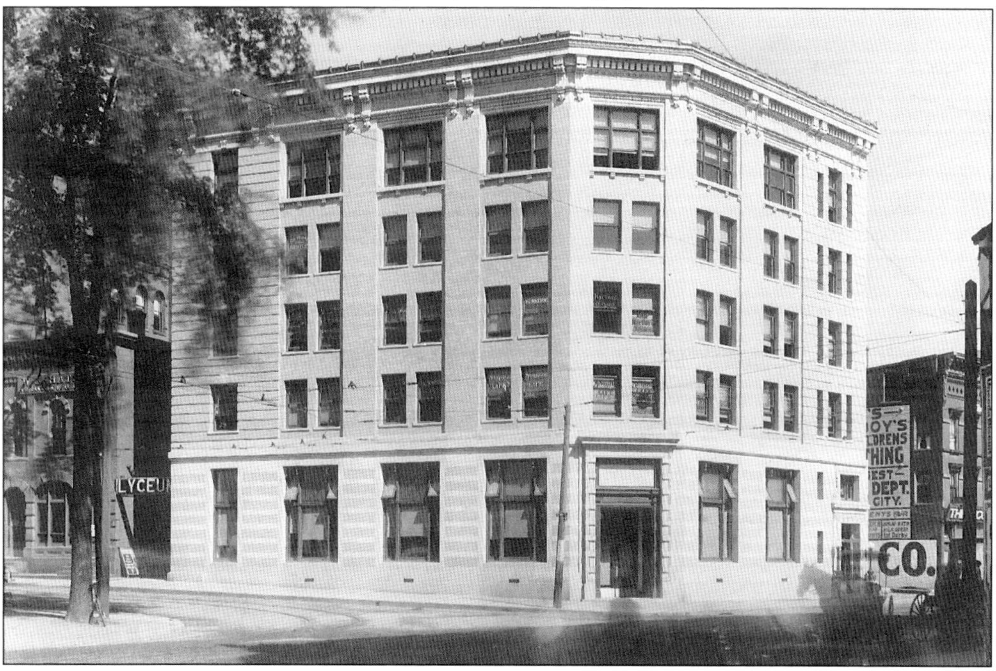

The New Britain National Bank. Designed by the firm of Davis and Brooks, this building was erected on the corner of West Main and Main Streets, *c.* 1907. Established in 1860, the bank was the oldest financial institution in the city. When it moved to 55 West Main Street, the Gates Building (as it is now known) housed offices and stores. (Local History Room, NBPL.)

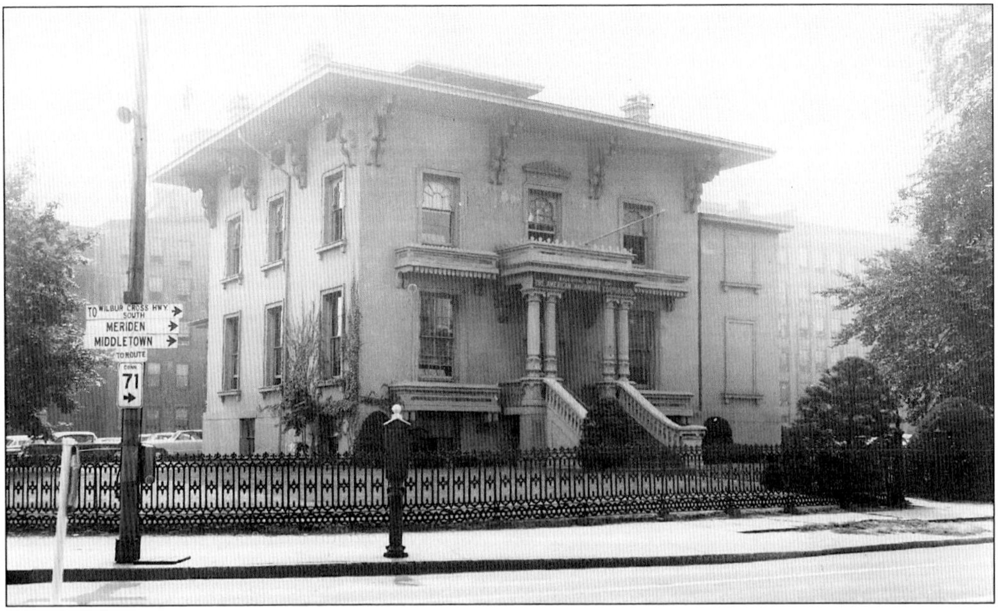

The American Hardware Corporation's executive office. This building on Franklin Square was formerly a private residence. Major industries Russell and Erwin, P. & F. Corbin, Corbin Cabinet Lock, and Corbin Screw merged in the early part of this century to form American Hardware. This, in turn, was purchased by the Emhart Corporation in the mid-1960s. (*Herald* photograph file.)

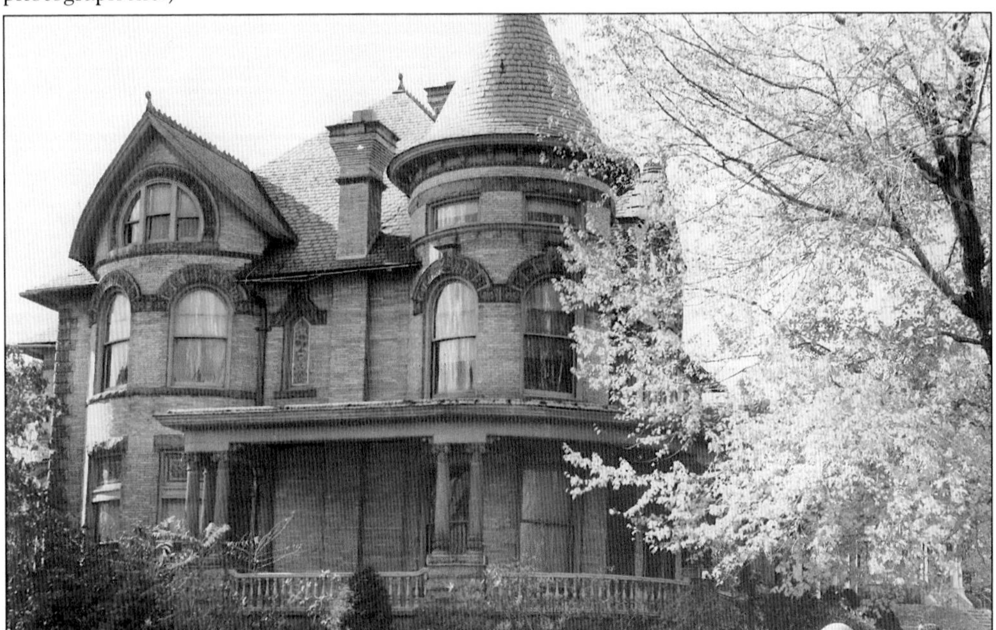

The law firm of Camp, Williams and Richardson, located in the William Cadwell residence. This dwelling was designed and built for William Cadwell's wife as a wedding gift in the 1890s. When Mr. Cadwell died, his wife continued to live here until her death in 1958. It was willed to the president of Beaton and Cadwell, who sold it to the current owners within a year. (Local History Room, NBPL.)

Four

When We Worshiped

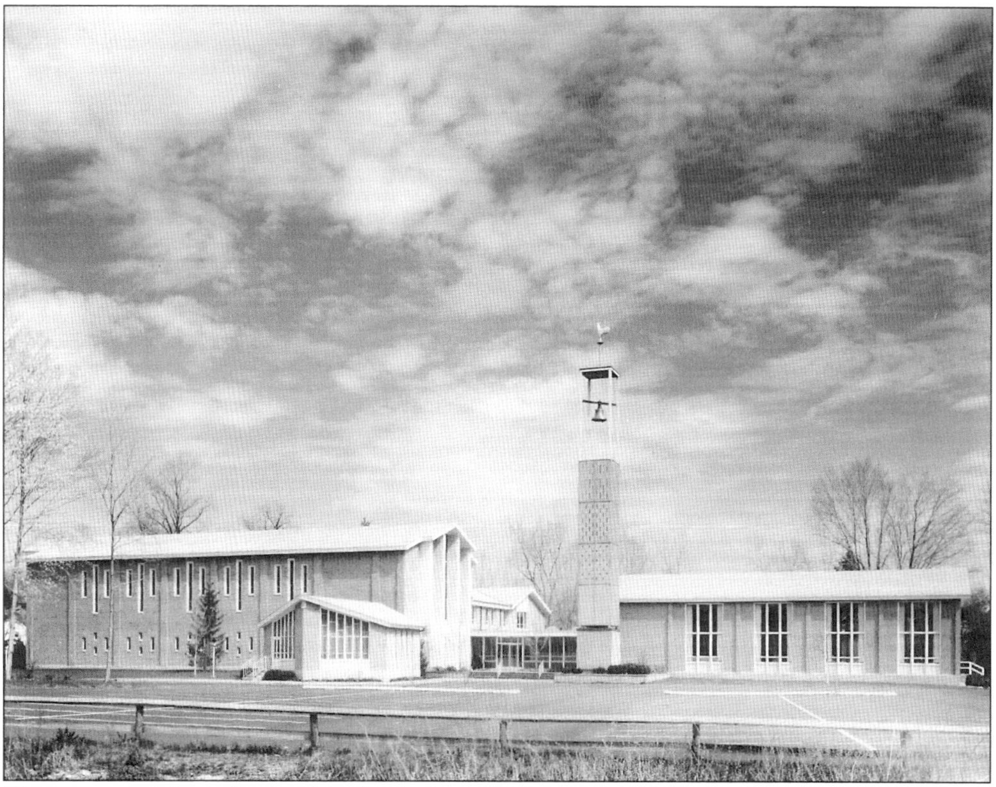

The present edifice of First Church of Christ, Congregational, located on Corbin Avenue. As the city celebrates its 125th anniversary, First Church is fast approaching its 240th. On April 19, 1758, the church was organized with Reverend John Smalley as its pastor. There are presently over fifty churches in the city, but First Church, led by the Reverend James Simpson, continues to be a community leader by allowing over seventy-five organizations to use its facilities for meetings. (First Church of Christ, Congregational.)

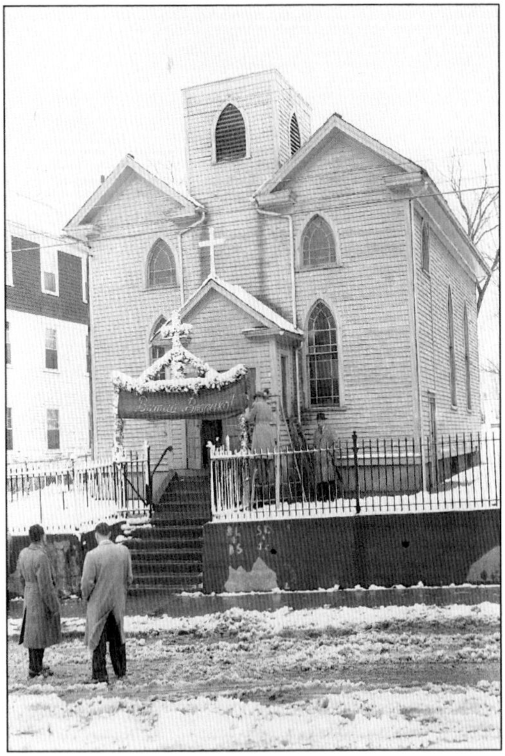

The old edifice of St. Josaphat Ukrainian Catholic Church in 1956. St. Josaphat's was organized in the early 1950s, but the church community dates back to the turn of the century. Purchasing the former Russian and Greek structure on Beatty Street, the congregation worshiped here before moving to Eddy Glover Boulevard in 1975. (*Herald* photograph file.)

St. Stephen's Armenian Apostolic Church on Tremont Street. Due to the large number of Armenians living in the area, land was purchased to erect this church. Although the parish went through a turbulent era in the early 1930s, matters were resolved and it remains active to this day. (*Herald* photograph file.)

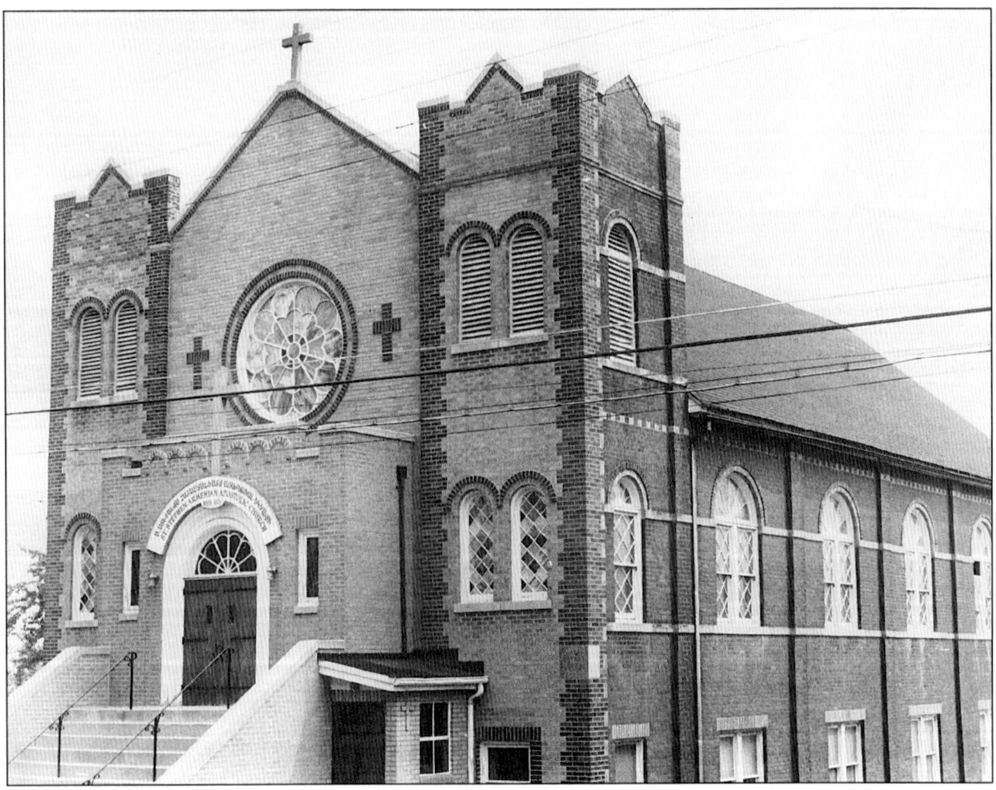

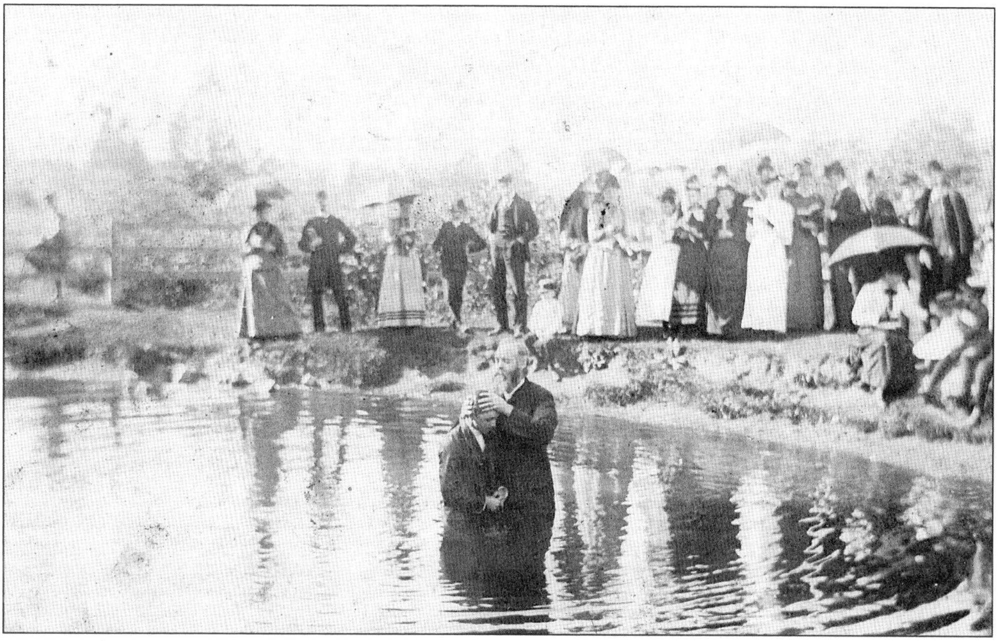

Reverend Hazeekia Davis of People's Church of Christ. Reverend Davis is shown here baptizing a parishioner by rite of immersion. The generous congregation raised $200,000 during it first fifty years (1888–1938). Of that amount, $75,000 went to foreign missions. (Local History Room, NBPL.)

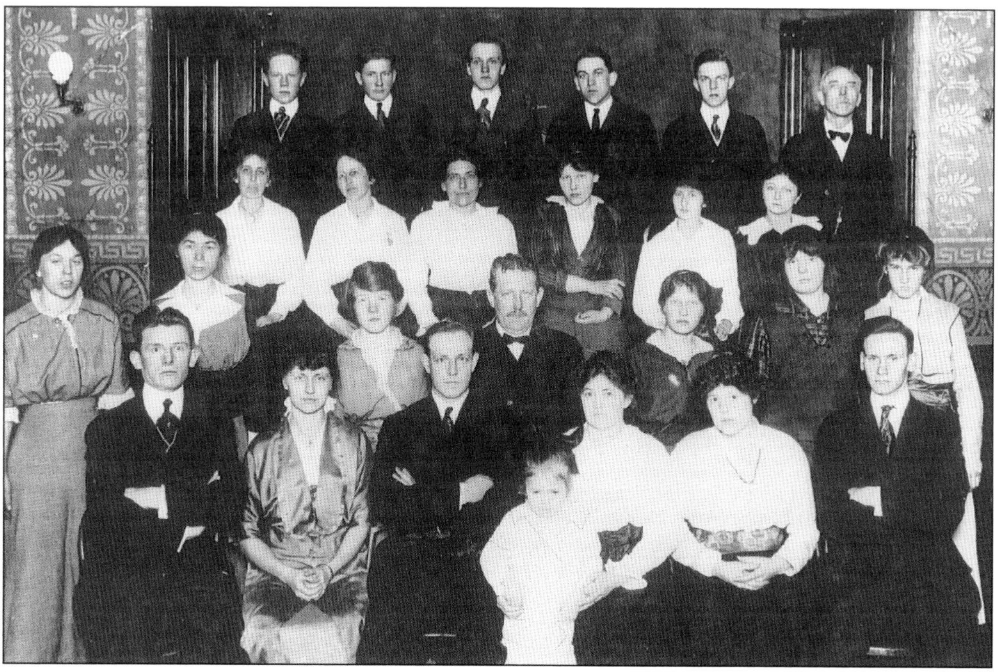

Parishioners of the Swedish Elim Baptist Church. The church, built in 1893, was the smallest Swedish church in the city. Early services were held at Reverend T. Clafford's home, Calumet Hall, and the First Baptist Church before the Elm Street structure was completed. In 1966, the parish built a new edifice in Kensington. (Mark Johnson.)

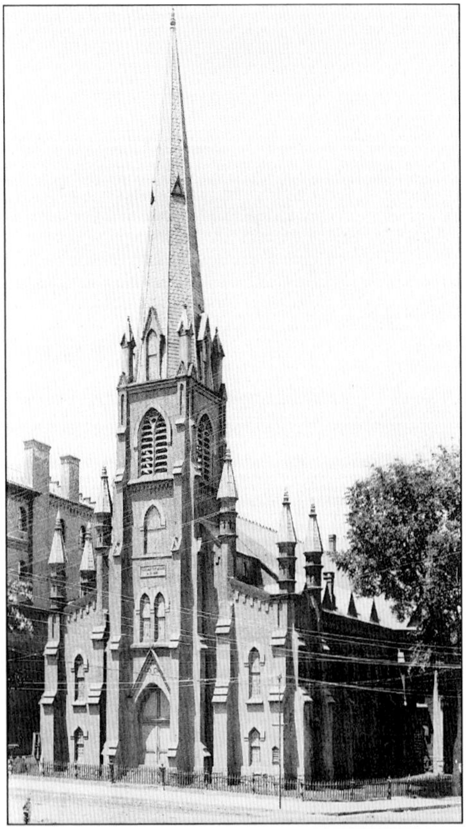

The third home of the First Baptist Church had a relatively short life. Built on the corner of Main and West Main Streets (now the site of the Gates Building), this structure was dedicated in 1870 and last services were held on March 4, 1906. A new church was built across from the public library. In 1974, First Baptist merged with South Congregational Church. (Local History Room, NBPL.)

Students of the Hebrew School in 1929. Teacher Moses Hartnan is seated among his pupils. From left to right are: (front row) Anna Lifshutlz, Mr. Hartnan, and Lee Ratner Birnbaum; (back row) Herbert Jaffe, Howard Levine, Louis Cohen, Louis Spector, Israel Rosensweig, and Elliot Lifshultz. The year 1996 marks the 100th anniversary of the Congregation B'Nai Israel. (Libbie Dunn Zucker.)

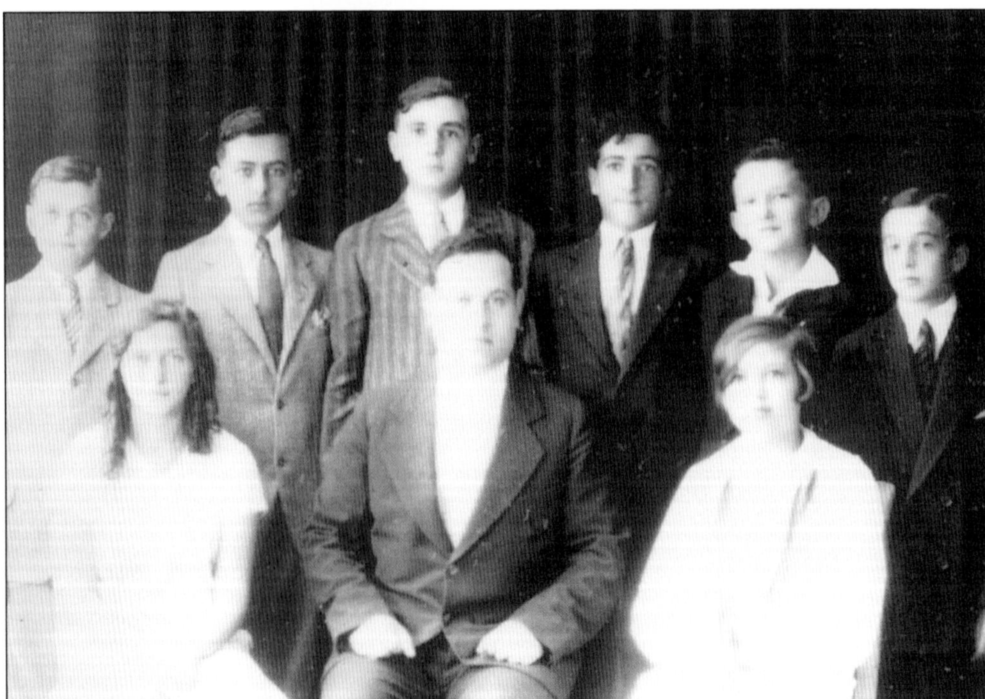

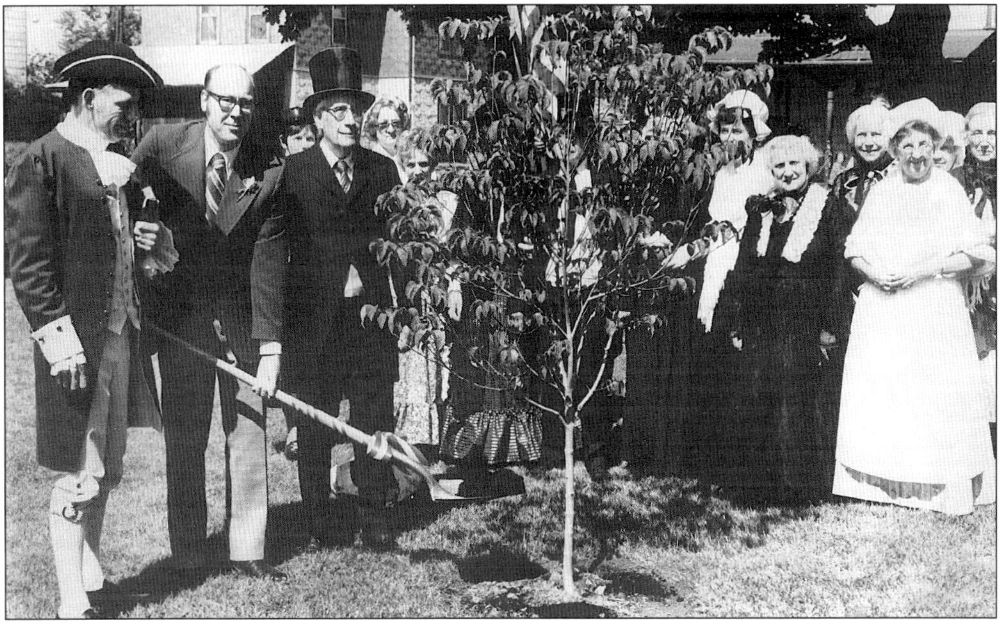

Stanley Memorial churchgoers, dressed in Colonial garb. Members celebrated the nation's birthday in 1976 by planting a bicentennial tree. In 1905, Mrs. Frederick North Stanley gave a gift of $10,000 in memory of her husband. These funds were used to build the chapel. It was dedicated on Easter Sunday in April 1906, but it was May of 1907 before the congregation of twenty-one people was formed. (*Herald* photograph file.)

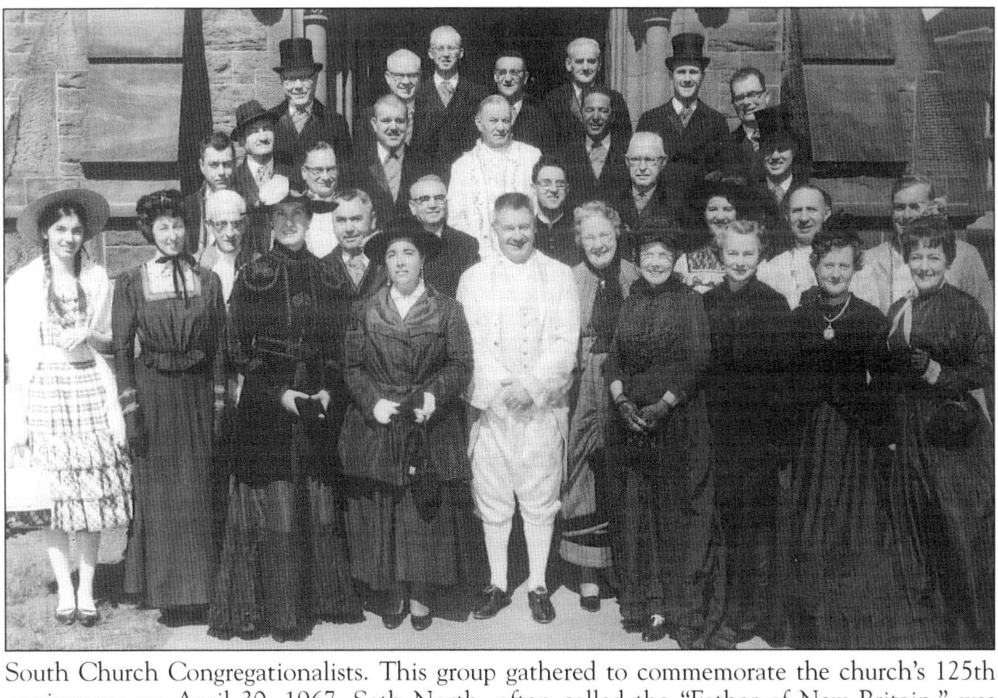

South Church Congregationalists. This group gathered to commemorate the church's 125th anniversary on April 30, 1967. Seth North, often called the "Father of New Britain," was instrumental in organizing the church in 1842. The current structure is made of Portland brownstone and was dedicated on January 16, 1868. (South Congregational Church.)

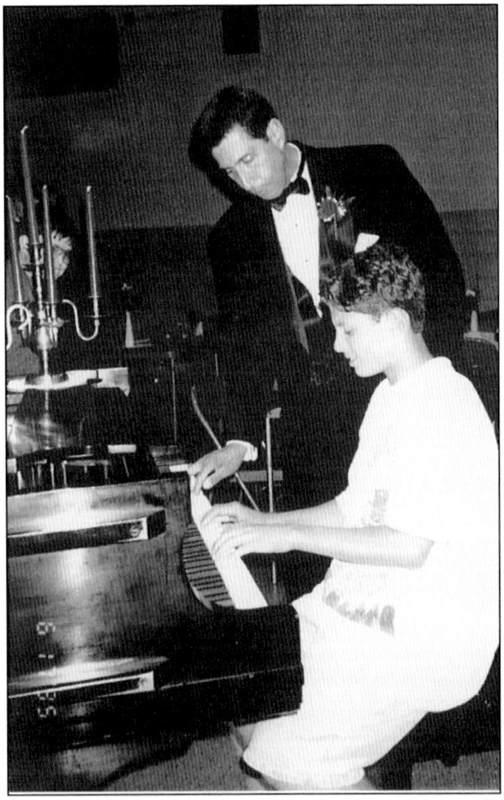

Rick Daddario and one of his twin sons prior to the 1995 piano marathon. A unique fund-raiser for St. Jerome's Church began in 1994, when gifted pianist Rick Daddario played piano non-stop for over twenty-four hours. During the two years the event has been held over $10,000 has been raised. Mr. Daddario has been the church organist for twenty-six years, a position he has held since the age of fourteen. (Rick Daddario.)

The interior of St. Ann's Church. Wedding photographs offer excellent opportunities to view churches. Many parishioners of Italian descent attend St. Ann's, which sponsors two popular annual events: the Easter Passion Play and the Italian Festa. (Fred Hedeler.)

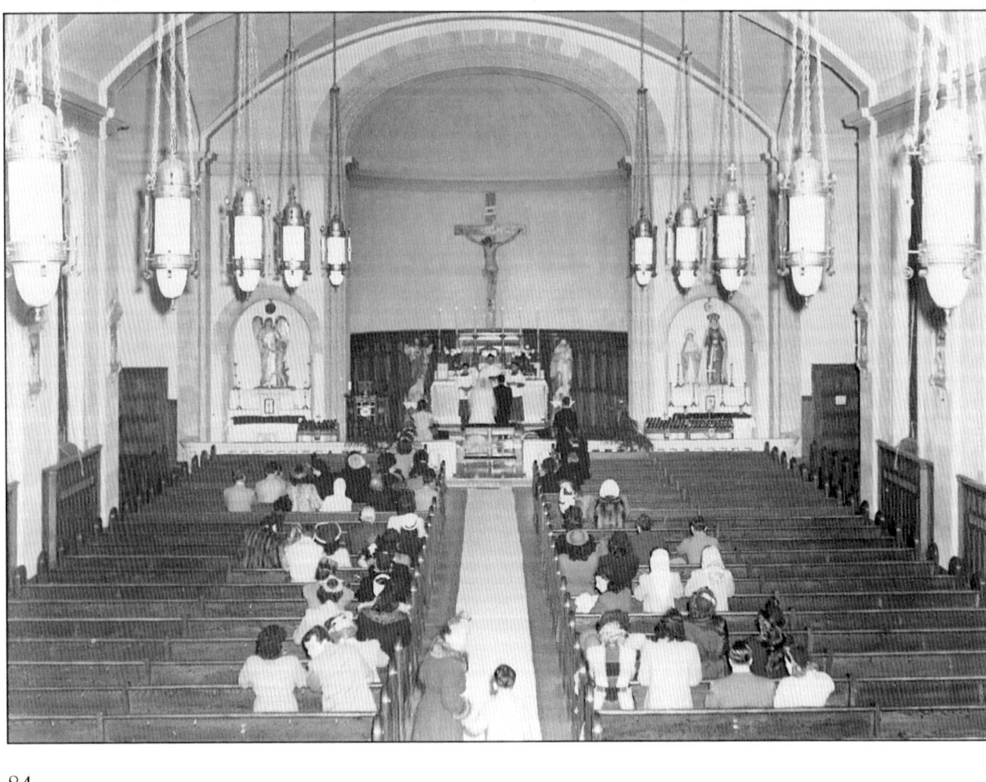

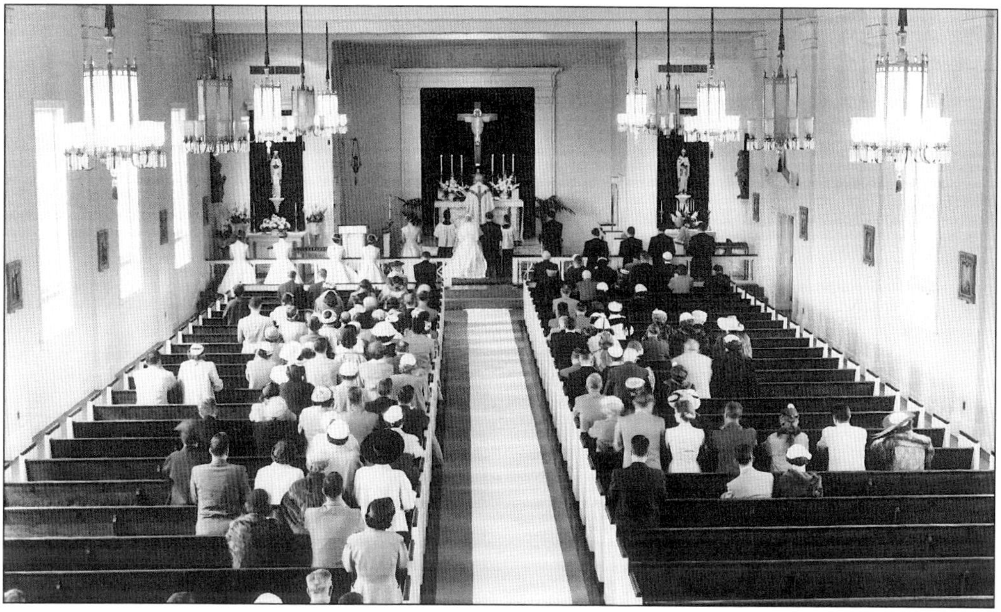

St. Maurice's Parish, named in honor of Bishop Maurice F. McAuliffe. The parish was established in 1946. When the Steele Street church was dedicated in 1949, it contained a 1,100-pound bell, cast in 1842, a gift from Walter Turner of Norwich, Connecticut. (Fred Hedeler.)

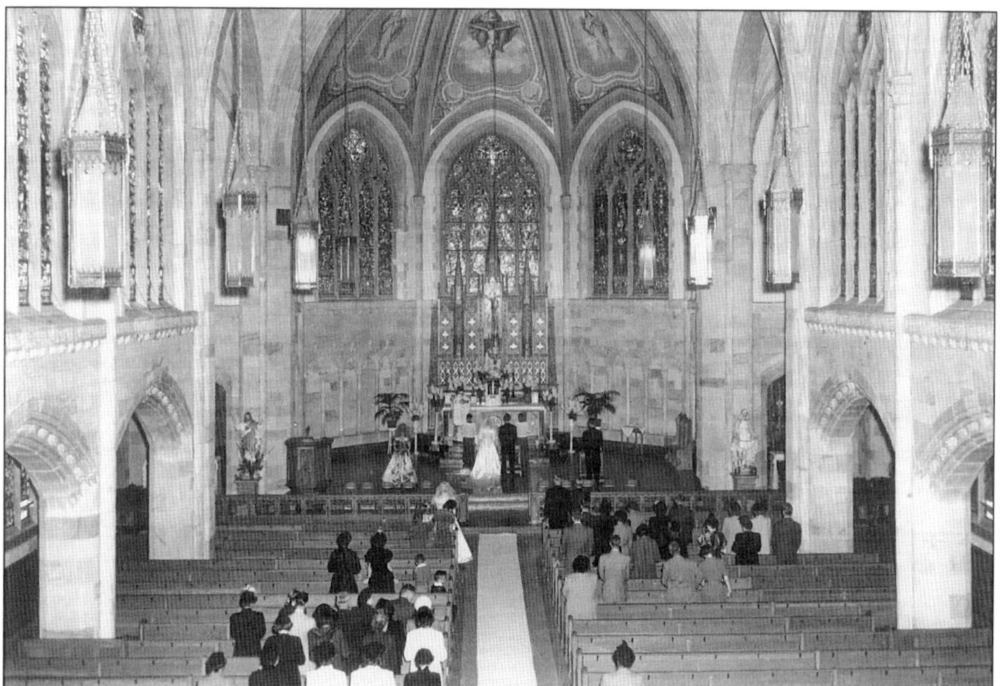

Wanda Stolarun and Stanley Dabrowski exchanging vows on September 16, 1950, in the beautiful Gothic-style Holy Cross Church. On November 3, 1927, the Bishop of Hartford sent a message to Father Stephen Bartkowski of Rockville, Connecticut, authorizing the organization of the church and appointing Father Bartkowski as its first pastor. (Wanda Stolarun Dabrowski.)

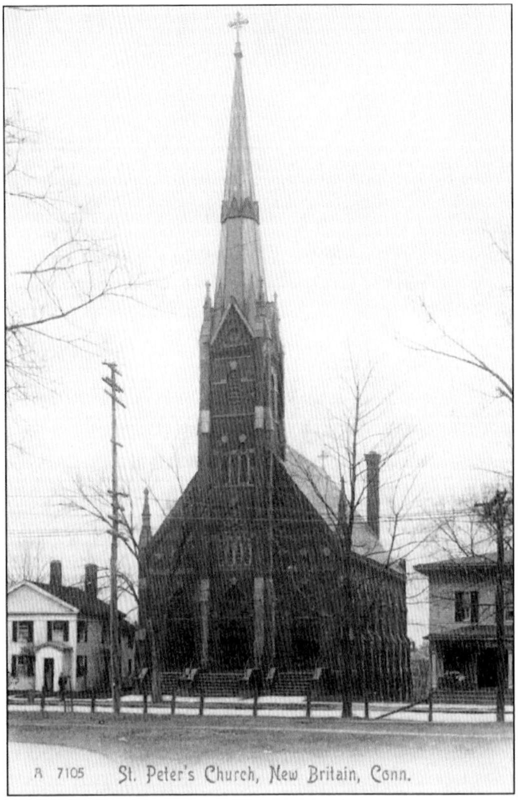

St. Peter's Church, located on Franklin Square. This church, which celebrated its 100th anniversary in 1990, holds the unique honor of having served two ethnic groups in the city: German and French. The first pastor of this parish was the Reverend Nicholas F.X. Schneider. (Local History Room, NBPL.)

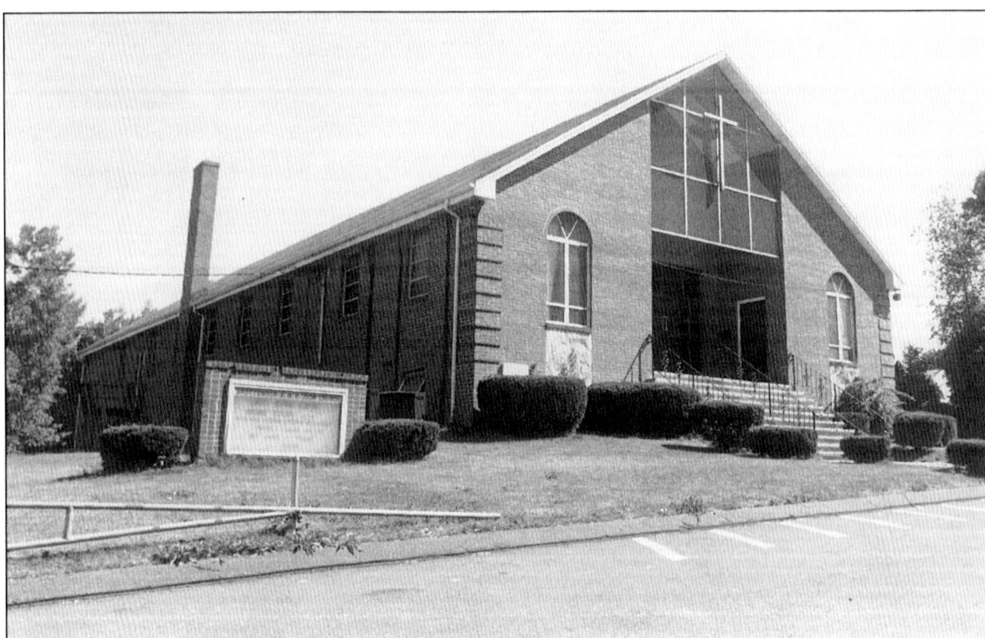

The current AME Zion Church on Crestwood Lane. What began as a mission in 1903 led to the formation of the A.M.E. Zion Church in May 1905. Originally on Church Street, the congregation moved several times before this structure was built. (*Herald* photograph file.)

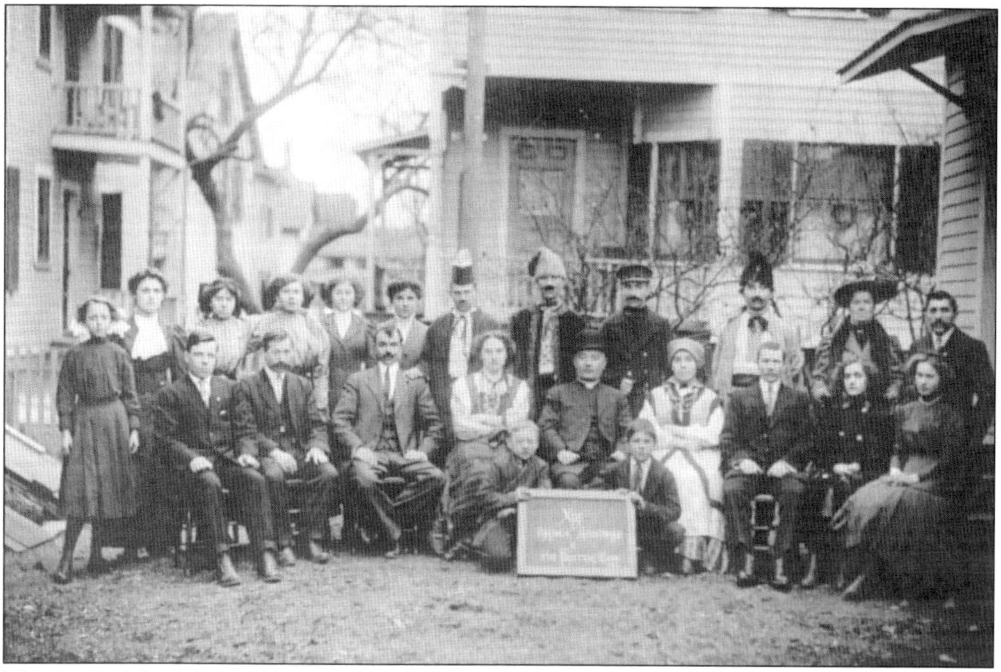

Members of St. Mary's Ukrainian Church, some in native dress. Faithful parishioners helped construct the Winter Street parish. The lower part of the church was designed by Clarence Palmer. A formal "burning of the mortgage" ceremony was held on January 28, 1945. (Ukrainian Educational Center.)

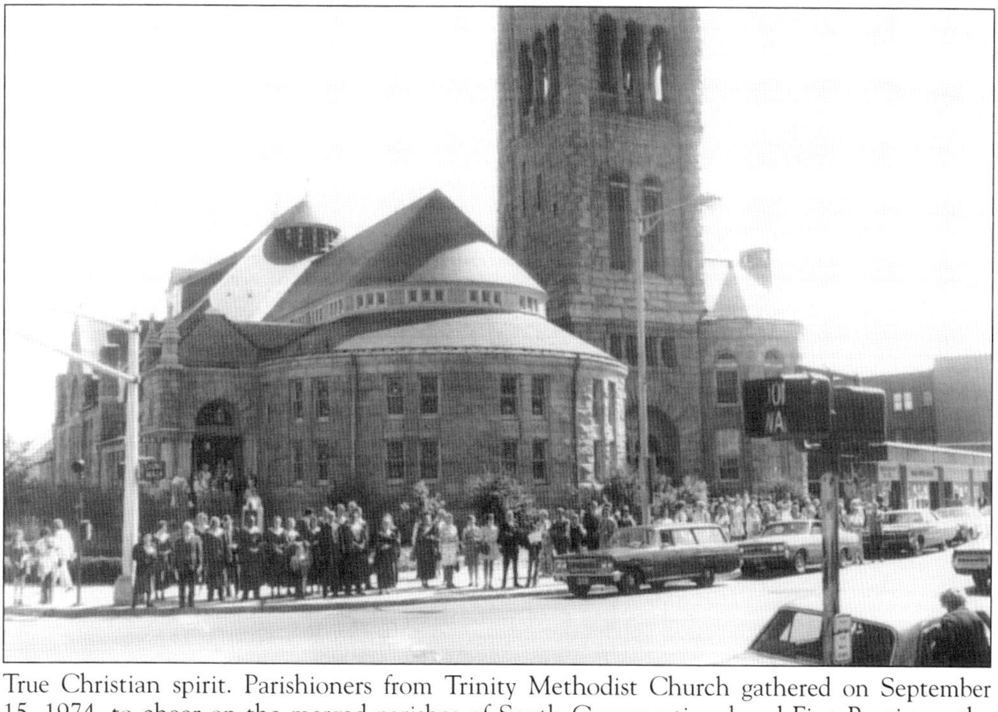

True Christian spirit. Parishioners from Trinity Methodist Church gathered on September 15, 1974, to cheer on the merged parishes of South Congregational and First Baptist as the procession passed by. Trinity's history dates back to 1815. (South Congregational Church.)

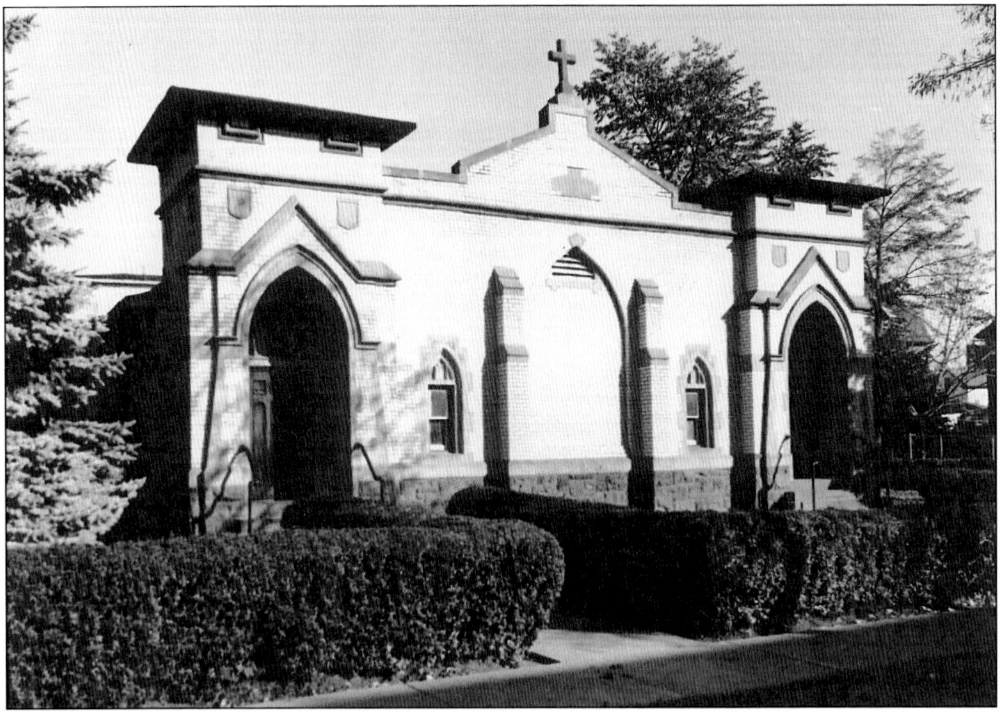

The little Slovak church of All Saint's. The parish was organized by Reverend Stephen A. Grohol, and in 1919, land was purchased to build the church. Reverend Grohol continued to serve until 1932, when he was transferred to Stratford. (All Saint's Church.)

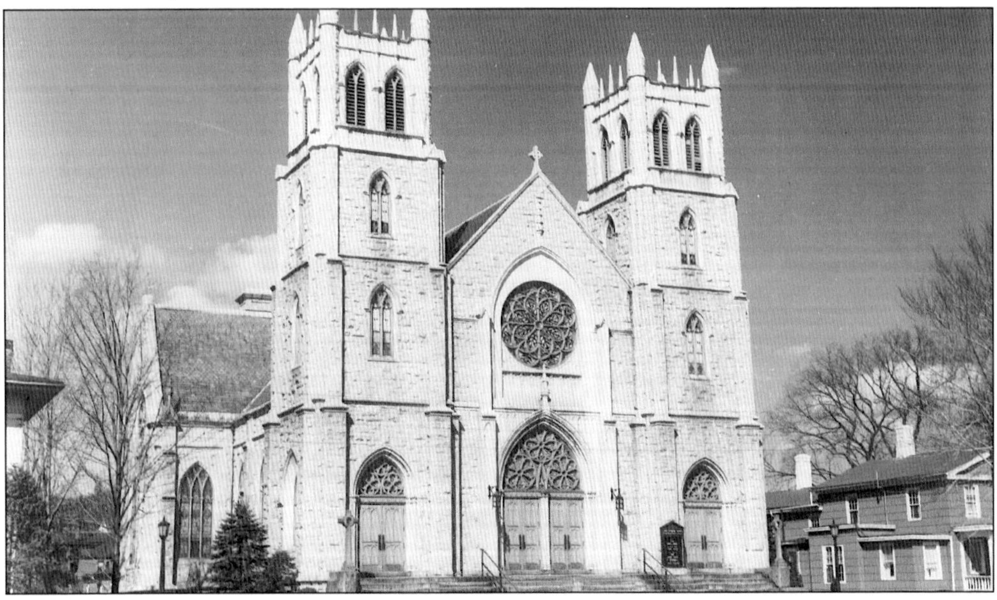

The First Lutheran Church of the Reformation. This magnificent structure was designed by William Cadwell and was dedicated on May 13, 1906. Once, twin spires graced the double towers. Although the south spire was struck by lightening in 1925 and repaired, it was apparent that both spires were endangered. In 1938, the congregation voted to remove the spires and reinforce the towers, which remain intact today. (Fred Hedeler.)

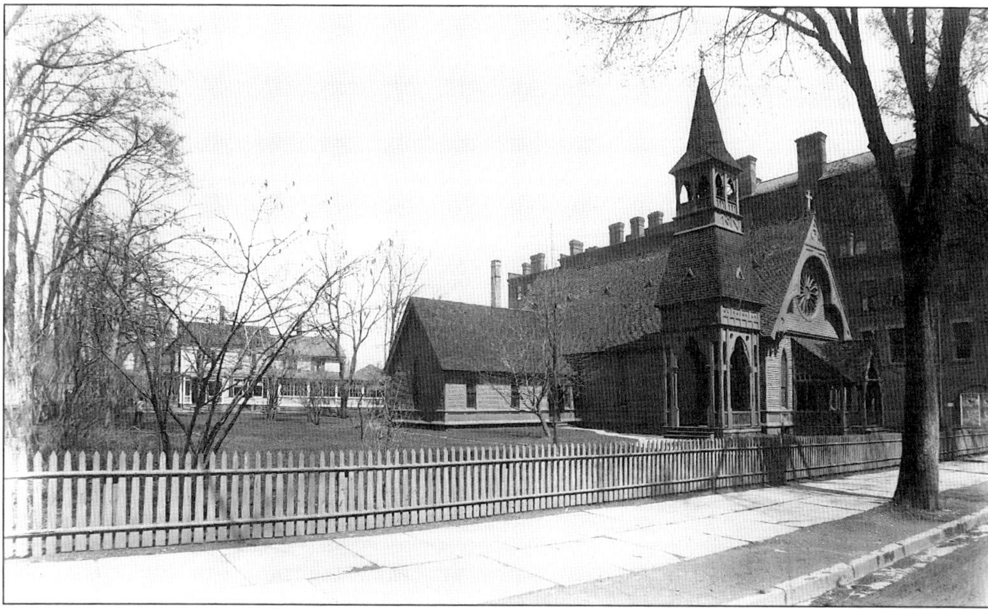

St. Mark's Episcopal Church on the corner of Main and Washington Streets. The church, organized in 1836, bought land for this structure, which was erected in 1848, for $6,300. The site was sold for $275,000 eighty-four years later. The current stone edifice was erected in 1921 and contains a beautiful rose window executed by William Morris & Co., Ltd., of London, England. (Local History Room, NBPL.)

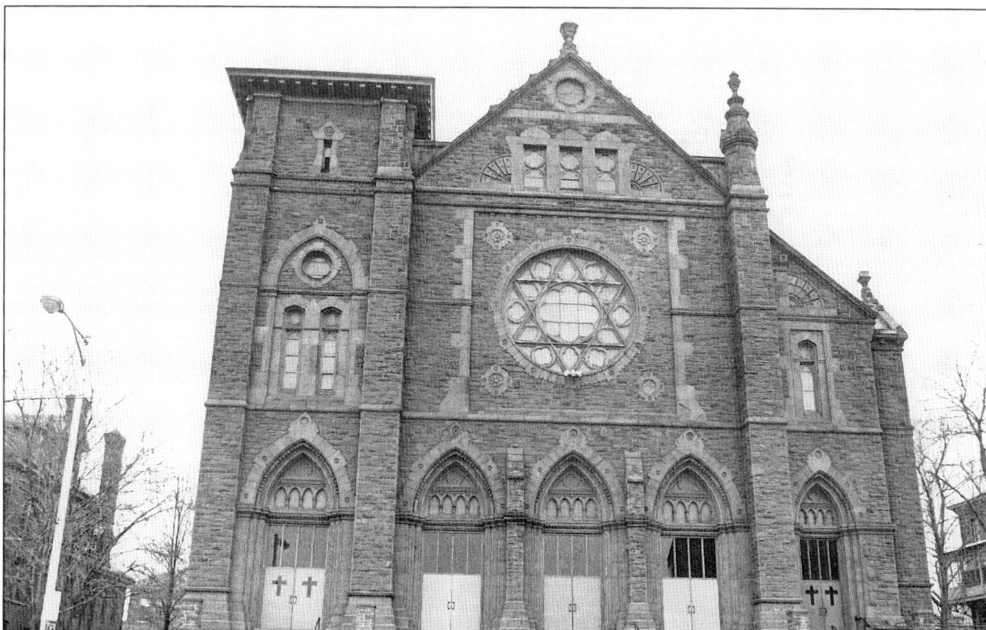

The Main Street building of St. Mary's. The first church, located on Myrtle Street, was dedicated in 1853. The current structure, completed in 1887, was gutted by fire in 1902 but rebuilt within thirteen months. Considered the "Mother Church," it originally served the Irish community. (Local History Room, NBPL.)

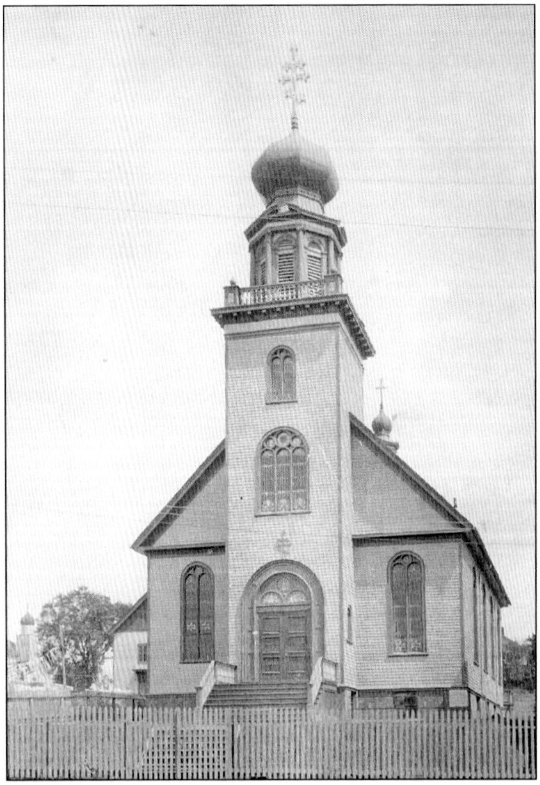

The Byzantine Catholic Church of the Holy Trinity. The turn of the century brought about the development of this new parish. The original wooden structure shown at left was built on Beaver Street and remained in use until fire destroyed it. Another wooden church replaced it until the current parish was erected in 1928. Frederick C. Teich of Hartford was the architect and the Harry Battistoni Co. was in charge of construction. The stained-glass windows were from Rambush of New York. (Mary Grip.)

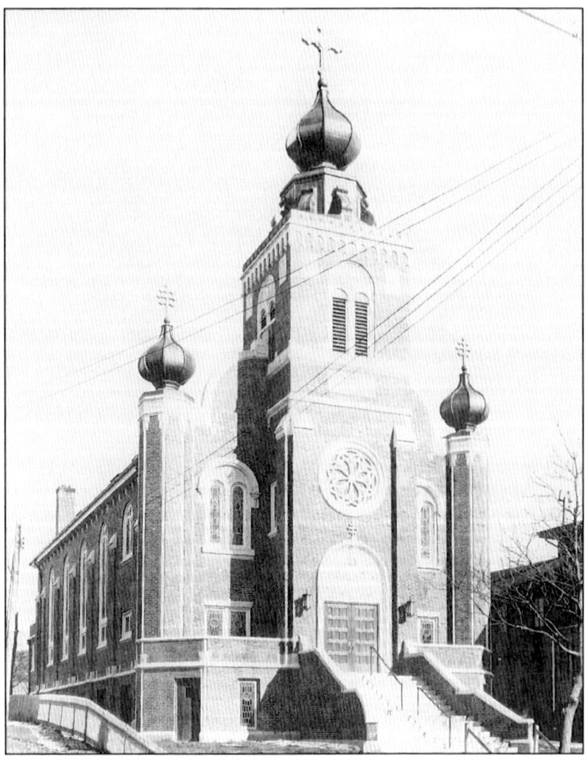

Five

Why New Britain?

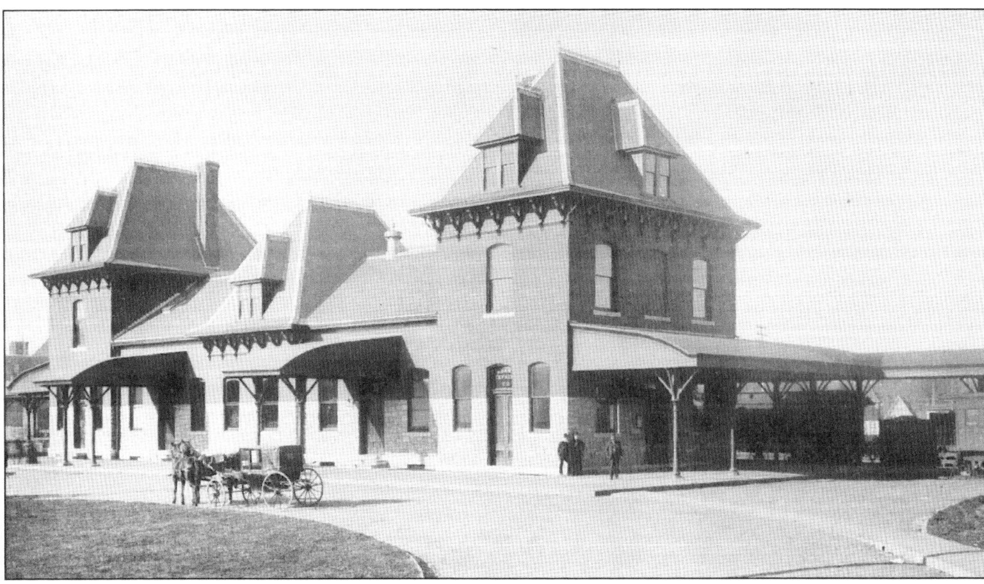

The railroad depot showing the Church Street entrance, *c.* 1898. The depot was built to accommodate increased railway traffic through the city. Passenger service ended in 1960. When the community was first settled, there was no railroad and no large body of water upon which to locate the industries. That the city became a major industrial center is a triumph of determination by the early entrepreneurs. (Local History Room, NBPL.)

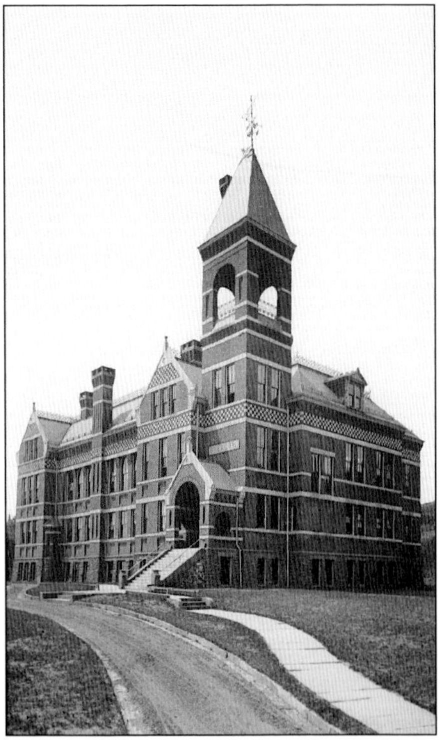

The State Normal School, one of the first in the nation. Established in 1850, the school's original building, located on the site of Central Junior High School, was abandoned when this structure was built on Hillside Place. It was designed by Warren R. Briggs. In the early 1920s the Normal School moved to the Stanley Street campus. (Local History Room, NBPL.)

The Hungerford residence on lower Main Street. This elegant residence once faced Main Street and contained an orchard and pasture on the grounds. It was owned by a prominent attorney and later turned over to the YWCA for administrative offices. By 1958 this structure and an adjacent dormitory were razed. (*Herald* photograph file)

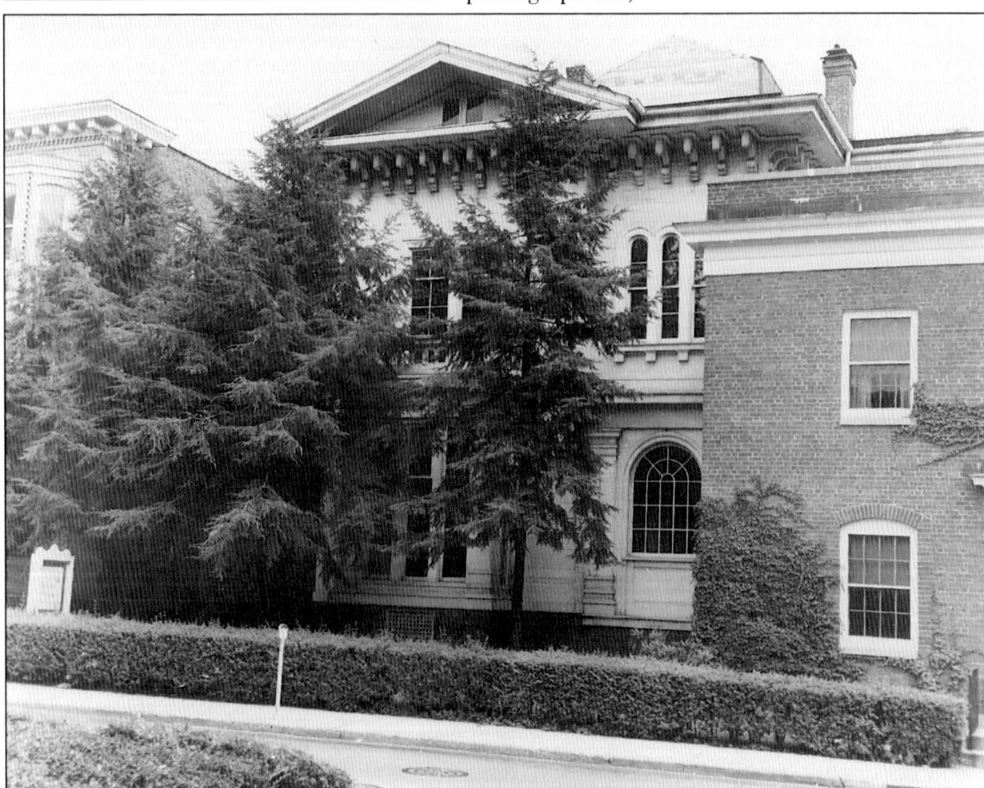

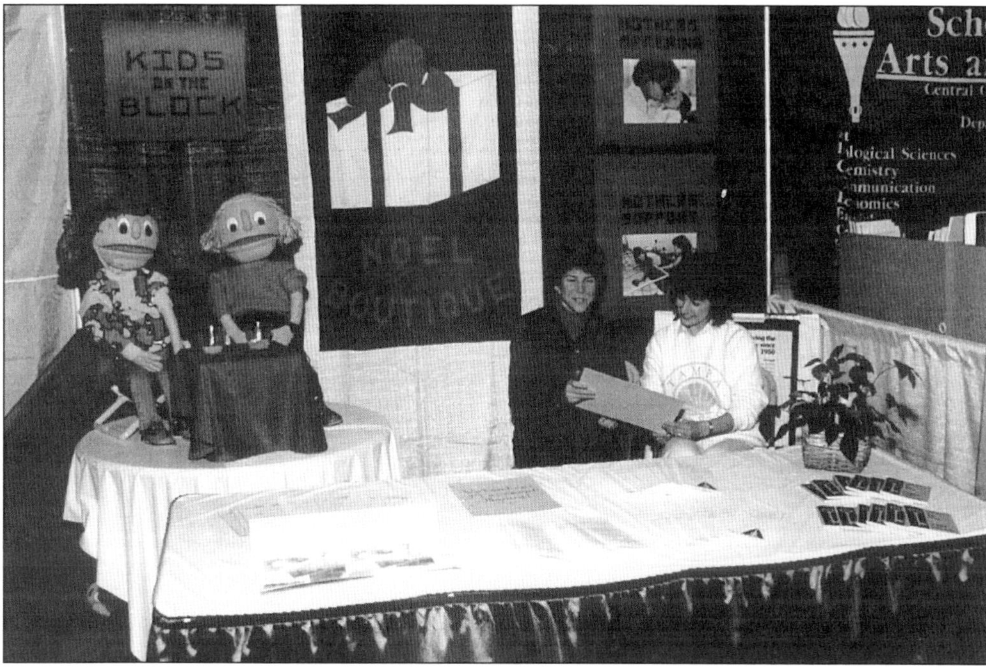

The Junior League's annual Noel Boutique holiday event, featuring their "Kids On The Block" program props. Incorporated in 1950, the Junior League of Greater New Britain strives to fulfill its mission of promoting educational and charitable activities through volunteerism. (Junior League of Greater New Britain.)

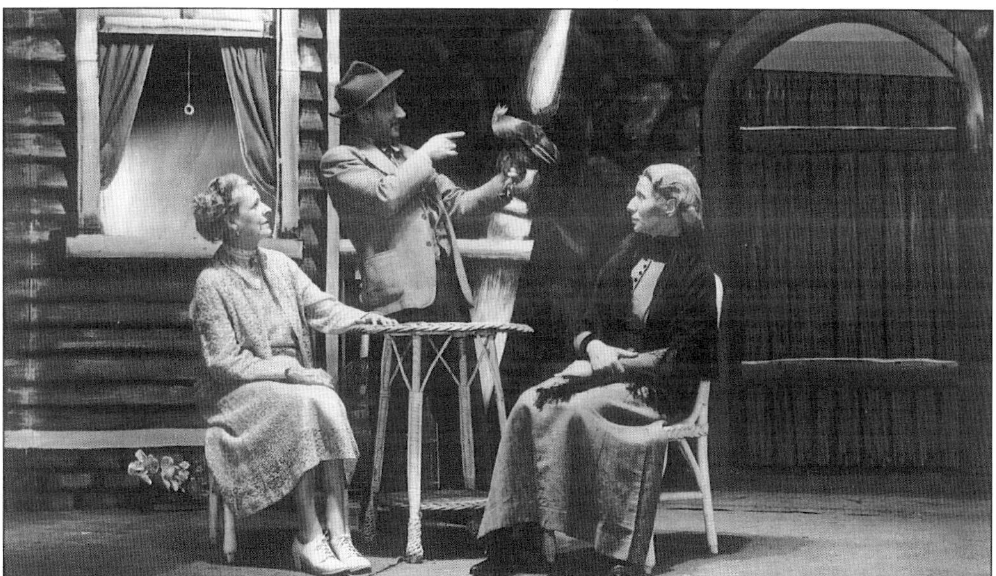

A scene from the Repertory Theatre's 1950 production of *Silver Whistle*. Adding to New Britain's rich cultural heritage, the Repertory's origins date back to the 1930s. In 1954, the Norden Street bungalow was purchased as the theater's permanent home. In addition to their regular season, the troupe also supports workshops and children's theatre. (Repertory Theatre of New Britain.)

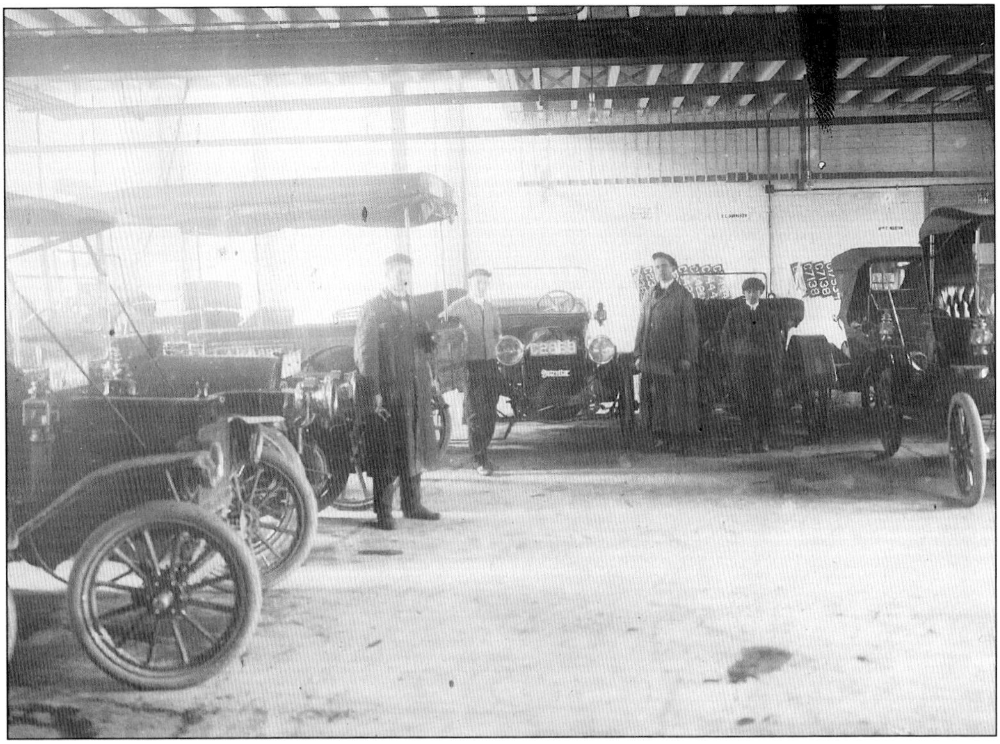

The interior of the Corbin Motor Vehicle Corporation factory in the 1920s. A 1910 ad for a Corbin proclaimed the car never wore out. Unfortunately, manufacturing costs exceeded retail prices and production of the Corbin ended by 1912. The garage remained operational until the 1930s. (*Herald* photograph file.)

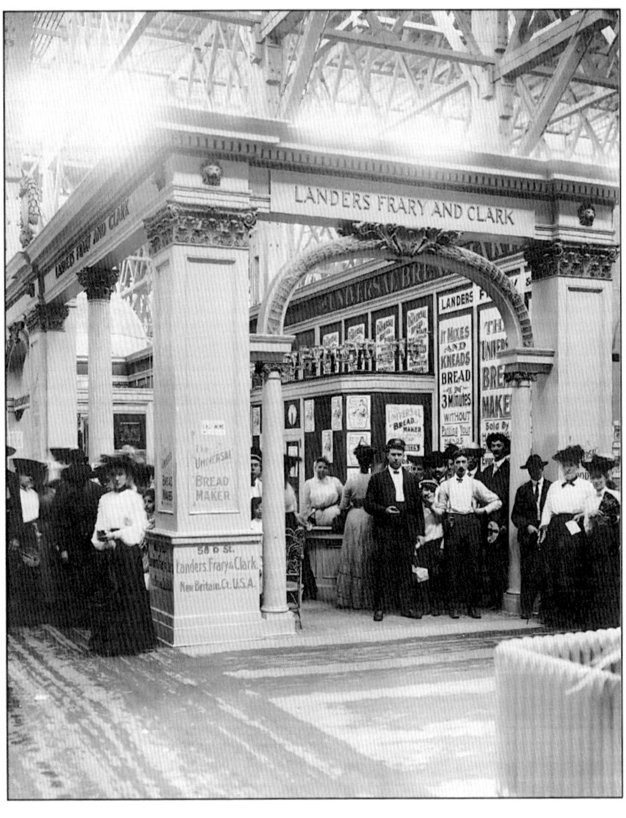

The Landers, Frary and Clark Co.'s exhibit hall at the St. Louis Exposition of 1904. This decorative hall was designed by the firm of Davis and Brooks. The bread maker, the focal point of the exhibit, took a gold medal—yet another example of the superiority of locally made products. (Local History Room, NBPL.)

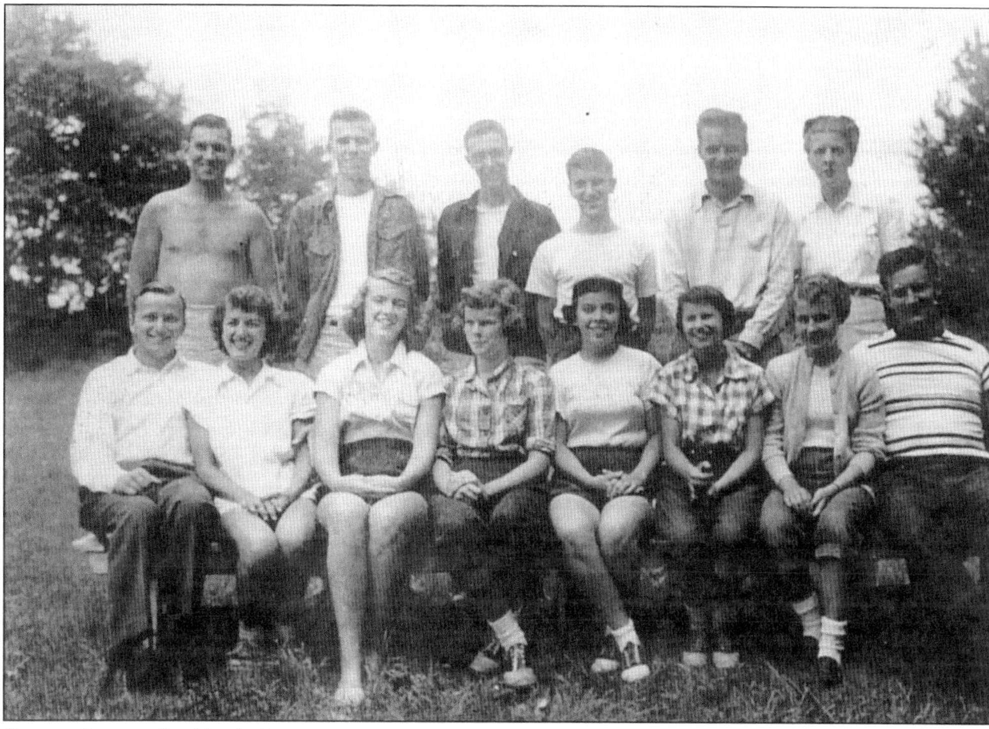

Counselors at the Fresh Air Camp in 1951. Children were given the opportunity to escape the city's heat and these young people made their stay enjoyable. Pictured are, from left to right: (front row) Lorin White, Louise Chandler, Joan Duffy, Shirley Watson, Nancy Clark, unknown, Fran Orms, and Tom Cummiskey; (back row) Dave Vogel, Ray Venberg, Al Ruscyk, Ernie Judd, Ron Zisk, and Dotty Parsons (nurse). (Ray Venberg.)

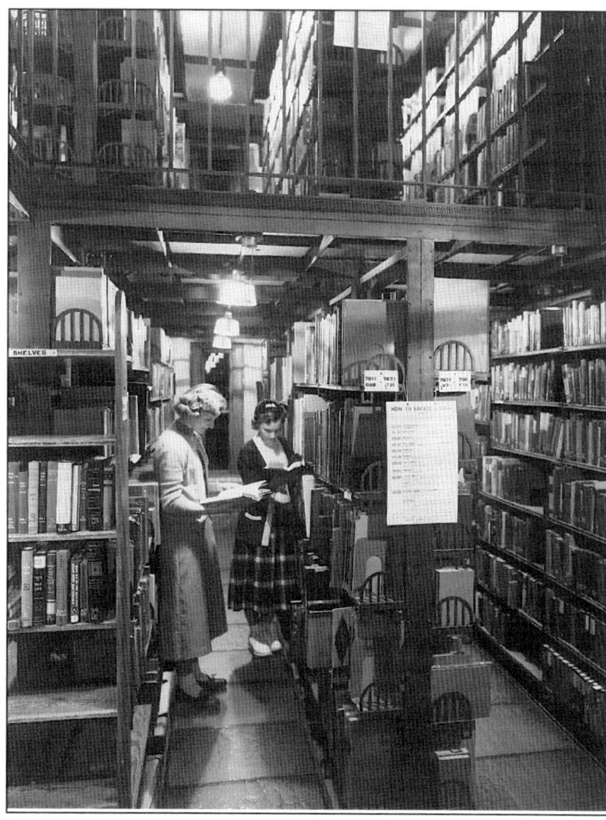

The glass-floored stacks at the New Britain Public Library. This building, the fourth home of the library, was erected in 1900 with funds from industrialist Cornelius B. Erwin's estate. In 1976 an addition was built that joined the Hawley Children's Library to the Erwin Building. The section shown here was demolished during renovation. (Irving Blomstrann.)

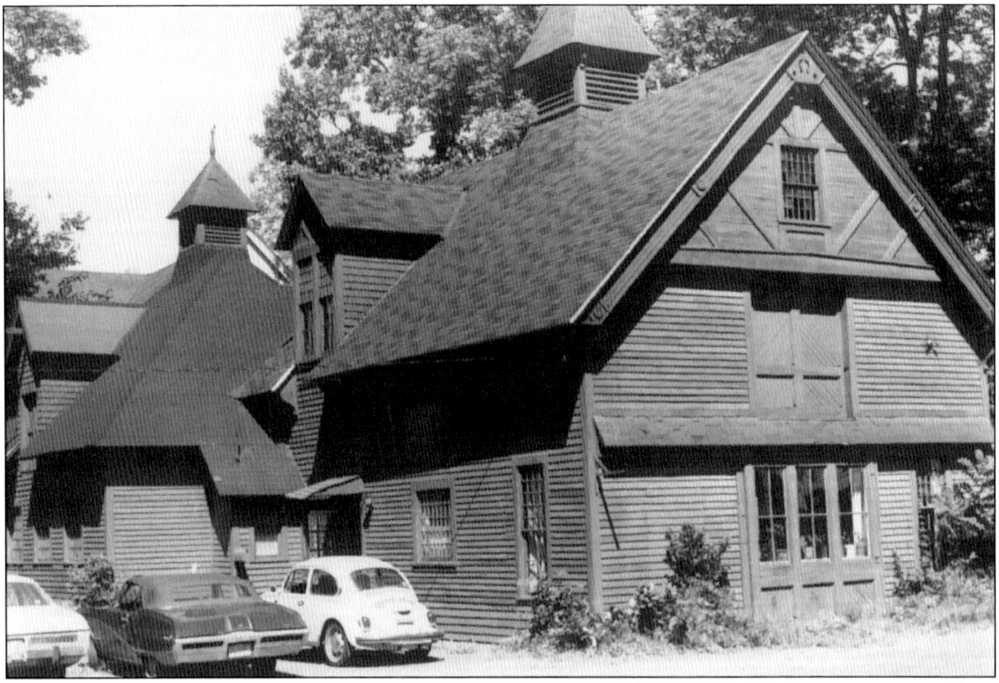

The Art League barn on Cedar Street. One of the oldest art leagues in the area, this organization promotes art through instruction and exhibits. The nineteenth-century barn was built by George Post. It was deeded to the Art League by the widow of Judge William C. Hungerford. (*Herald* photograph file.)

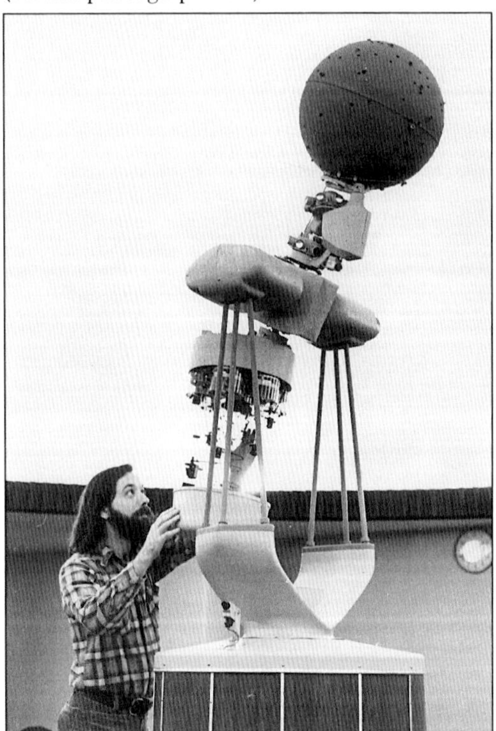

The Spitz planetarium projector at Central Connecticut State University in 1974. The school is enhanced by the Copernican Space Science Center, which houses the largest public telescope in New England, a planetarium, and a museum. Established as the State Normal School, it has become a key element in the state university system. (*Herald* photograph file.)

The Boys' Club basketball team of 1946–47. Founded in 1891, the Boys' Club has expanded its horizons and is now known as the Boys' and Girls' Club. The photograph shows, from left to right: (front row) Vern Baker, Biff Masciotra, Joe Zaleski, Joe Sardo, and Jim Petruzella. (back row) unknown, Ed Stawarz, unknown, Frank Paul, and Ed Krawiec. (Eleanor Hahn Zaleski.)

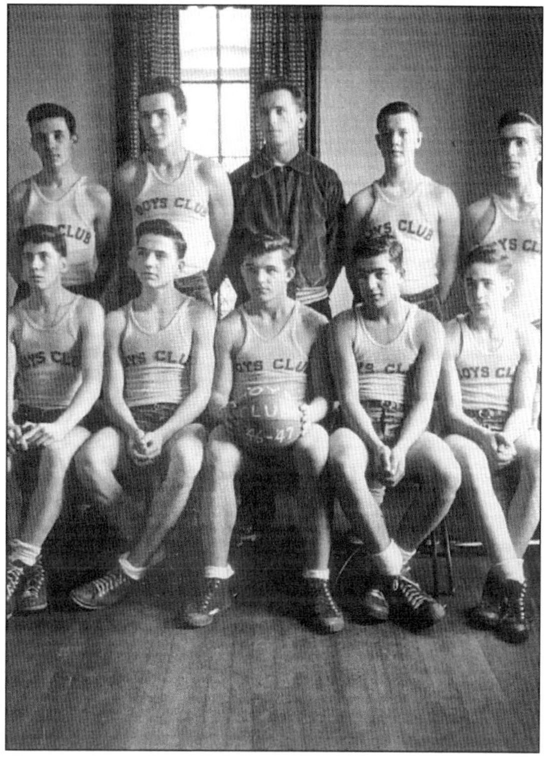

The Municipal Recreation Junior Basketball Champions, the Washington Cougars, in 1949. Pictured are, from left to right: (front row) S. Drenzek, H. Kowalewski, R. Zisk, and R. Drenzek. (back row) R. Czarnecki, R. Drzala, R. Butkiewicz, A. Rusczyk, and W. Kloskowski. (Local History Room, NBPL.)

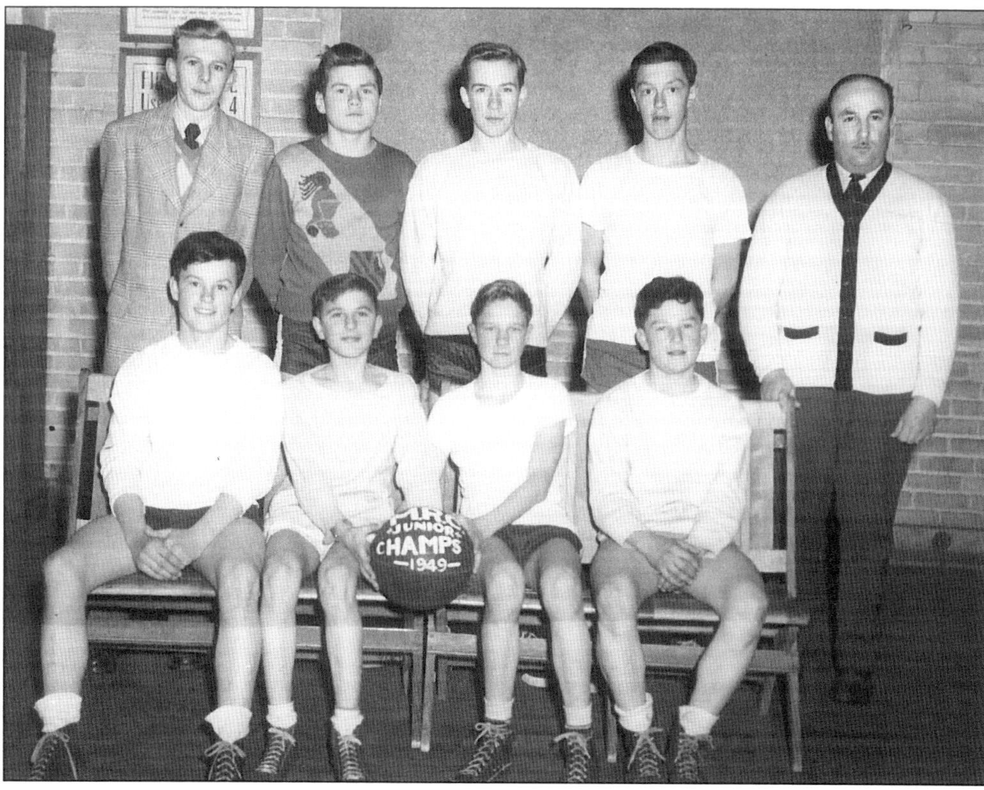

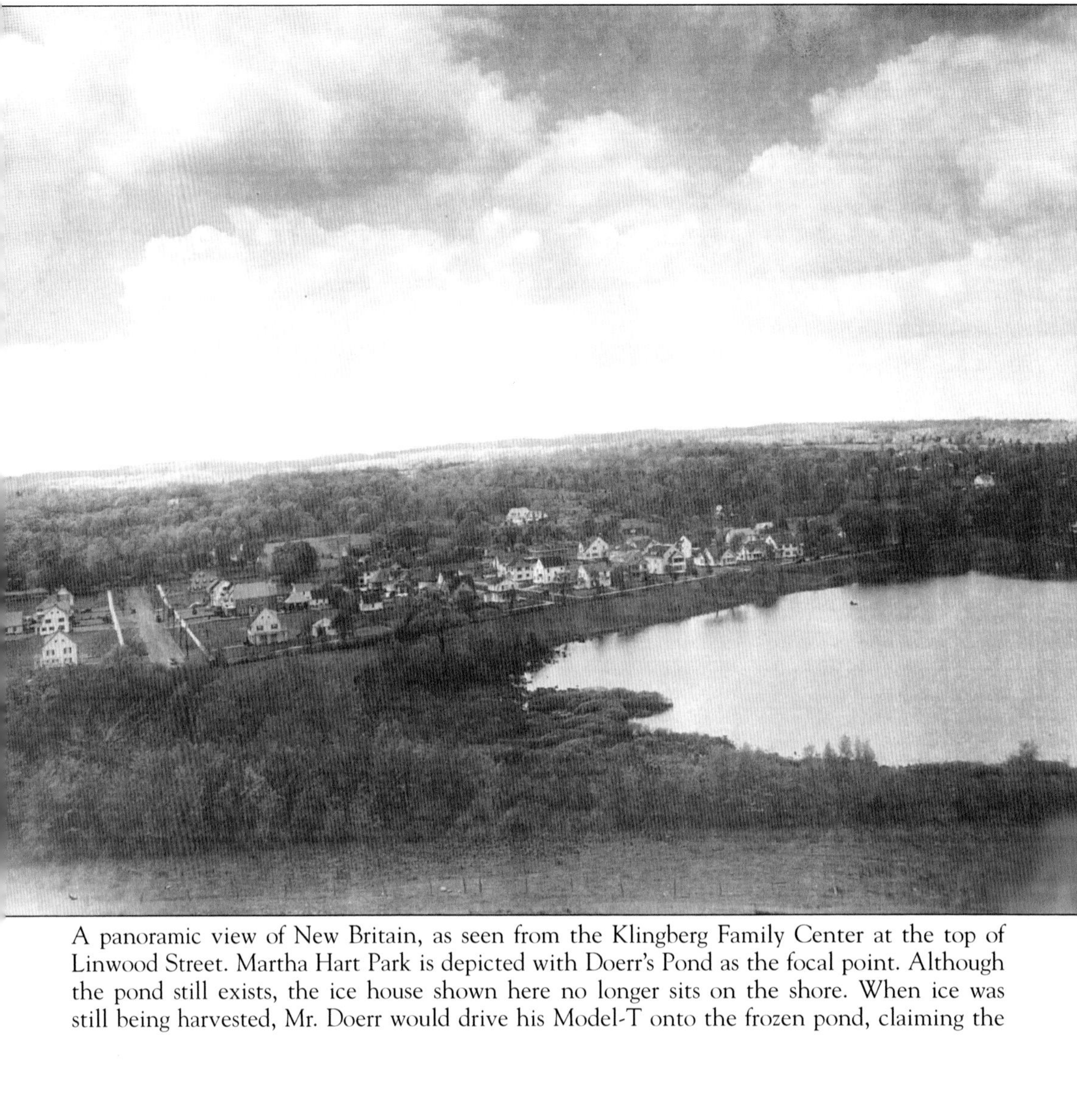

A panoramic view of New Britain, as seen from the Klingberg Family Center at the top of Linwood Street. Martha Hart Park is depicted with Doerr's Pond as the focal point. Although the pond still exists, the ice house shown here no longer sits on the shore. When ice was still being harvested, Mr. Doerr would drive his Model-T onto the frozen pond, claiming the

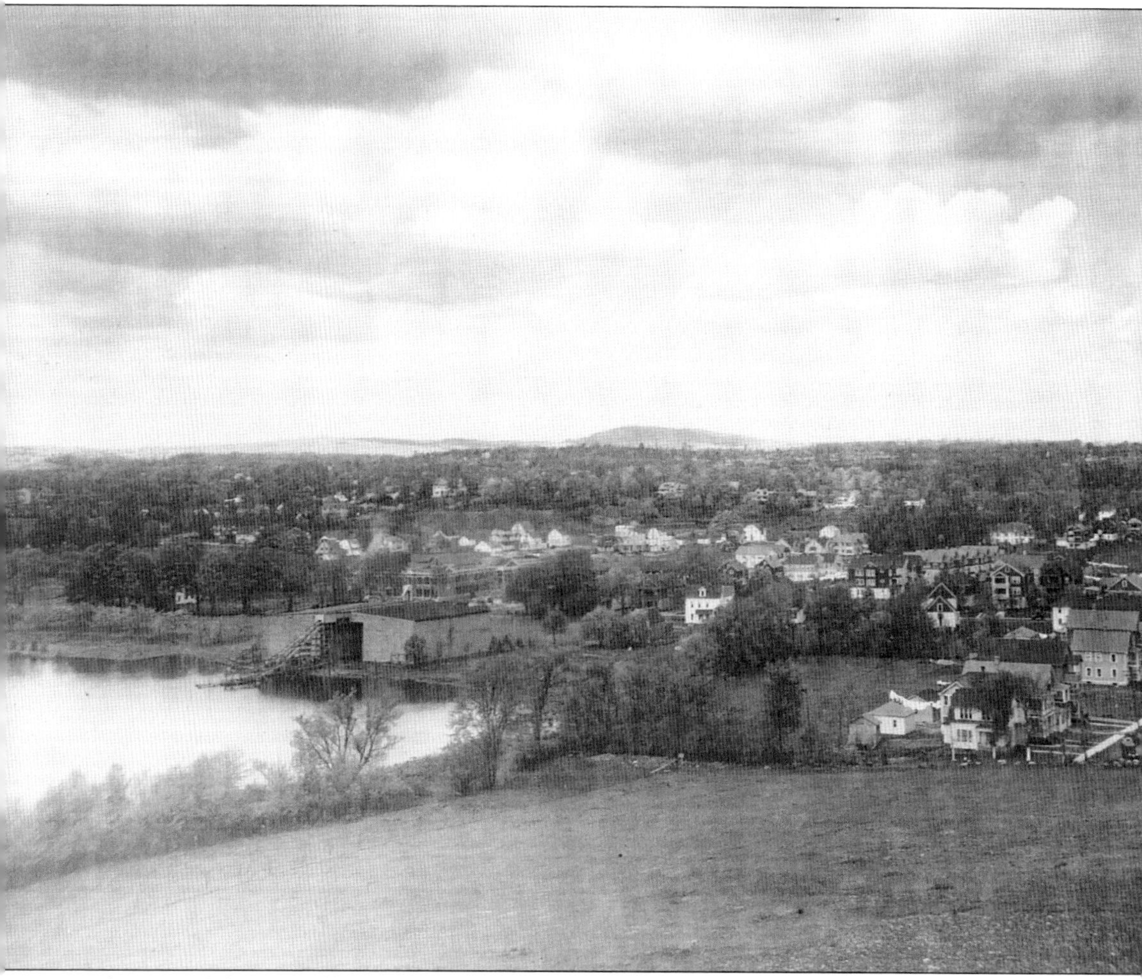

vibration of the car collapsed air bubbles in the ice. He called this method "crop cultivation." The introduction of mechanization led to the death of natural ice harvesting. Industrialist Ethelbert Allen Moore deeded 32 acres of land, including the pond, to the city to be used as a public park. It is named after his wife, Martha Hart. (Klingberg Family Center.)

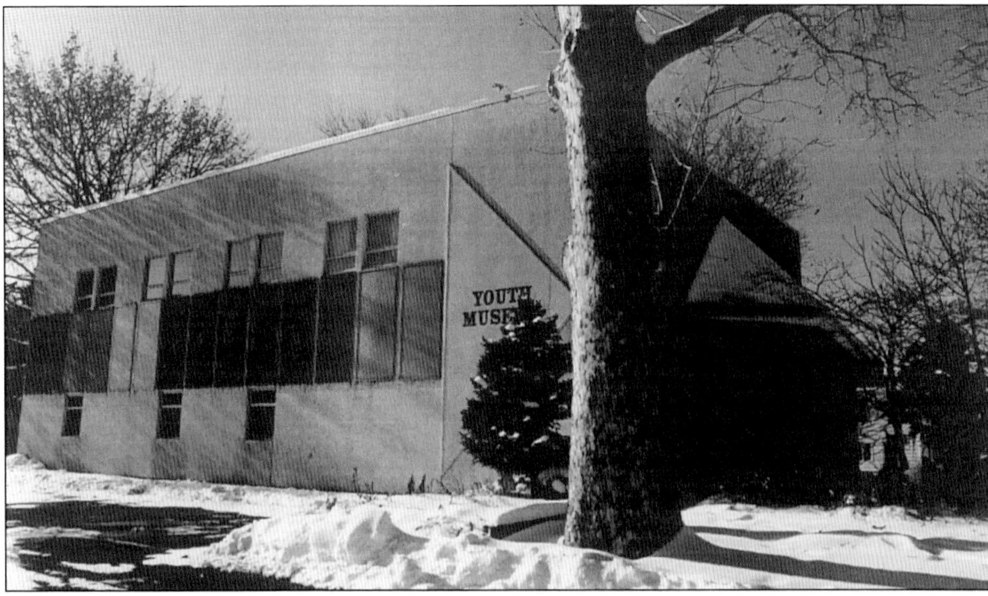

The Youth Museum, a division of the New Britain Institute, at 30 High Street. The core collection began with donations from Eugene Schmidt (mounted birds) and James Shepard (shells, minerals, and fossils). Originally called the Museum of Natural History, exhibits occupied the top floor of the library until another room was prepared on the ground floor in 1956. In 1976 the organization gained its own building where today superb exhibits and programs continue to educate and entertain area residents. (Deborah Pfeiffenberger.)

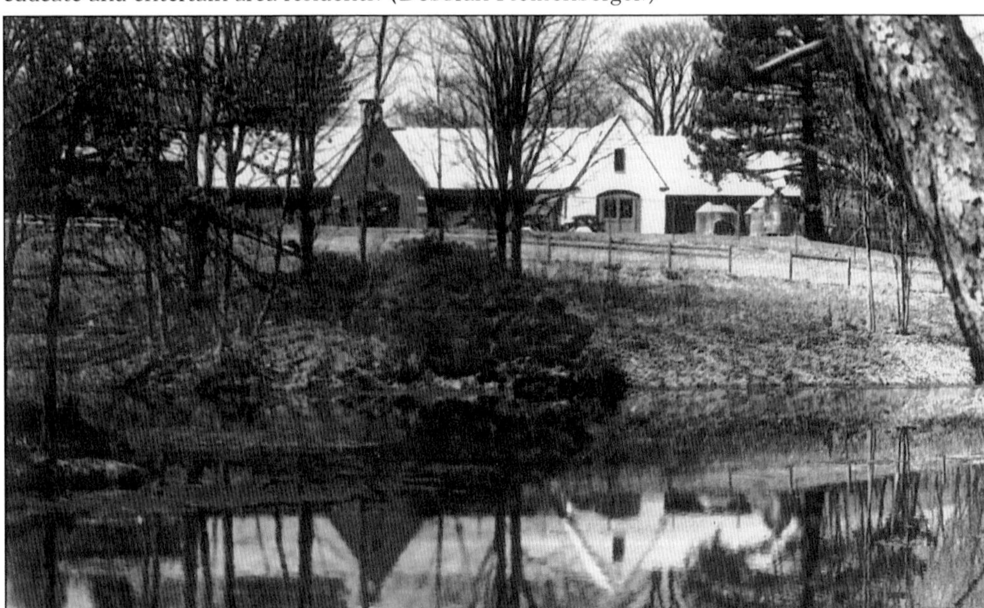

The Hungerford Educational Outdoor Center. A demand for outdoor educational activities led to the acquisition of the old Hungerford stables in Berlin. In 1984, this became the Hungerford Educational Outdoor Center, run under the directorship of the Youth Museum. Farming implements, natural history specimens, and live animals are all part of this wonderful "hands on" museum. (Deborah Pfeiffenberger.)

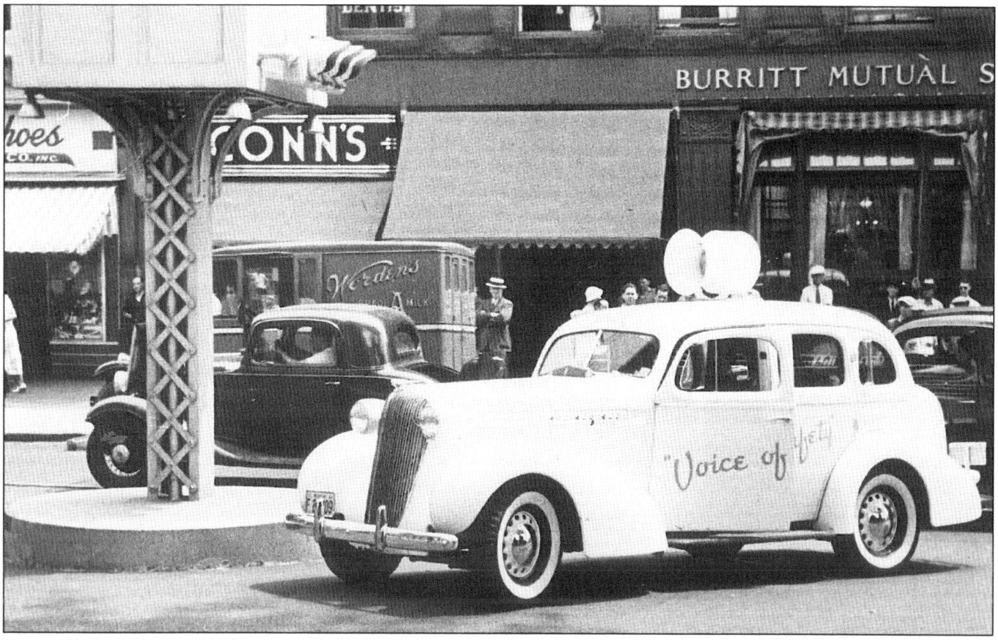

Two of New Britain's busiest thoroughfares. In the above photograph of Main Street, c. 1936, the traffic tower and accompanying "Voice of Safety" automobile can be seen. The intersection of Main and West Main Streets, where the tower was located, remains one of the most congested corners in the city. Central Park, on the southwestern corner, was like a rural haven compared to the other three, which were occupied by the Gates Building, the Booth Block, and the First Church. The bottom photograph of West Main Street in the 1920s shows the Capitol Theater marquee, the Hotel Burritt, and the incredible amount of traffic traversing the street. (*Herald* photograph file/Gordon Alling.)

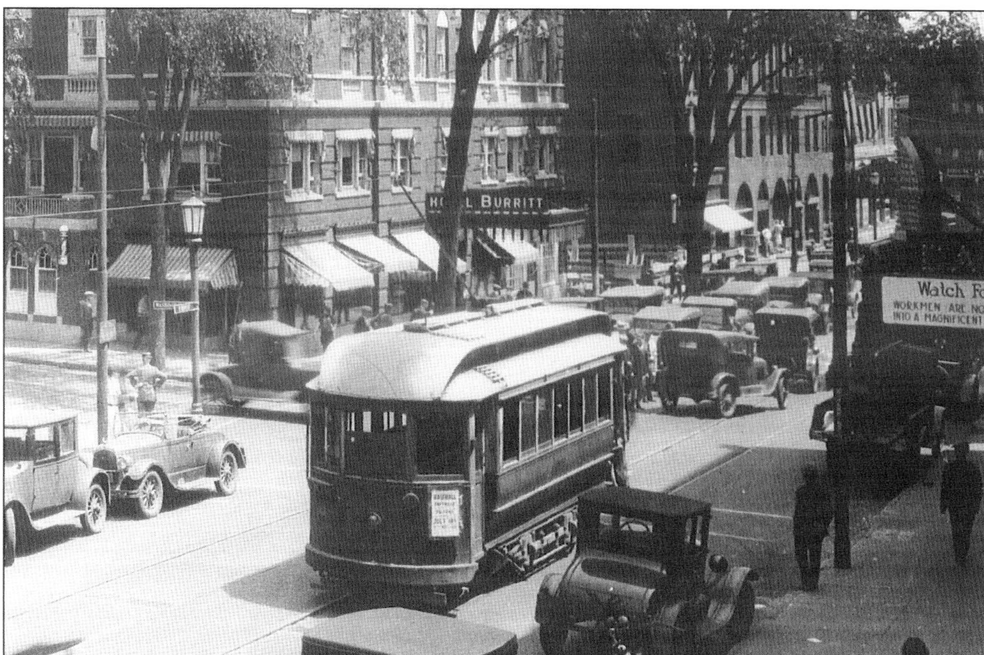

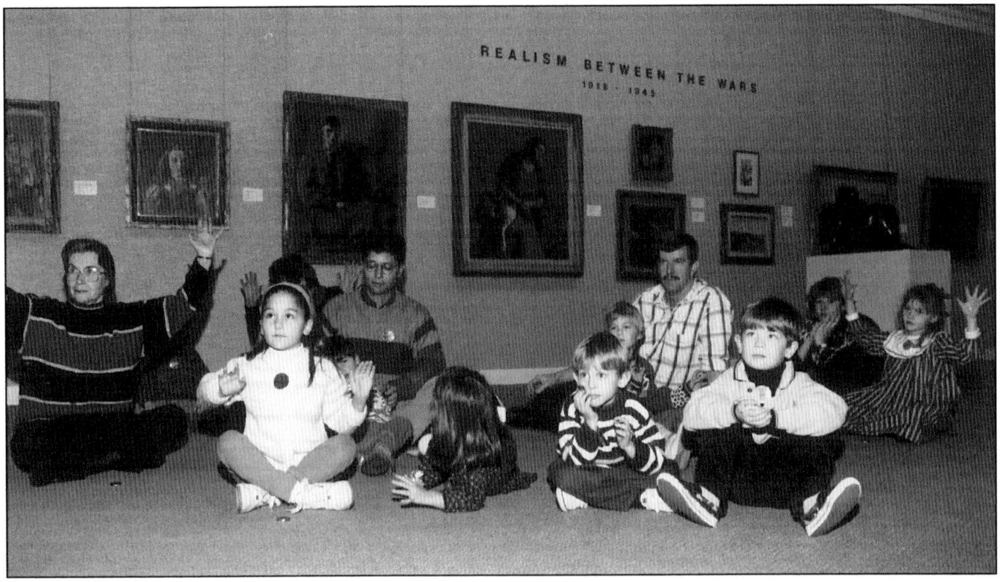

Docent Lois Penney (far left) and a group of children and parents in one of the weekly programs offered by the New Britain Museum of American Art. John B. Talcott donated $25,000 to start an art collection at the New Britain Institute at the turn of the century. The collection was transferred in the 1930s to the former of home of Grace Judd Landers on Lexington Street, pictured below. (New Britain Museum of American Art.)

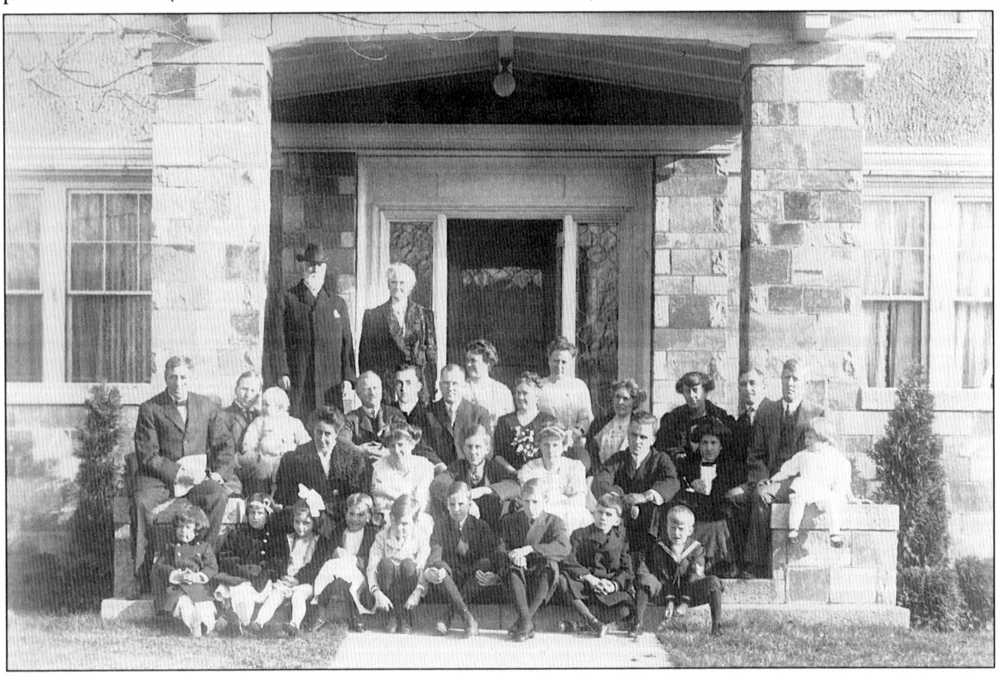

Thanksgiving 1910. This was an occasion for the family of William H. Hart, chair of Stanley Works, to gather on the front steps. The structure then belonged to Grace Judd Landers prior to becoming the home of the New Britain Museum of American Art. It seems appropriate that the location for one of the finest collections of American art in the country was once occupied by one of New Britain's industrial giants. (Local History Room, NBPL.)

Six

How We Served

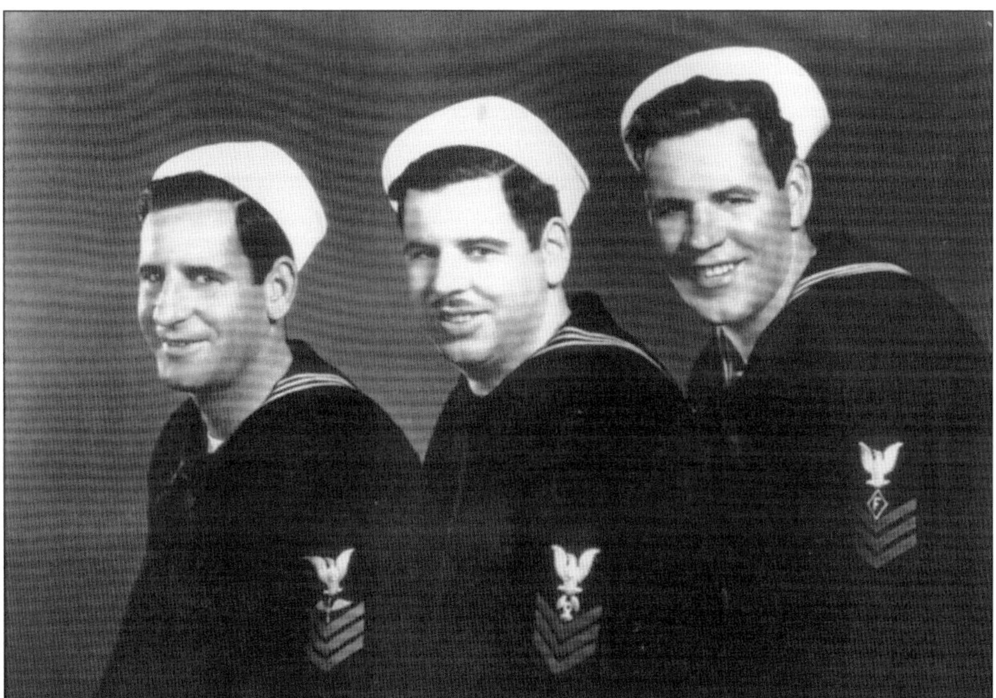

Three McKeon brothers, James, Wilfred, and Edward. All enlisted during World War II. Like the McKeons, many New Britain families saw several children from one family go off to war. For over two hundred years, even before our incorporation, local residents have served in all branches of the military. (Patricia McKeon Marinelli.)

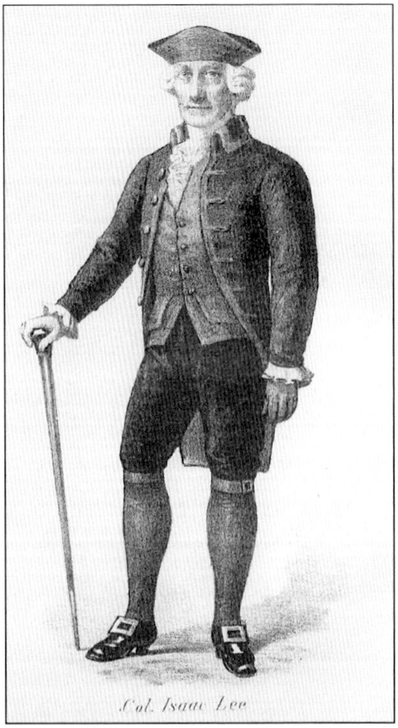

Colonel Isaac Lee (1717–1802). Service in the Revolutionary War was among his many contributions. He was active in the formation of local government and religious societies in Farmington, Berlin, and locally. Credited with naming New Britain (after Great Britain), Colonel Lee married three times and died at the age of eighty-six. (Local History Room, NBPL.)

Fairview Cemetery superintendent Emil F. Schall. Mr. Schall is shown here checking notes against the gravestone of Joseph H. White, who was reputed to be one of the youngest Union soldiers to serve in the Civil War. He was only nine years old when he enlisted. Returning home safely, he died in 1907. (*Herald* photograph file.)

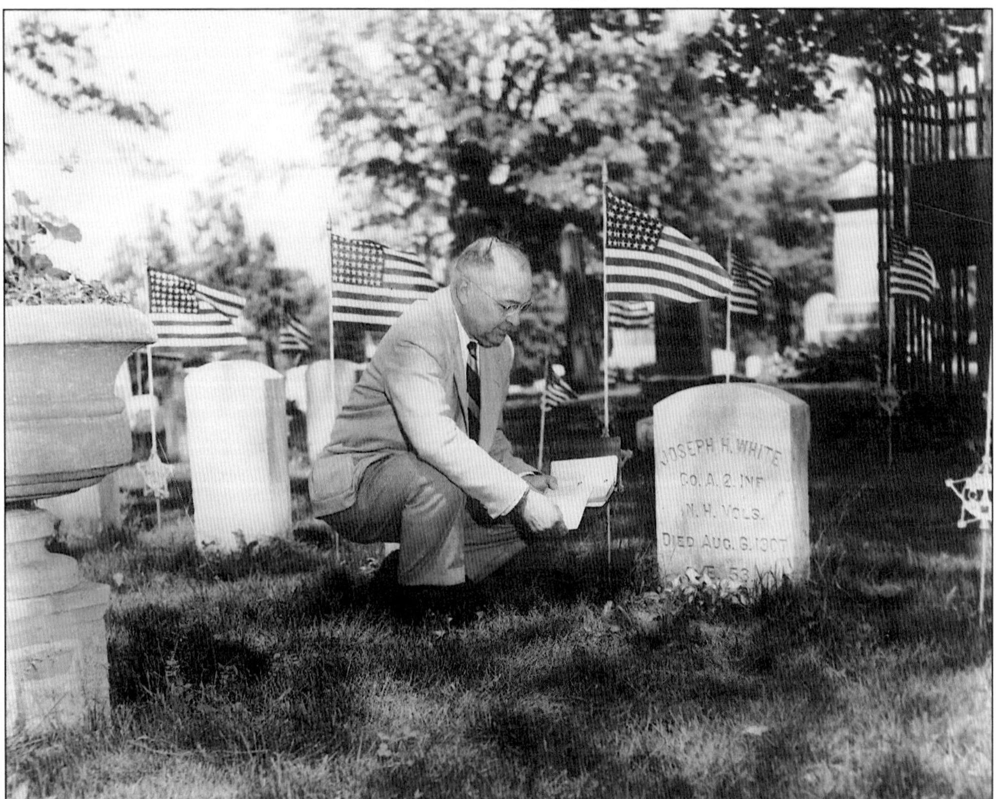

Reverend Lyman S. Johnson at home on Roxbury Road. Born in 1838, Reverend Johnson recorded his recollections of the Civil War in a seventy-seven-page memoir. His keen observations brought the horrors of war to life. After his discharge, he continued to reside in New Britain until his death in 1932, at age ninety-three. (Local History Room, NBPL.)

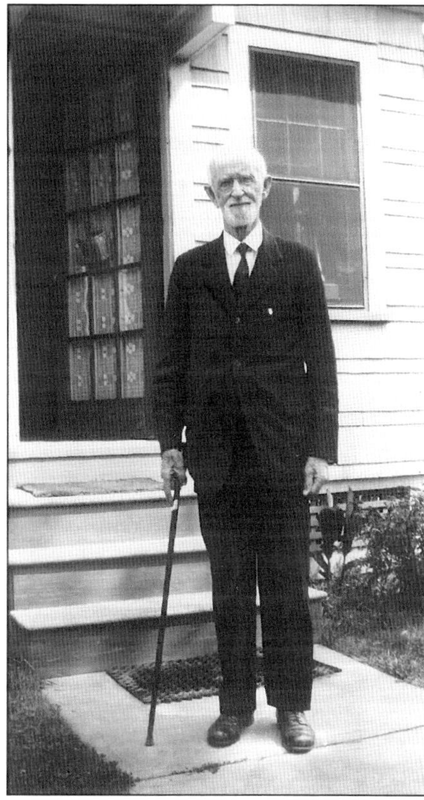

Surviving members of the GAR (Grand Army of the Republic), Stanley Post #11. Organized in 1867, this post was the fourth instituted in the state. It peaked in 1890 with 228 members. Five New Britain Stanleys fought in the Civil War; three of them died. The post was named in honor of Theodore, who died as a result of wounds received at the Battle of Fredericksburg. (Local History Room, NBPL.)

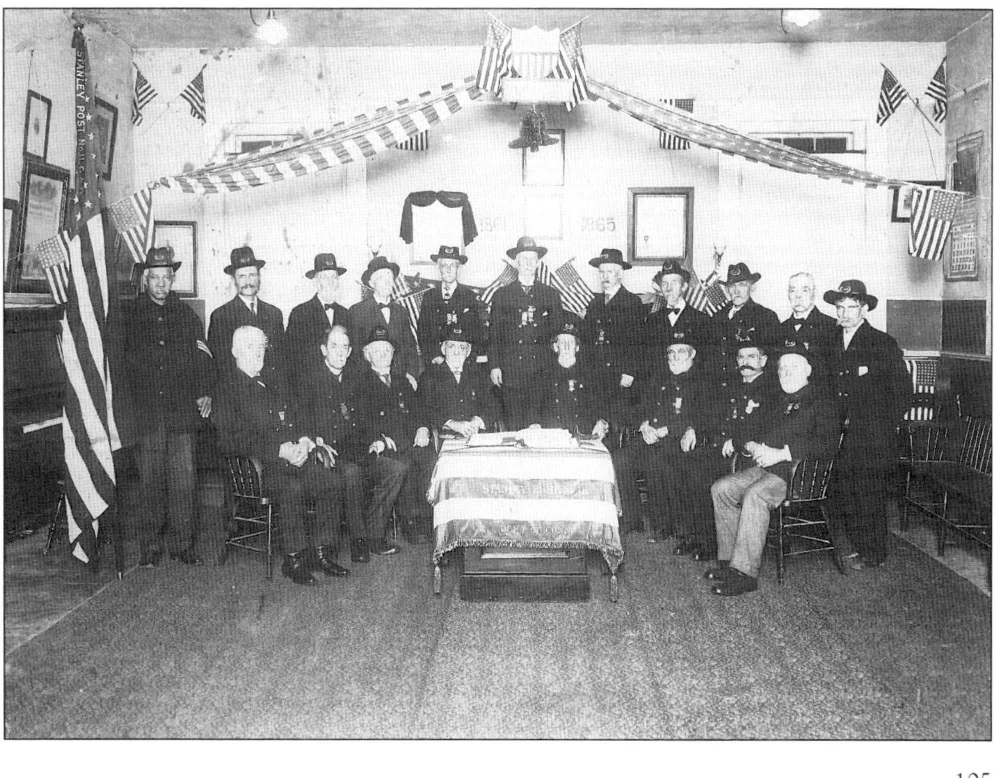

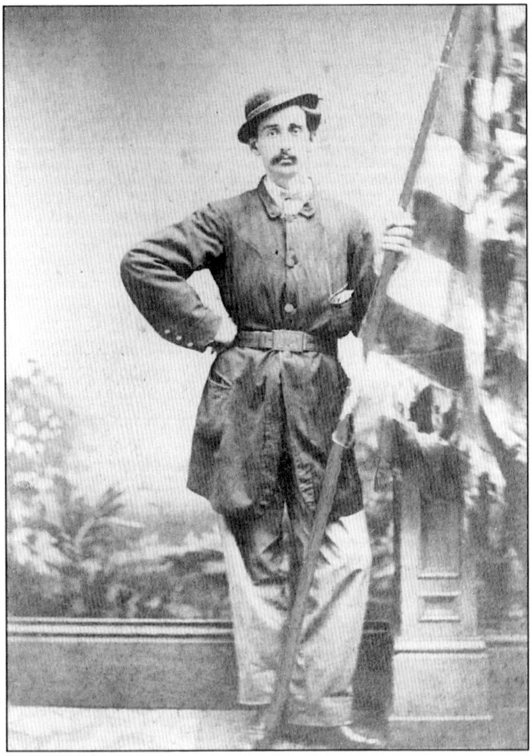

Julius O. Deming as a young man serving in the Civil War and as an elderly man, just before his death on February 21, 1918. Sergeant Deming served in the 1st Connecticut Volunteers and the 6th Regiment. In later years he served as commander of the GAR post. The last local Civil War veteran was Dr. Thomas Mulligan, who died at age ninety-five in 1936. The flag that was draped over the coffin of every New Britain Civil War veteran who died between 1911–1936 was buried with Dr. Mulligan. Ironically, as a young man, Dr. Mulligan was so ill that it was feared he would die. Having recovered, he entered service in August 1862 and remained in the war until its end in 1865, without suffering any wounds. (Local History Room, NBPL.)

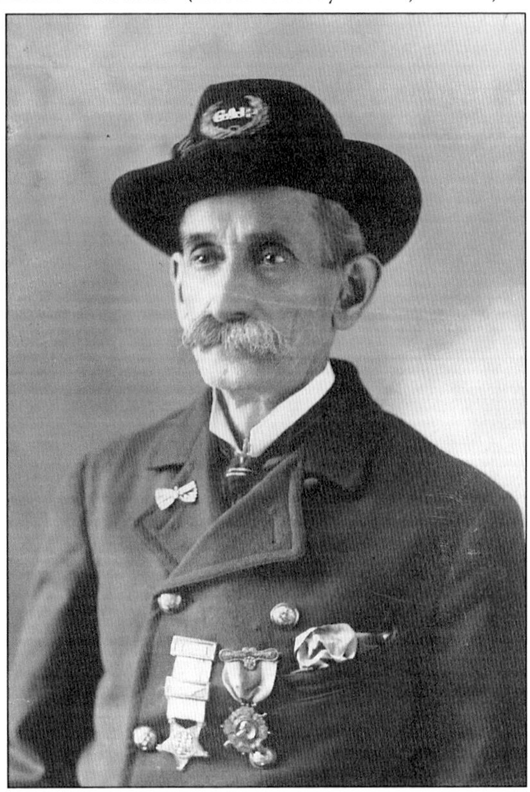

The Spanish-American War Memorial in Willow Brook Park. Dedicated on June 27, 1927, the ceremony was preceded by a parade. The designers of the monument were Delbert Perry and Earl Bishop. Mrs. Sarah Magson, widow of Samuel Magson, first commander of A.G. Hammond camp, United States American War Veterans, unveiled the monument. (Local History Room/NBPL.)

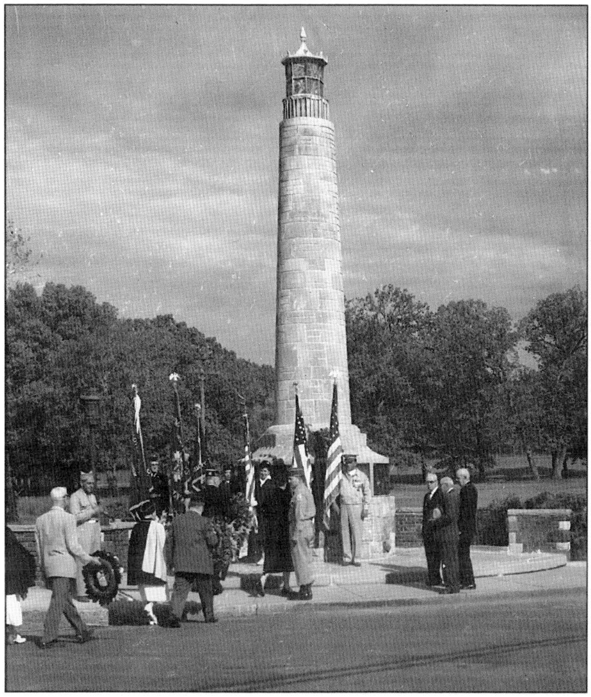

The first patients at the New Britain General Hospital. As can be seen here, the first patients were veterans of the Spanish-American War. The monument pictured here was based on the Morro Castle lighthouse in Havanna Harbor. (Frank Fraprie, New Britain General Hospital Archives.)

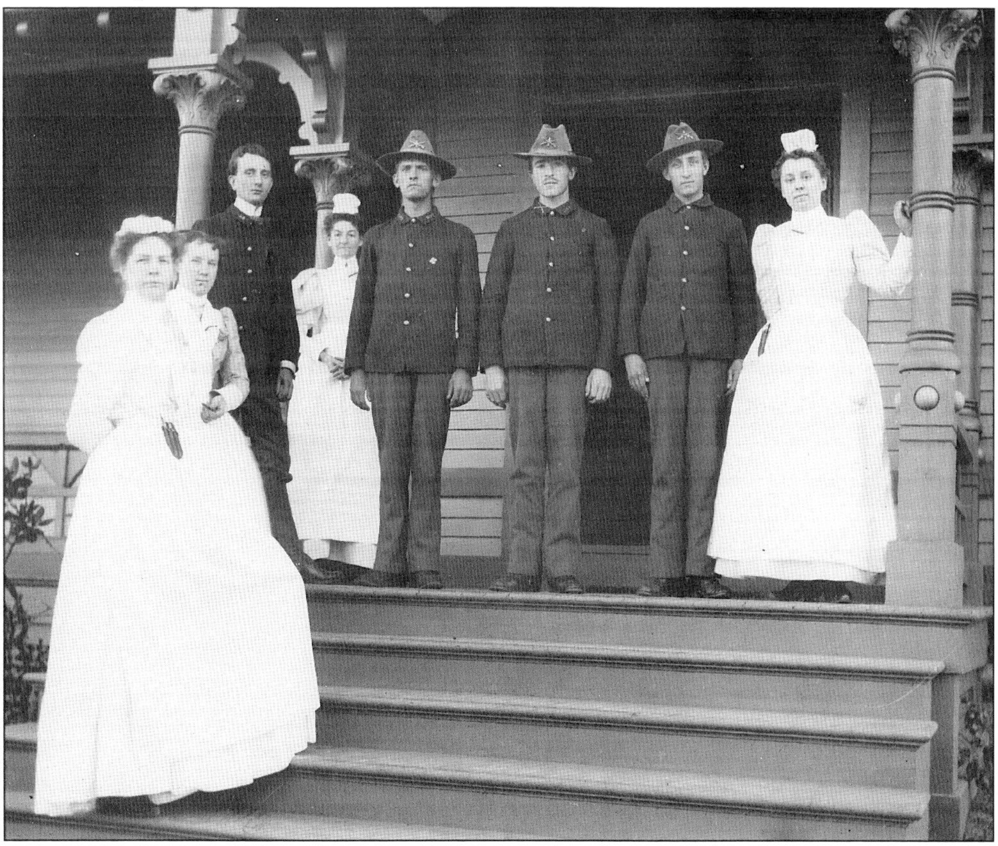

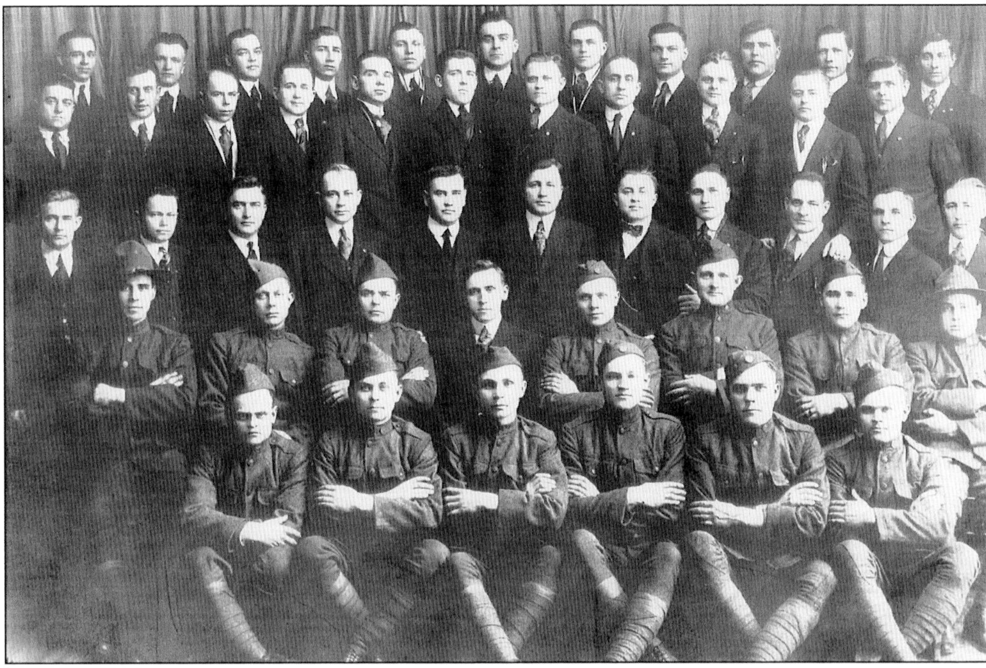

St. Andrew's parish members, including veterans of World War I. The cornerstone for the monument in Walnut Hill Park was laid in July 1927. Mayor Gardner Weld placed war relics into a strong box and dropped it into a hollow stone at the base of the monument. The monument was dedicated on September 22, 1928. (St. Andrew's Church.)

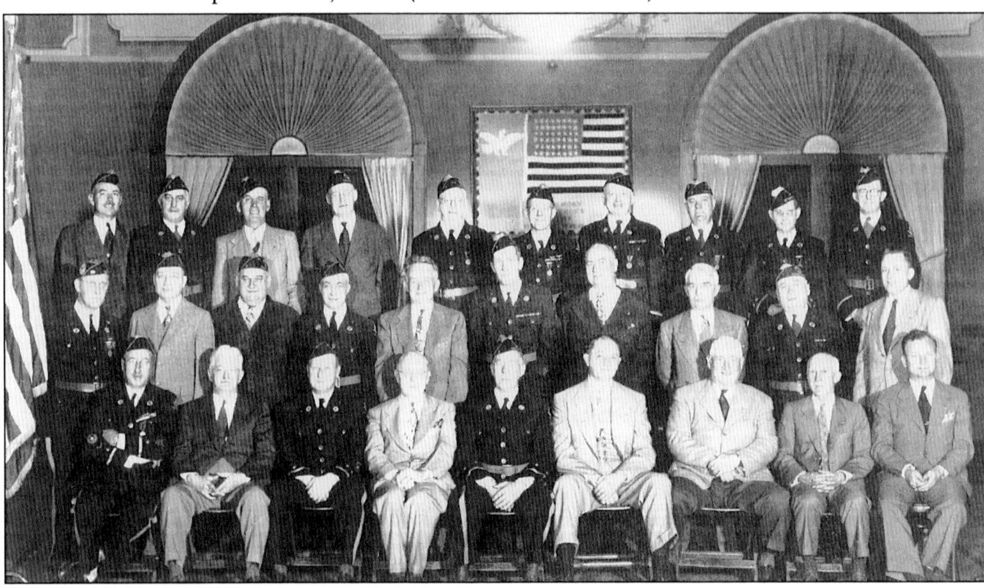

Twenty-five commanders of the American Legion, Eddy Glover Post #6, in 1947. Pictured are, from left to right: (front row) G. Weld, J. Jackson, W. Squires, E. Ogren, A. Petts, H. Ginsburg, N. Avery, M. Pease, and H. Gwiazda; (middle row) L. Chevalier, E. Schall, M. Andrews, H. Scarborough, M. DeCalvin, W. Shaw, E. Stack, and R. Lekston; (back row) R. Sakalowski, H. Mitchell, C. Coons, J. Anderson, J. Fienburg, L. Browki, J. Welch, I. Good, N. Provost, and W. McEnroe. (Ed LaMire.)

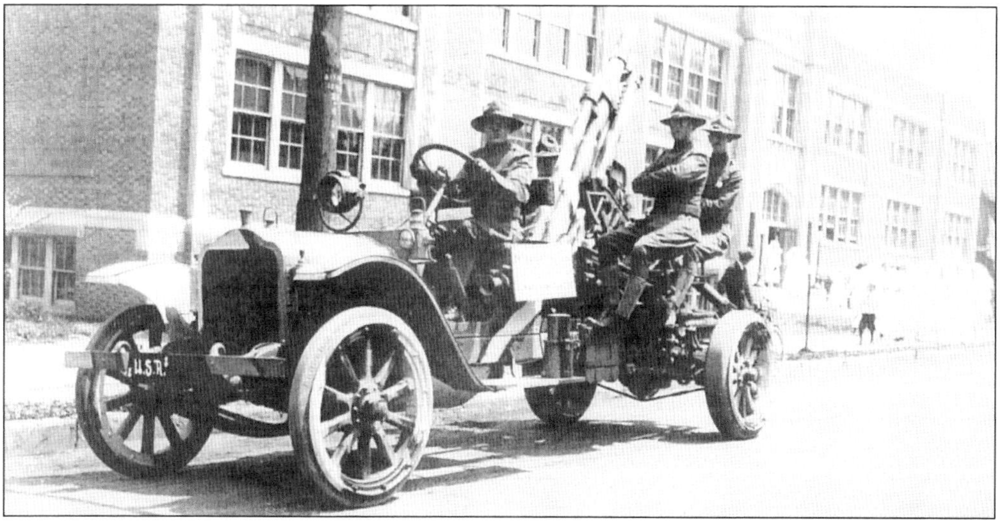

The first Armistice Day parade passing by the old high school. When the war ended in 1918, New Britain celebrated with a closing of schools and factories and with church bells chiming throughout the city. In subsequent years, celebrations were more subdued and marked with parades and solemn ceremonies. Armistice Day became Veterans Day, a time when we remember all those who have served. (Mr. and Mrs. William Bonney.)

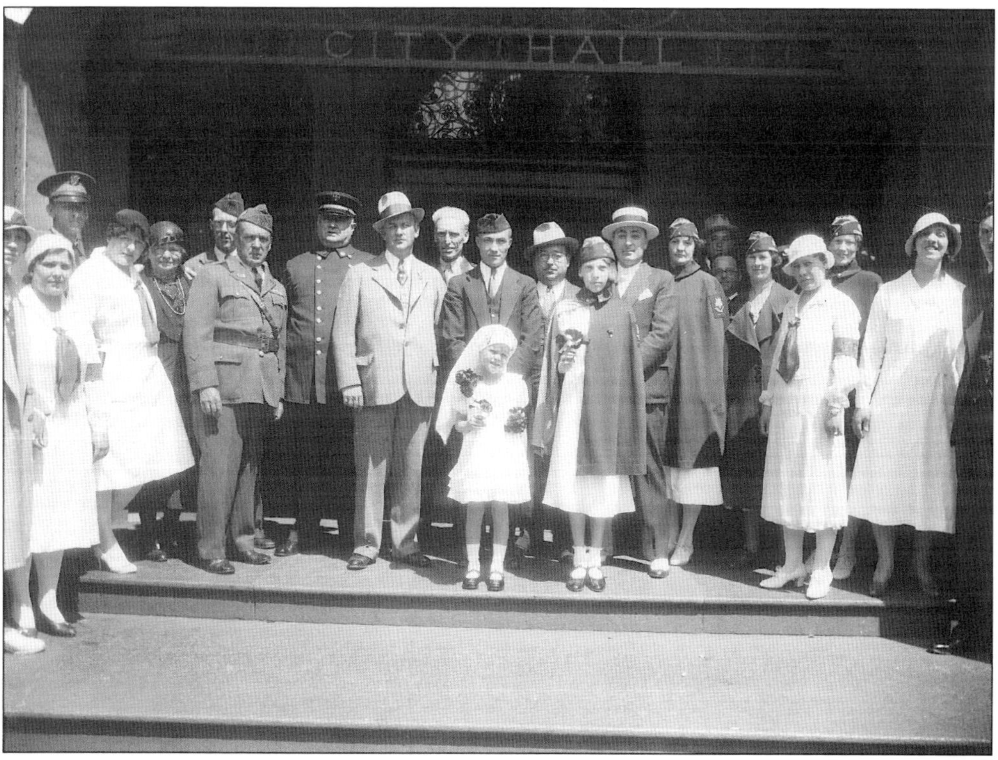

World War I veterans with members of the VFW and American Legion poppy committees. The two children represented the poppy queens. The little girl with the veil was the VFW poppy queen, while the young lady with the cape was the American Legion representative. (John Melechinsky.)

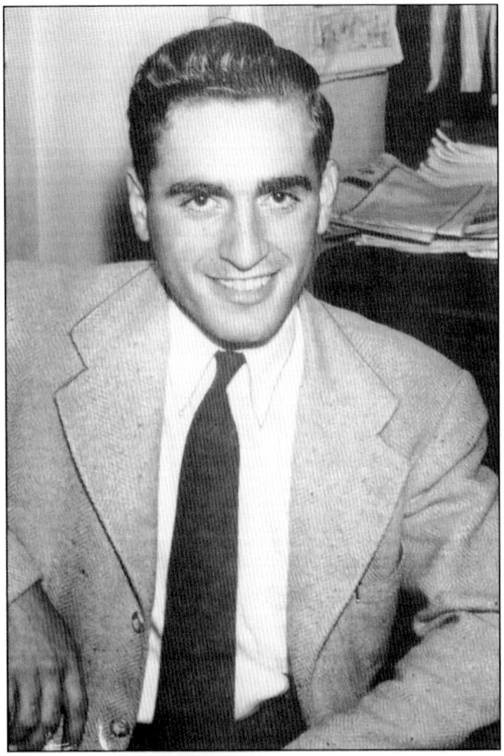

John D'Amato. While working as assistant manager of the Embassy Theater in July 1941, Mr. D'Amato heard unexpected news: he and another resident, Gunnar Carlson, were the first two local men selected for the draft. Within a matter of months, the country would enter World War II. (John D'Amato.)

The men of Company I, 169th Infantry, in October 1941 at Camp Blanding, Florida. From here they proceeded to Camp Shelby in Mississippi and were then shipped out overseas. According to Commander Alfred "Fritz" Casella, Camp Blanding offered "the best barracks we were to have in five years!" Ninety percent of this company hailed from New Britain. (169th Infantry.)

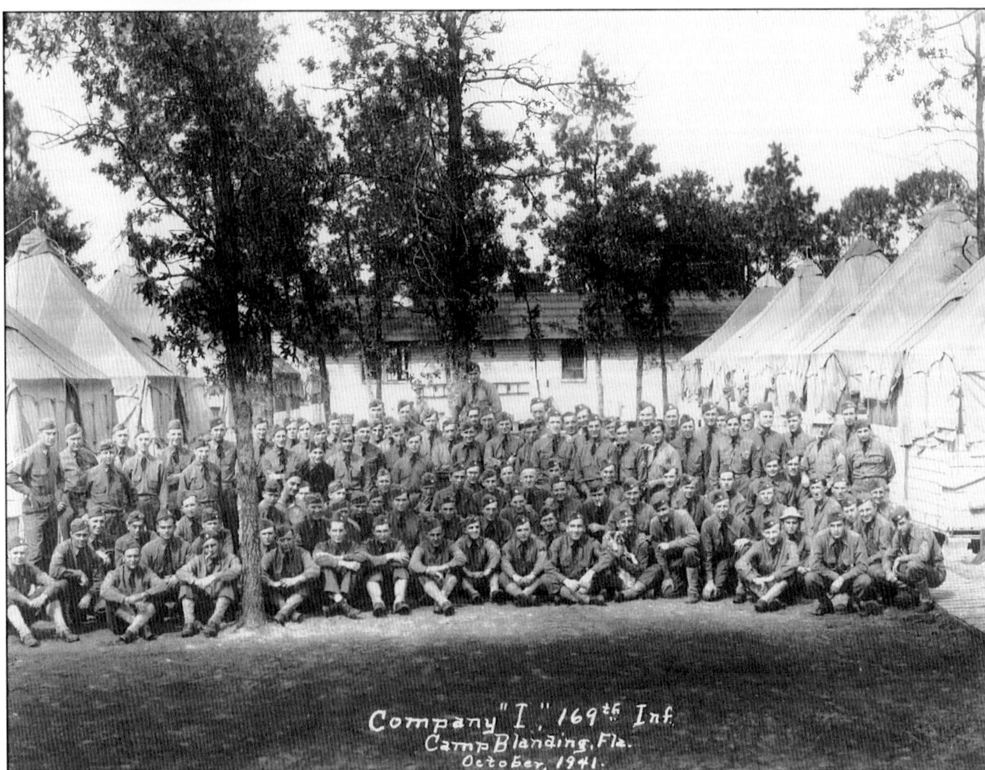

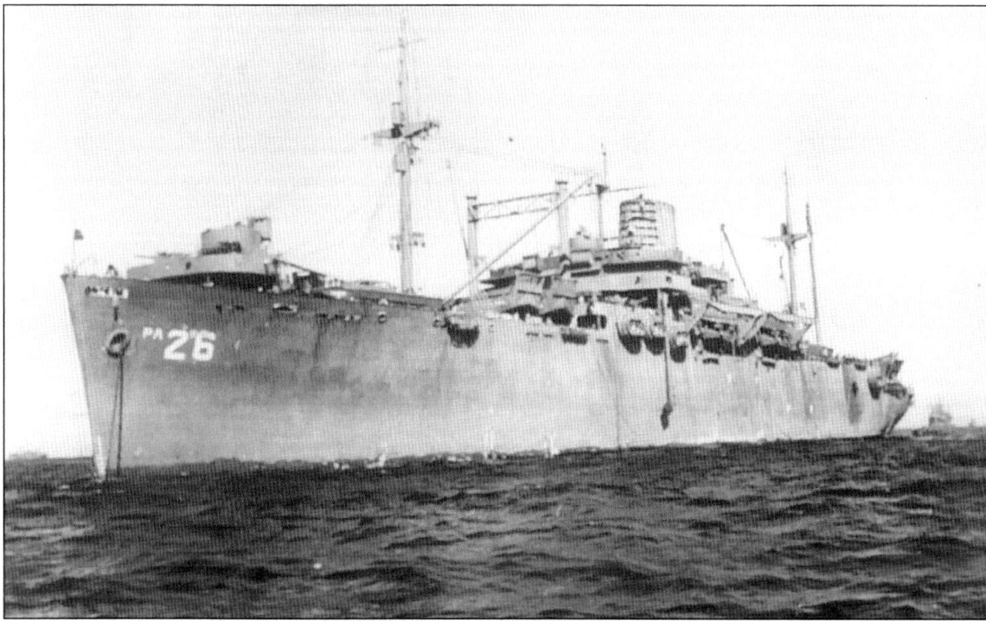

The USS *Samuel Chase*, better known as the "Lucky Chase," manned by a crew of the U.S. Coast Guard. The ship survived dive bombers, magnetic mines, and torpedo attacks by mere yards. It played a vital role during the invasion of Normandy and Okinawa. Two New Britain neighbors met unexpectedly aboard the *Chase*. Pictured below, on the left, Bruno "Bernie" Muraca, Seaman 1st Class, shows Army PFC Gnerino D'Amato the intricacies of tying knots. Prior to the war, the men lived within two blocks of one another on Oak Street. (Bernie Muraca.)

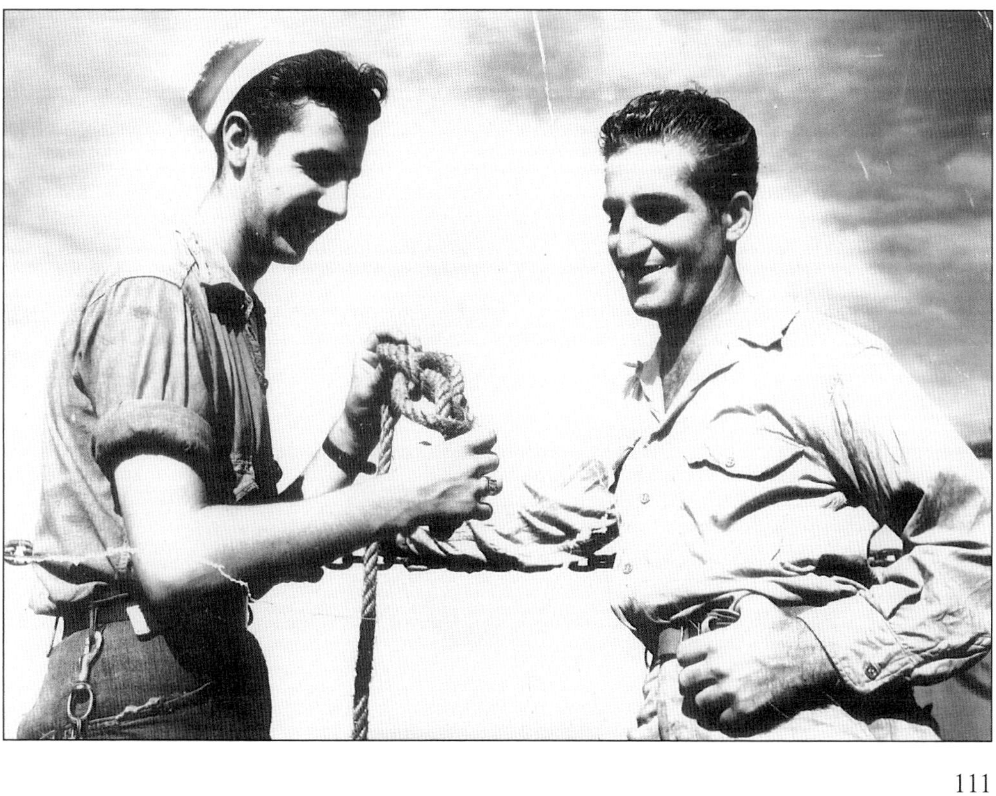

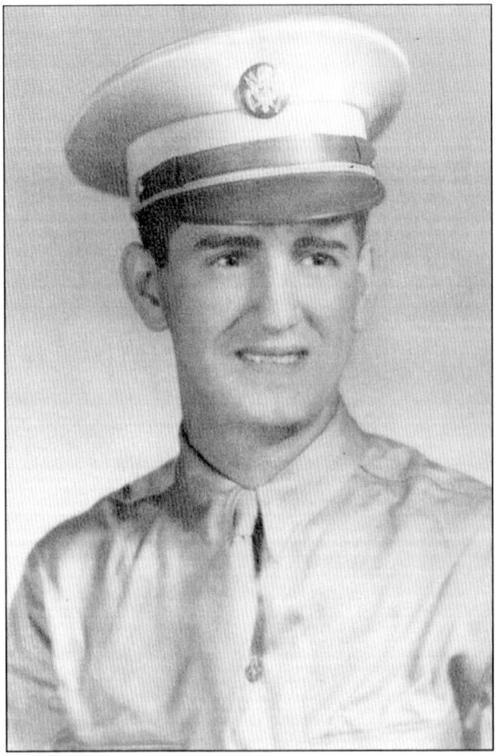

James J. (Dimitrius) Morris. Wounded at the Battle of the Bulge, he died on January 12, 1945. He was the first New Britainite sent home for burial. On November 5, 1947, his body was escorted by Sgt. James L. Miller of the 82nd Airborne. He was buried with full military honors the following day. Thus began the long process of bringing home the city's deceased. (Flossie Morris Sfiridis.)

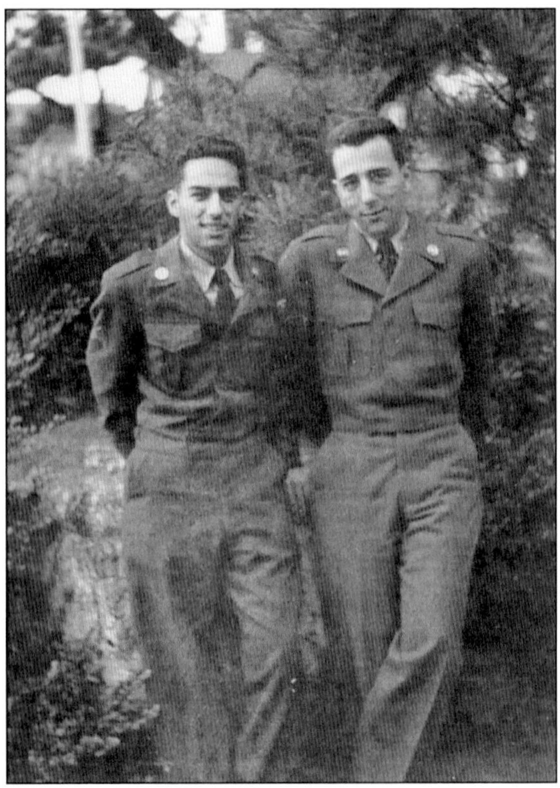

Fred Elia and Ted Fusaro. Proving it is truly a "small world," these friends met on R&R in Japan during the Korean War. One was affiliated with the U.S. Army, the other with the Air Force. The Korean Conflict is often referred to as the "forgotten war." (Ted Fusaro.)

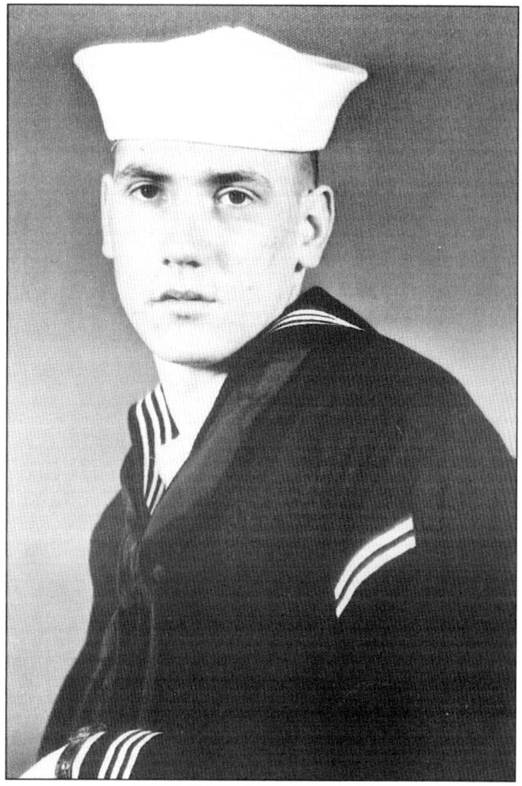

David A. Wasel. Tragically, David lost his life during peacetime when he went down with 128 others on the USS *Thresher* on April 10, 1963. The nuclear-powered attack submarine was built in at Portsmouth Naval Shipyard. In 1984 his parents, Mr. and Mrs. John Wasel, were invited and attended the dedication of Thresher Hall on the Naval Base New London in Groton. Locally, a fitting memorial was dedicated to David A. Wasel on April 9, 1967, when the reservoir was named after him. (Katherine Nadolny Wasel/Local History Room, NBPL.)

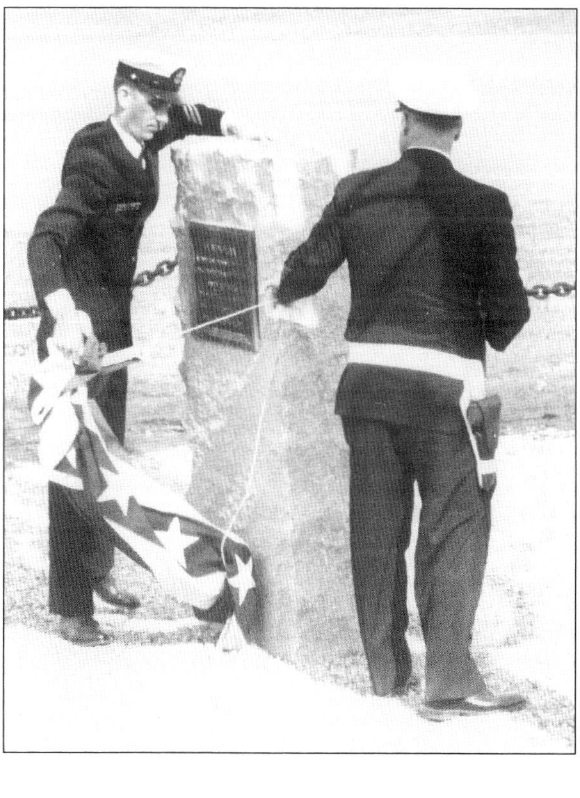

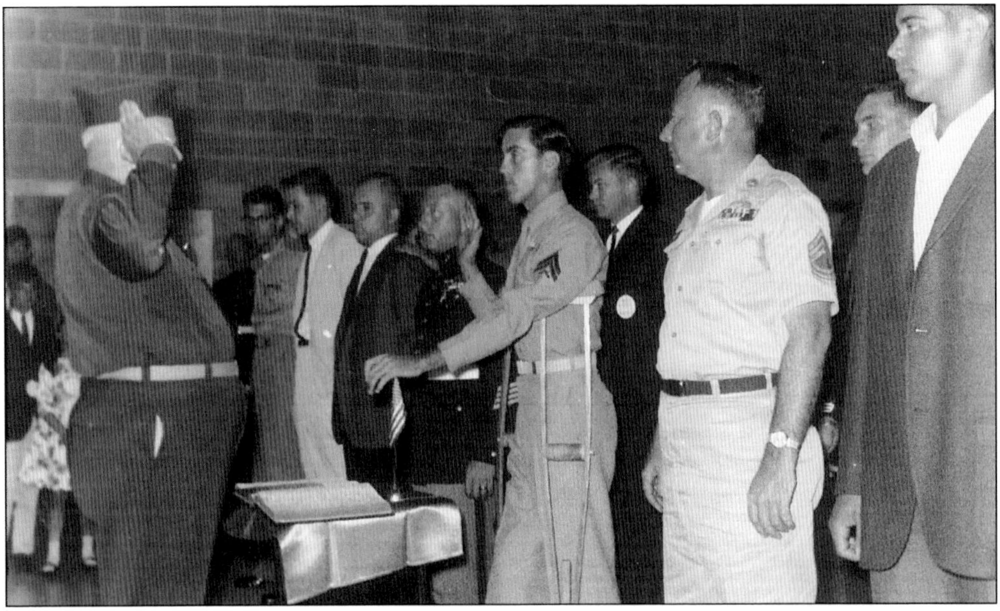

Entering into the VFW. Donald Pelletier Jr. (on crutches) and other veterans are shown here being sworn into the VFW by Post Commander Raymond C. Frost, a World War I veteran. Severely wounded in the line of duty, Pvt. Pelletier would become the first Vietnam veteran to serve as marshal of the Memorial Day parade in 1967. (Christine Cocores Balint.)

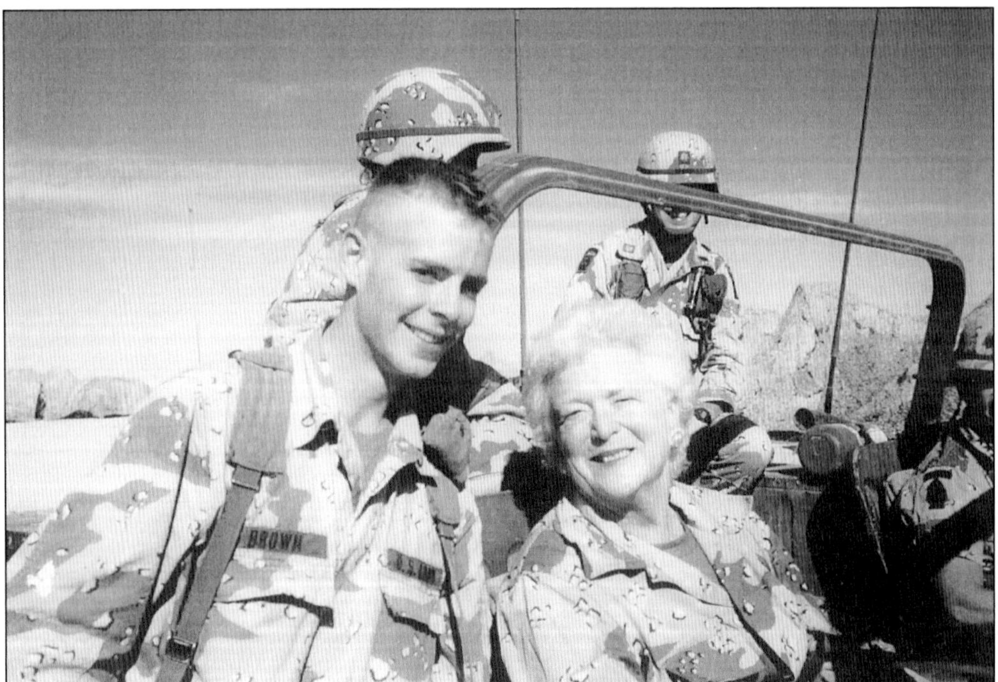

PFC Jeff Brown of the Army's 101st Airborne Division, the "Screaming Eagles," with First Lady Barbara Bush during the Persian Gulf Conflict. Pvt. Brown served in the Gulf seven months and took part in airborne assaults into Iraq. He returned home at the end of the conflict, in time to celebrate his twenty-first birthday. (Mr. and Mrs. Sidney DeBoer.)

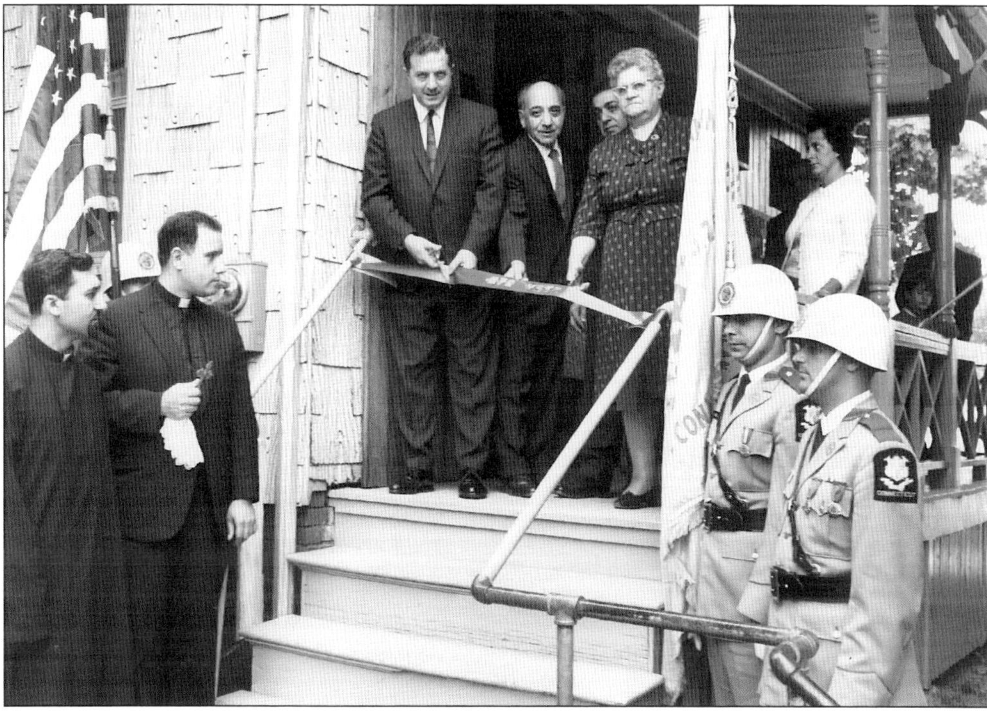

The Hartunian Tufankjian Post of Armenian veterans of Connecticut. Mayor Paul J. Manafort cuts the ribbon at the Hartunian Tufankjian Post of Armenian veterans of Connecticut. The post, just one of New Britain's many veterans groups, was located at 80 Rockwell Avenue. (John Melechinsky.)

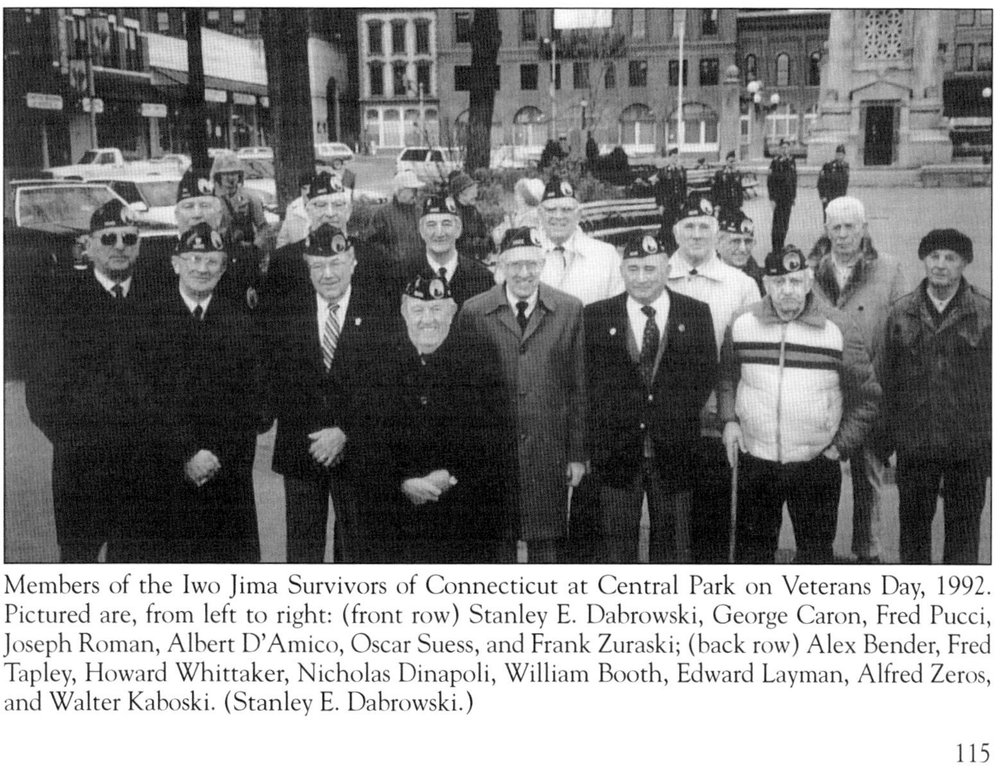

Members of the Iwo Jima Survivors of Connecticut at Central Park on Veterans Day, 1992. Pictured are, from left to right: (front row) Stanley E. Dabrowski, George Caron, Fred Pucci, Joseph Roman, Albert D'Amico, Oscar Suess, and Frank Zuraski; (back row) Alex Bender, Fred Tapley, Howard Whittaker, Nicholas Dinapoli, William Booth, Edward Layman, Alfred Zeros, and Walter Kaboski. (Stanley E. Dabrowski.)

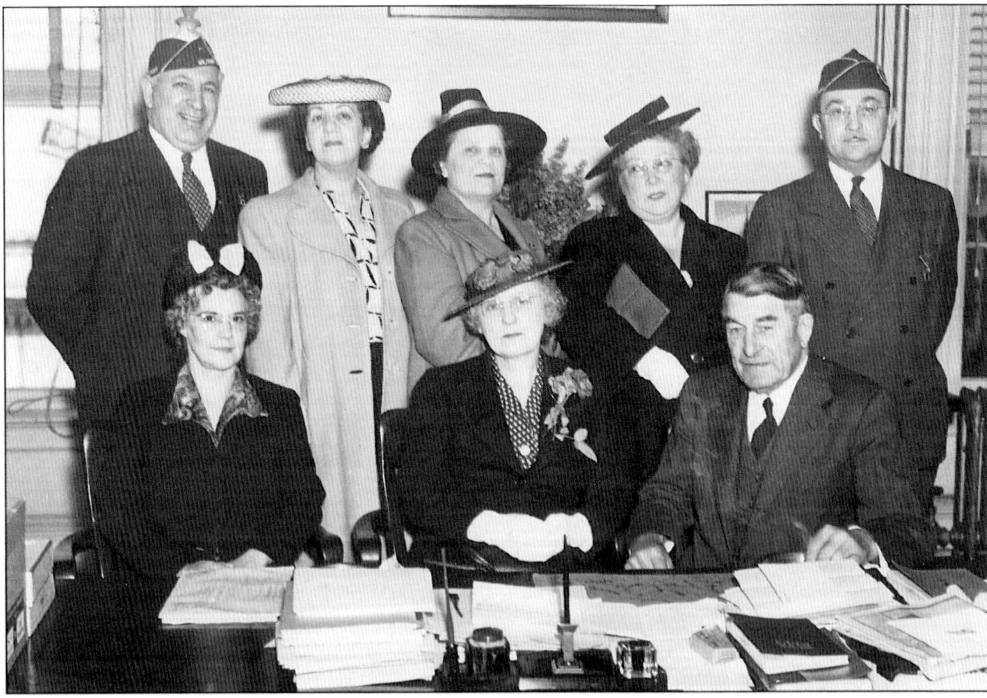

New Britain Chapter #51, Military Order of the Purple Heart, and Mayor George Quigley (first row). The chapter, founded in 1936, would start a woman's auxiliary in 1942. Stella Shumsky (third from left, back row) was the first president. The name of the order changed to the Frederick Fleischauer Chapter in honor of one of New Britain's youngest servicemen who was gassed during World War I. (Local History Room, NBPL.)

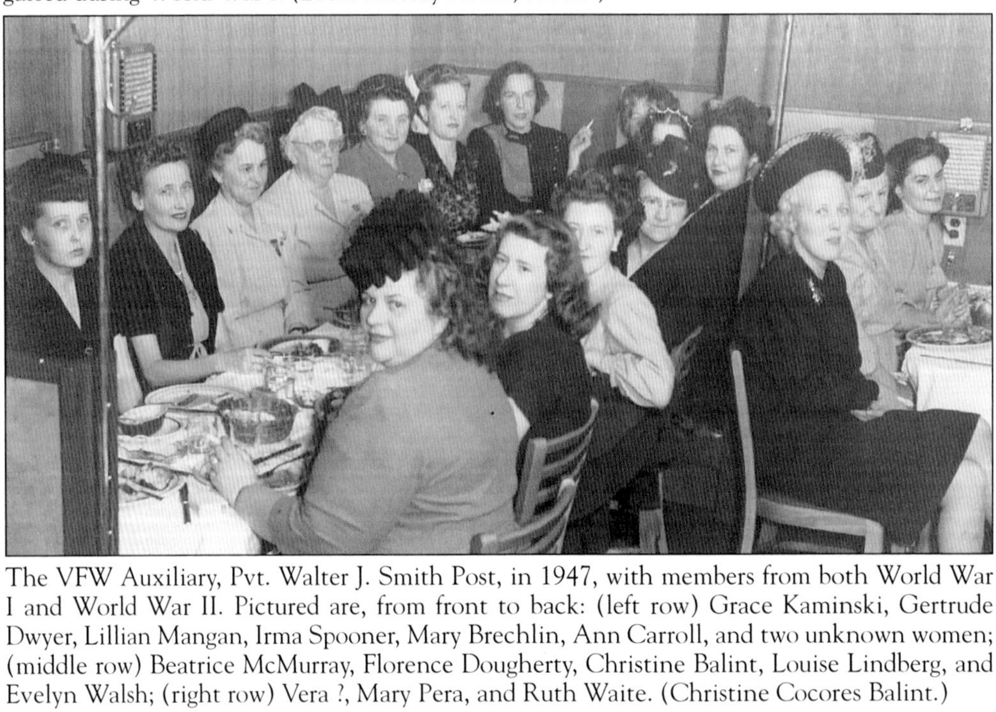

The VFW Auxiliary, Pvt. Walter J. Smith Post, in 1947, with members from both World War I and World War II. Pictured are, from front to back: (left row) Grace Kaminski, Gertrude Dwyer, Lillian Mangan, Irma Spooner, Mary Brechlin, Ann Carroll, and two unknown women; (middle row) Beatrice McMurray, Florence Dougherty, Christine Balint, Louise Lindberg, and Evelyn Walsh; (right row) Vera ?, Mary Pera, and Ruth Waite. (Christine Cocores Balint.)

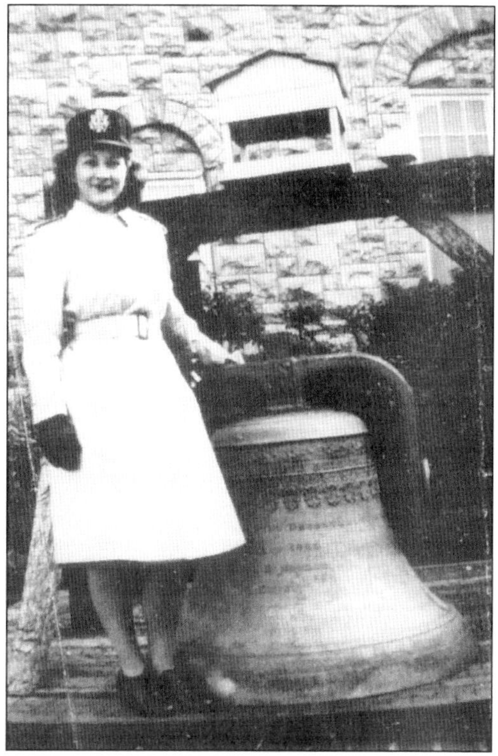

Frances Walshin Honeyman, psychiatric nurse. Mrs. Honeyman served in Memphis, Tennessee, during the war. She was in the Army Nurse Corps, stationed at Kennedy General Hospital, and continues to be active in the Sgt. Henry Berson Post #56 of the Jewish War Veterans. (Frances Walshin Honeyman.)

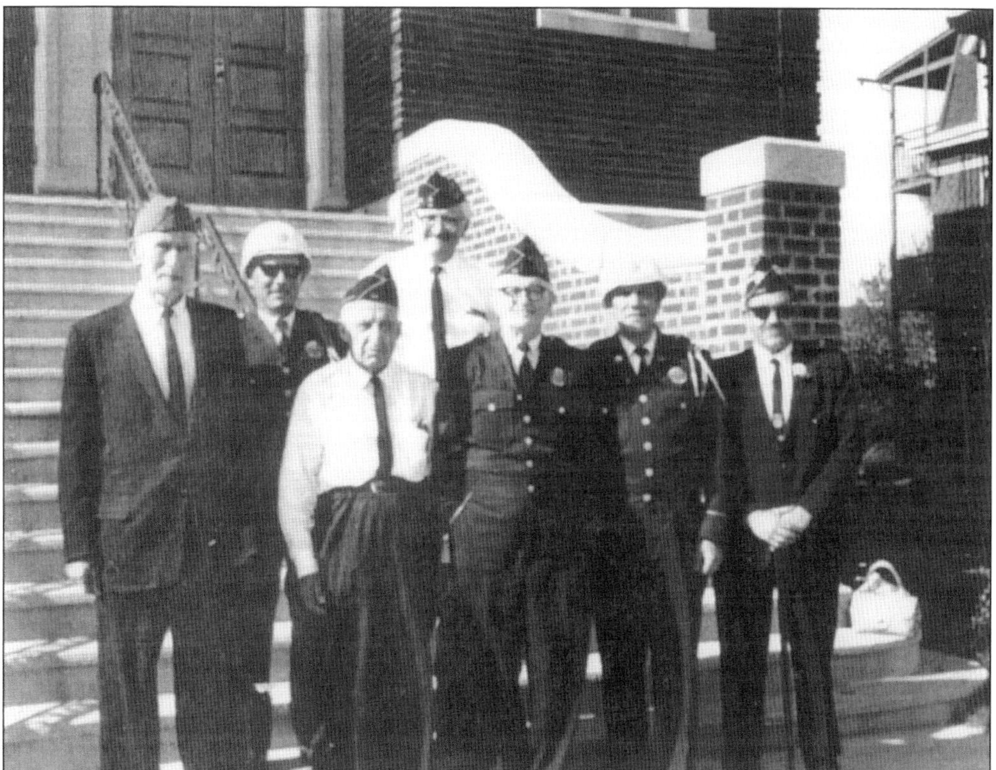

Jewish War Veterans on the steps of the Tephereth Israel Synagogue on Winter Street, following a Loyalty Day parade in 1969. Shown from left to right are: (front row) Max Edelson, Dave Fogelson, Morris Burros, Ben Firestone, and Nate Perry; (back row) Manny Hirsch and Ed Honeyman. (Mr. and Mrs. Ben Firestone.)

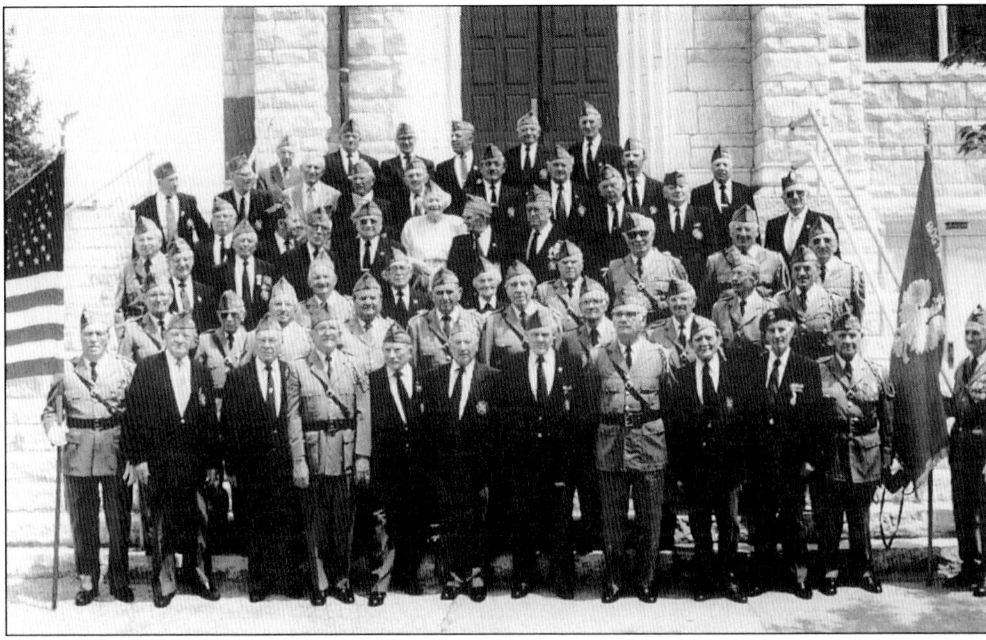

General Joseph Haller Post #111 and the Ladies Auxiliary. Members of the post have exemplified the meaning of caring and giving since the organization's inception in 1920. Funds have been raised for the Polish Orphanage, disabled veterans, and flood victims, among other causes. Jan Noniewicz, the post's historian, said the following about the Veterans Home, erected on the site of the old Bartlett School at the corner of Broad and Grove Streets: ". . . when the Veterans will no longer be here, they will have a living monument; if someone should enter these doors to rest, he'll do so in comfort, perhaps remembering that the Polish Army Veterans once lived and worked here." (Haller Post/Paul Dabrowski.)

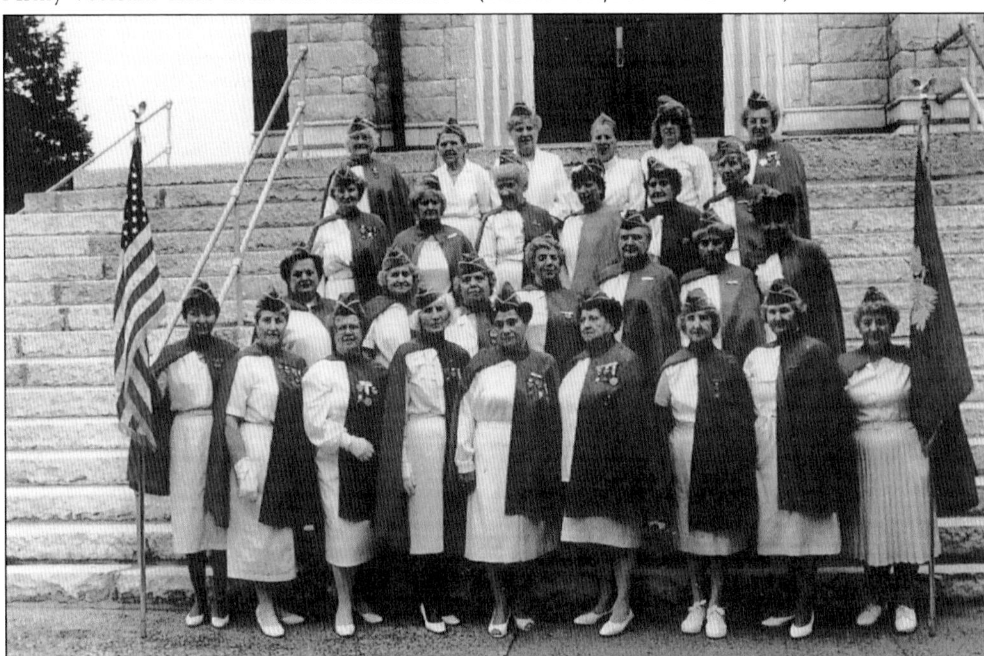

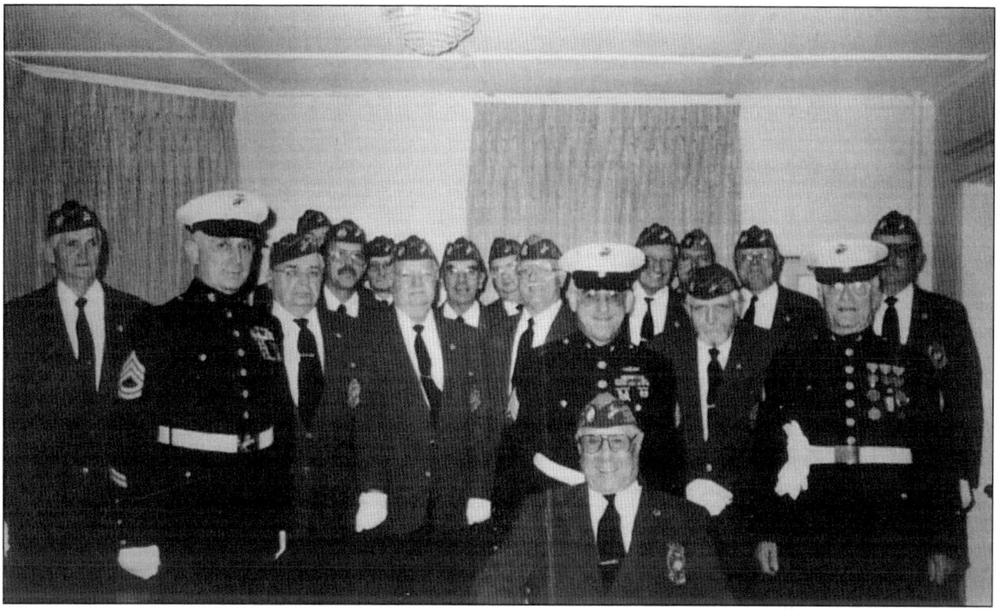

The City Marine Corps League. The league reorganized in 1991 after the Blodgett Roy Detachment had been dormant for thirty years. The new charter was received on October 16, 1991. Pictured are, from left to right: T. Contessa, E. Occhi, C. Pietras, P. Maykut, N. Raymond, J. Vandrilla Jr., A. Lavoie, F. Bongiovanni, N. Musk, E. Herrington, R. Clarke, J. Shettie, R. Hamilton, D. Fisk, J. Lynch, L. Gentile, R. Wearne, and Comdt. J. Westergom (seated in front). (John Westergom.)

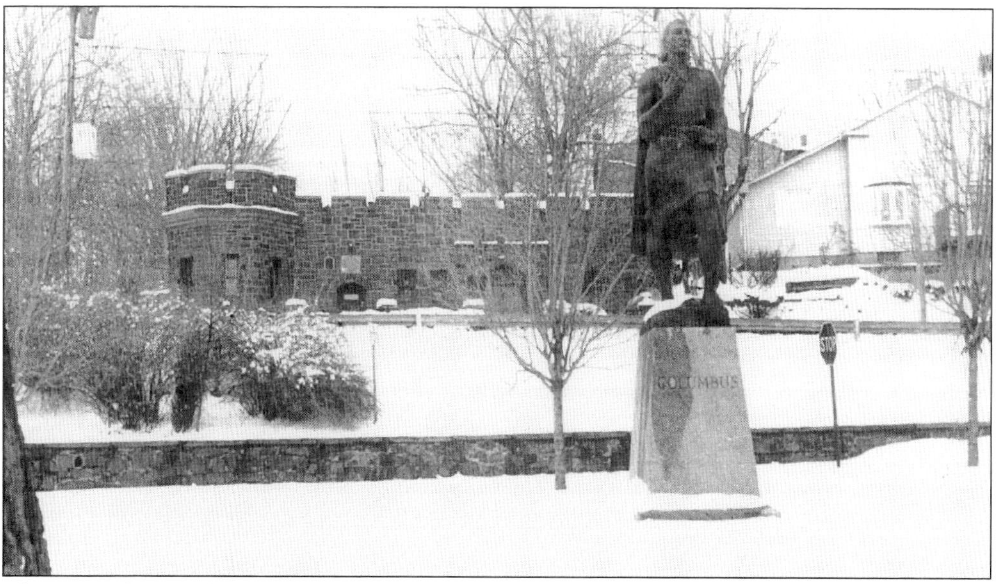

The Bernadino-Badaloto Post at 36 North Street and the Columbus Monument in McCabe Park. In 1930, veterans from World War I met to organize a local chapter of Italian-American veterans. It was named after Nicola Bernadino, the first soldier of Italian descent killed in action. Dedication of their headquarters, which resembles a castle, took place in 1943. Ten years later, the name of World War II veteran John N. Badalato was added to the post's name. (Frank Rocco and Paul J. Manafort.)

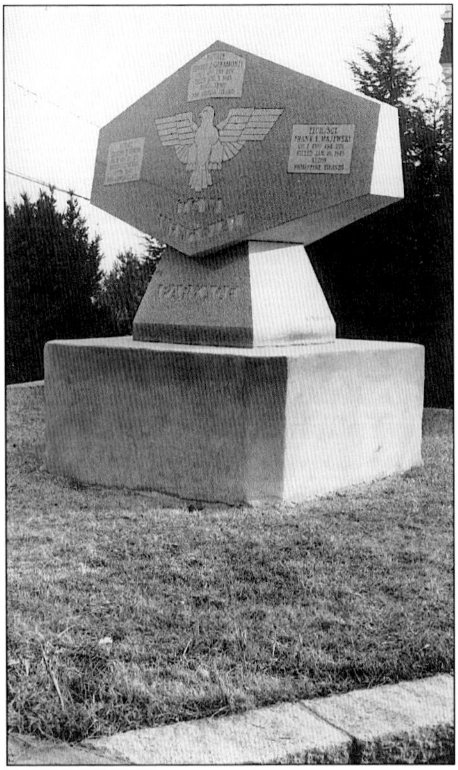

The TGM Memorial Monument. This monument was erected in honor of Pvt. Stanley Todzia, Pvt. Edward Giramonti, and Tech. Sgt. Frank Majewski, of the 169th Regiment, 43rd Division. The Northwestern TGM Post originated as an athletic club in 1936 and deactivated in 1941. Following World War II, the post reactivated as a veteran's group and continues to flourish today. (*Herald* photograph file.)

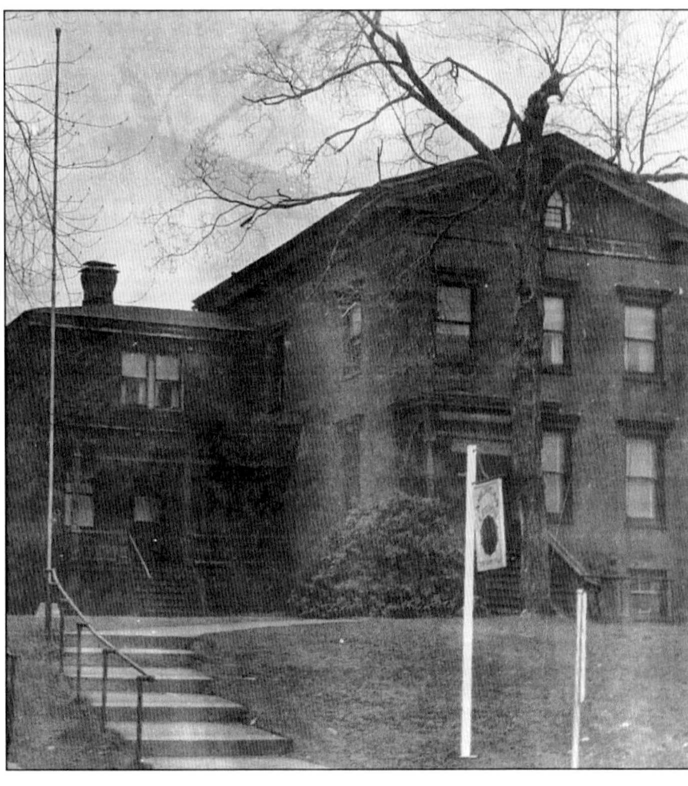

The Eddy Glover Post #6, American Legion headquarters, on Washington Street. The post is named after Lieut. Leslie Eddy and Lieut. Joseph Glover, both of whom died during World War I. The Washington Street structure was dedicated on May 26, 1926. (Ed LaMire.)

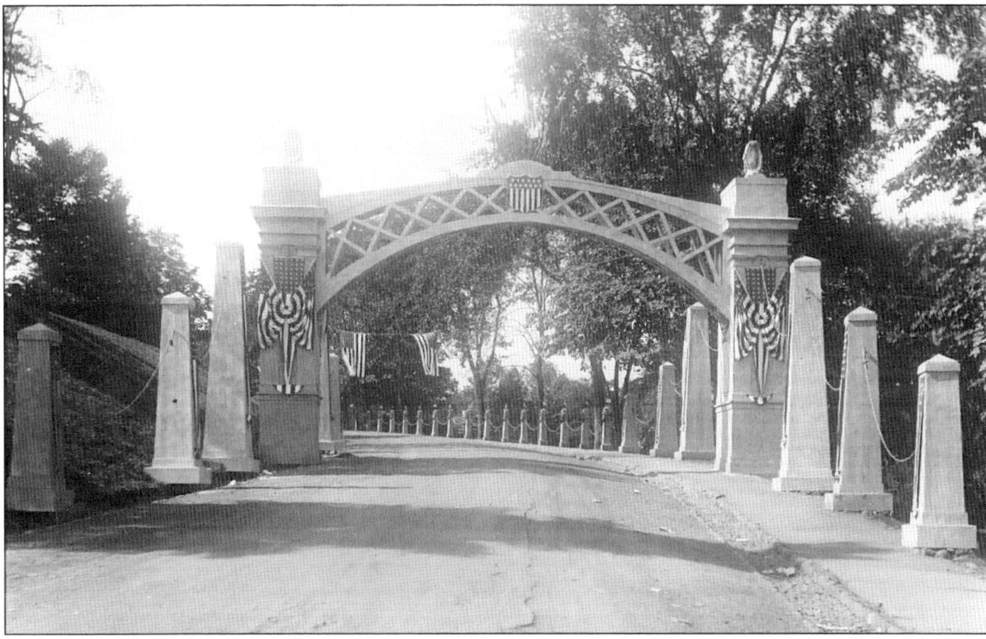

The Memorial Arch and Court of Honor decorated for New Britain's "Welcome Home" program held on September 19, 1919, in Walnut Hill Park. Within ten years, a permanent monument (shown below), designed by H. VanBuren Magonigle, was erected. Delivering the dedication speech, Charles F. Smith offered the following: ". . . may the city which it overlooks cherish it, guard it, beautify it and keep it from harm. . . as often as men's eyes shall be lifted up to it may they think of all that it signifies and of what in times of peace is their own duty as citizens to a city and country for which these brave men gave their lives." (Local History Room, NBPL.)

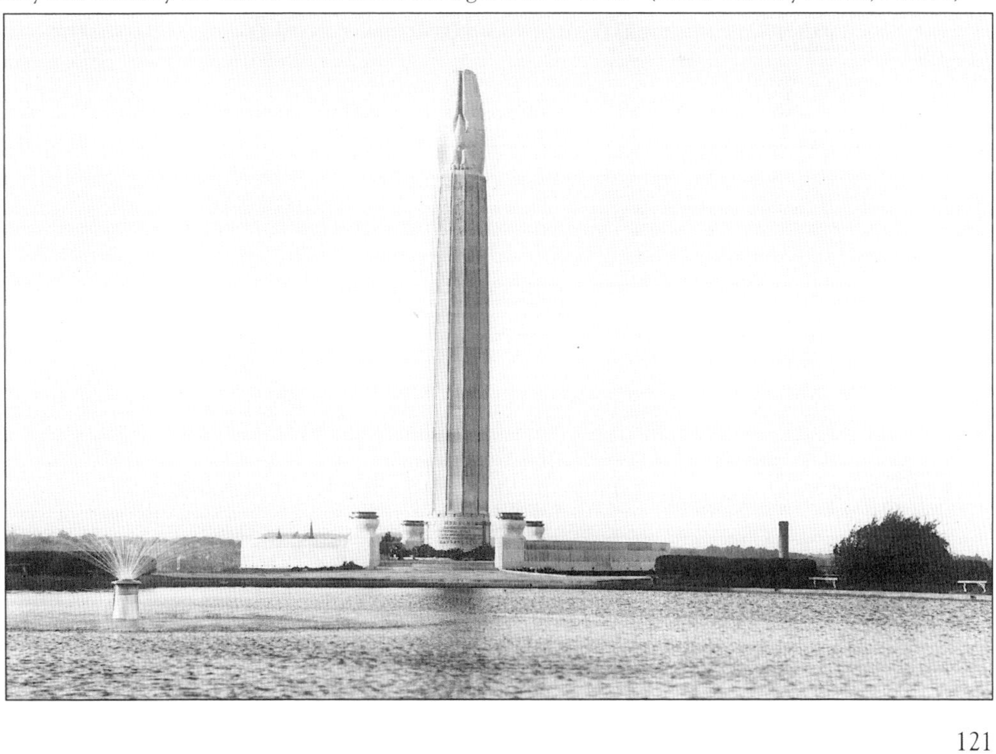

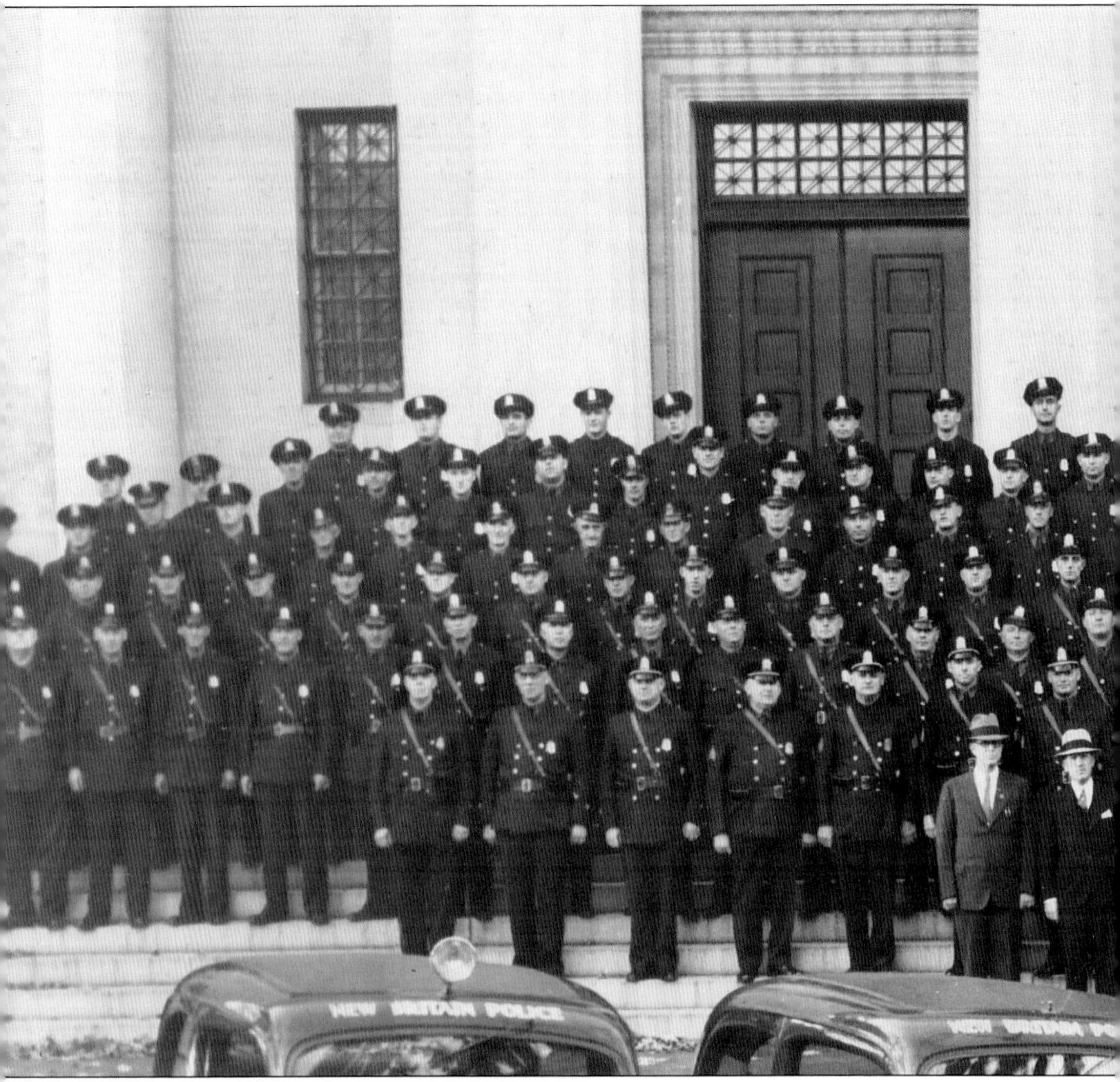

The New Britain Police Department on the steps of the Masonic Hall, which would later become Temple B'Nai Israel. When New Britain received its city charter in 1870, provision was made for the Common Council to appoint "a captain of police, not exceeding three active policemen and such other supernumerary policemen as they shall deem proper not exceeding

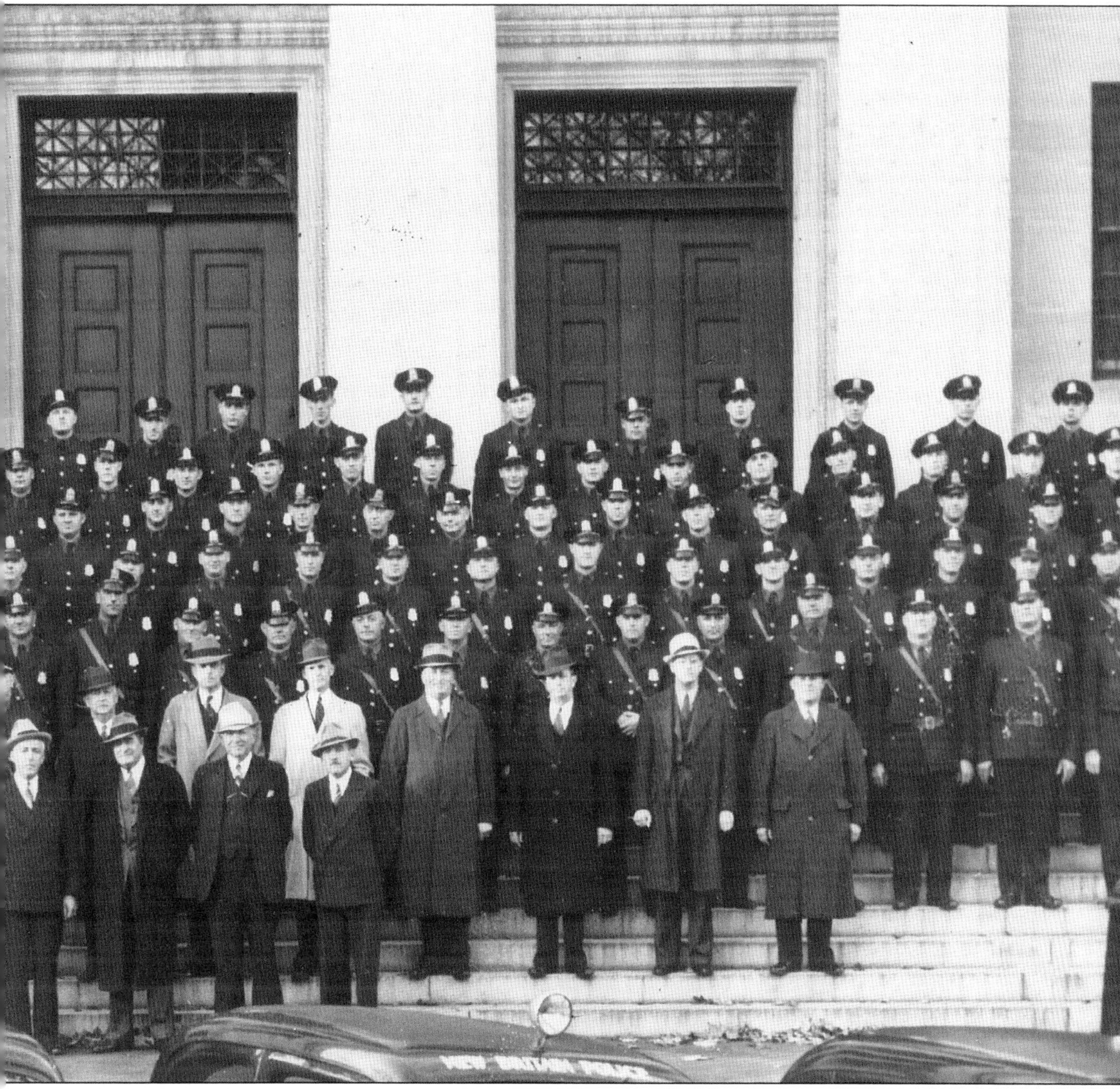

twenty. . ." The first captain was A.W. Spaulding, and his force consisted of Lafayette Craw, P.J. Flannery, and Patrick Lee. Eighteen supernumeraries were also appointed. (Local History Room, NBPL.)

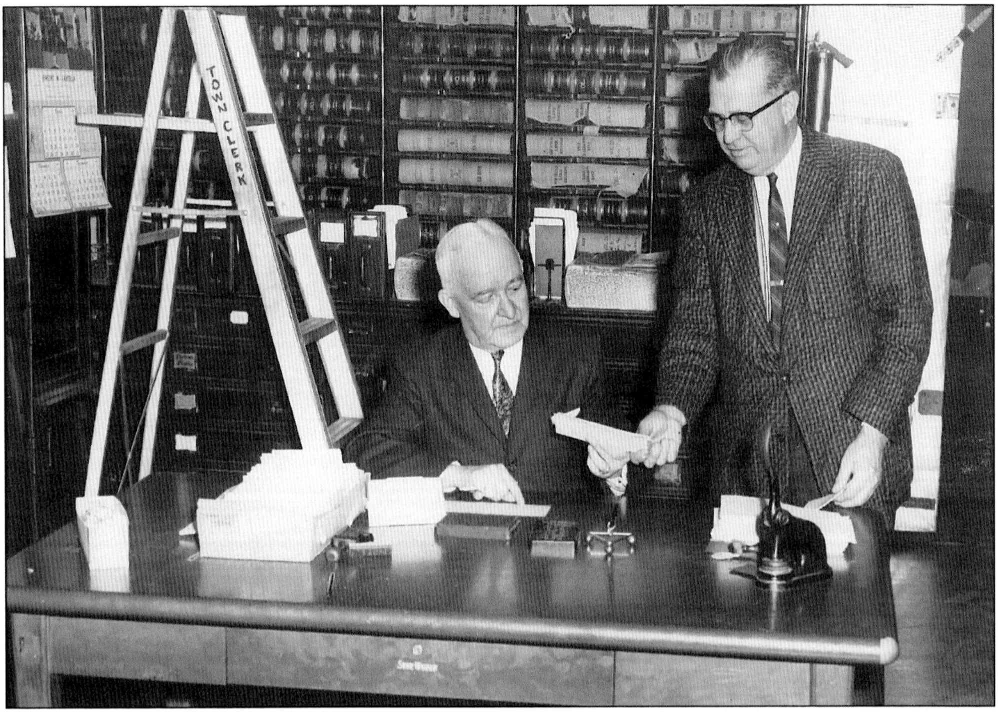

Harry Scheyd (left), the town clerk, and George Paris in the town clerk's vault. Part of serving the city entails record-keeping, as performed by the town/city clerk. Real estate titles, births, and deaths are among the volumes of material that must be preserved. (Local History Room, NBPL.)

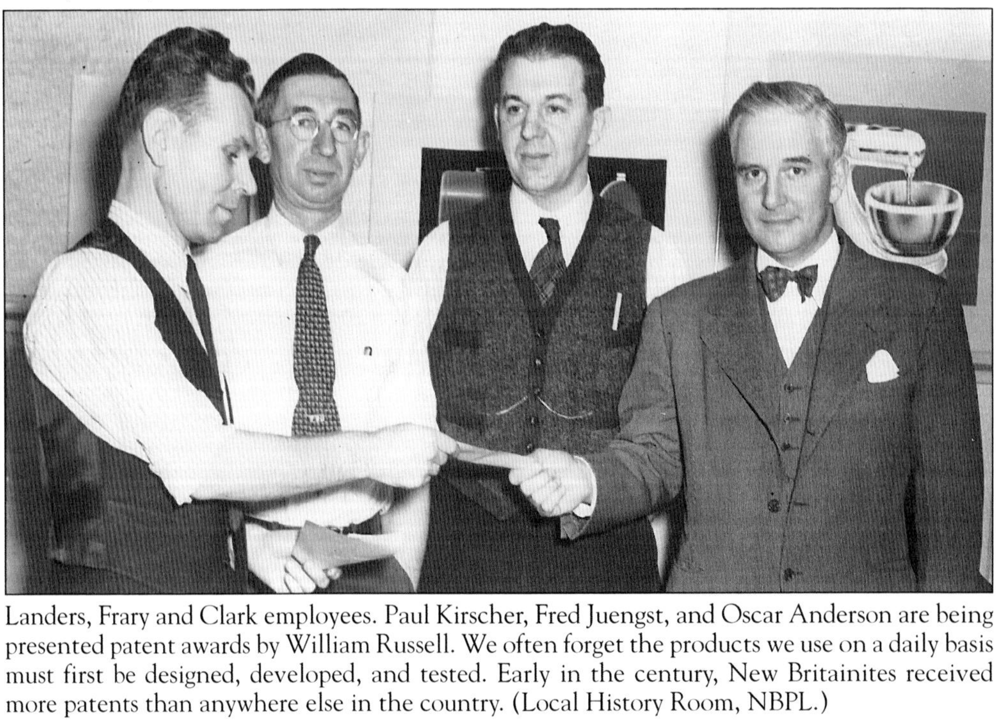

Landers, Frary and Clark employees. Paul Kirscher, Fred Juengst, and Oscar Anderson are being presented patent awards by William Russell. We often forget the products we use on a daily basis must first be designed, developed, and tested. Early in the century, New Britainites received more patents than anywhere else in the country. (Local History Room, NBPL.)

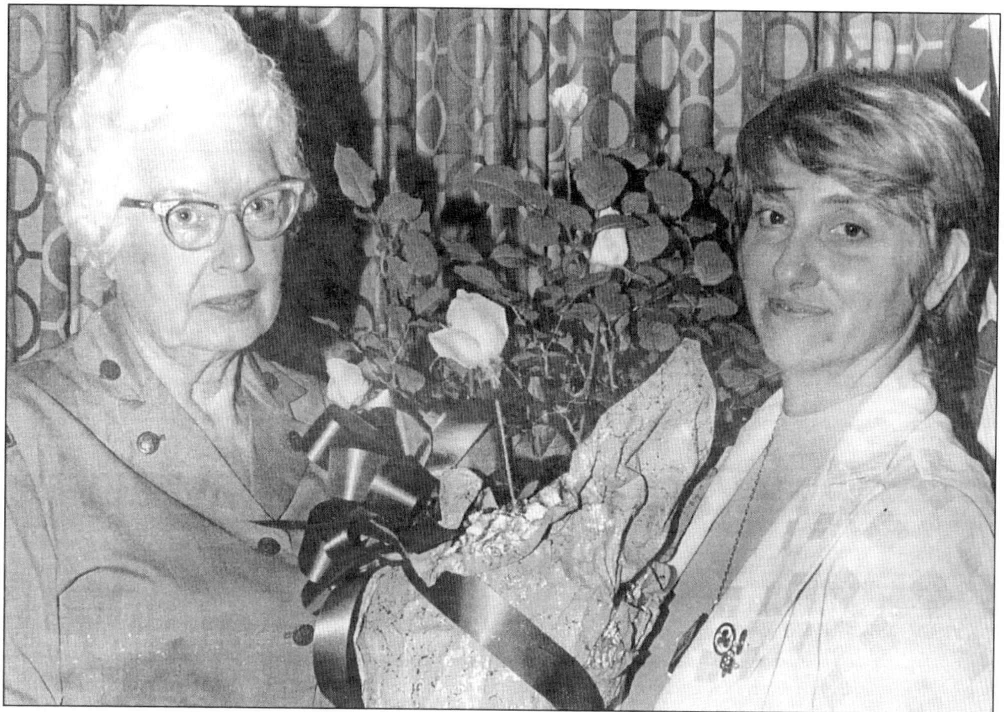

Mabel Bonney (left). Whether working with the Boys' Club, the Esther Stanley Chapter of the DAR, or the Girl Scouts, Mrs. Bonney has devoted years of her life to New Britain organizations. She was awarded a seventy-year pin from the Girl Scouts. Both her mother and her daughter were also active in scouting. (Mr. and Mrs. William Bonney.)

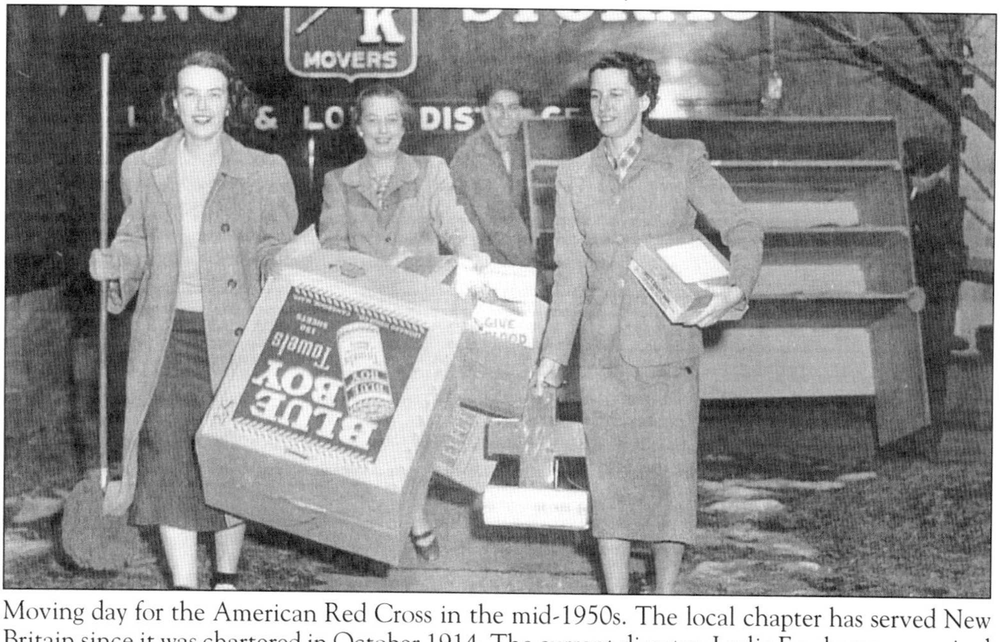

Moving day for the American Red Cross in the mid-1950s. The local chapter has served New Britain since it was chartered in October 1914. The current director, Leslie Eza, best summarized the community spirit evoked by the agency: "All we ask is someday if you have the opportunity that you help someone else. We help people help other people." (American Red Cross.)

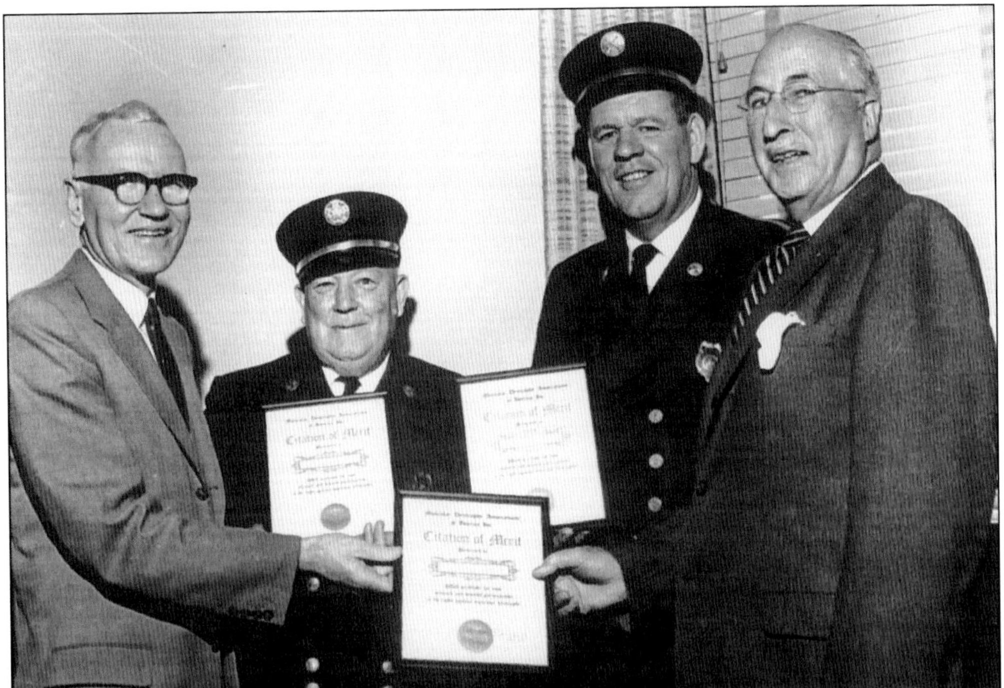

Certificates of merit. Joe Burns (left) of the Muscular Dystrophy Association presents certificates of merit to Chief Scarlett, Deputy Chief Edward McKeon, and Gardner Weld of the *New Britain Herald*. In addition to their busy jobs, these men found the time to help battle this crippling disability. (Artemese Blanchette McKeon.)

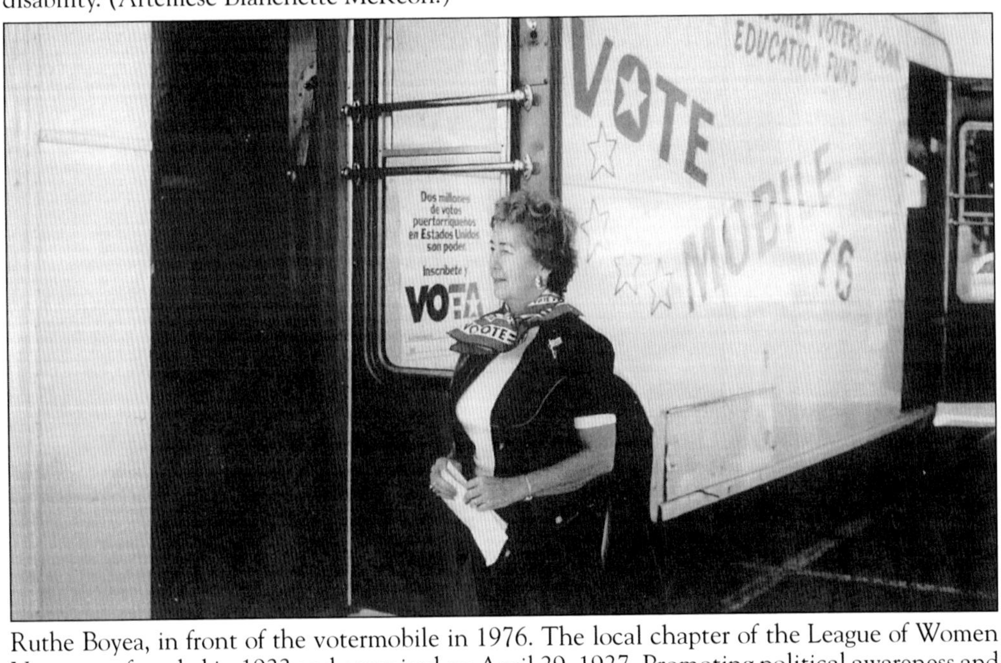

Ruthe Boyea, in front of the votermobile in 1976. The local chapter of the League of Women Voters was founded in 1922 and organized on April 29, 1927. Promoting political awareness and active participation in local government are goals the League continuously strives to achieve. (Douglas Boyea.)

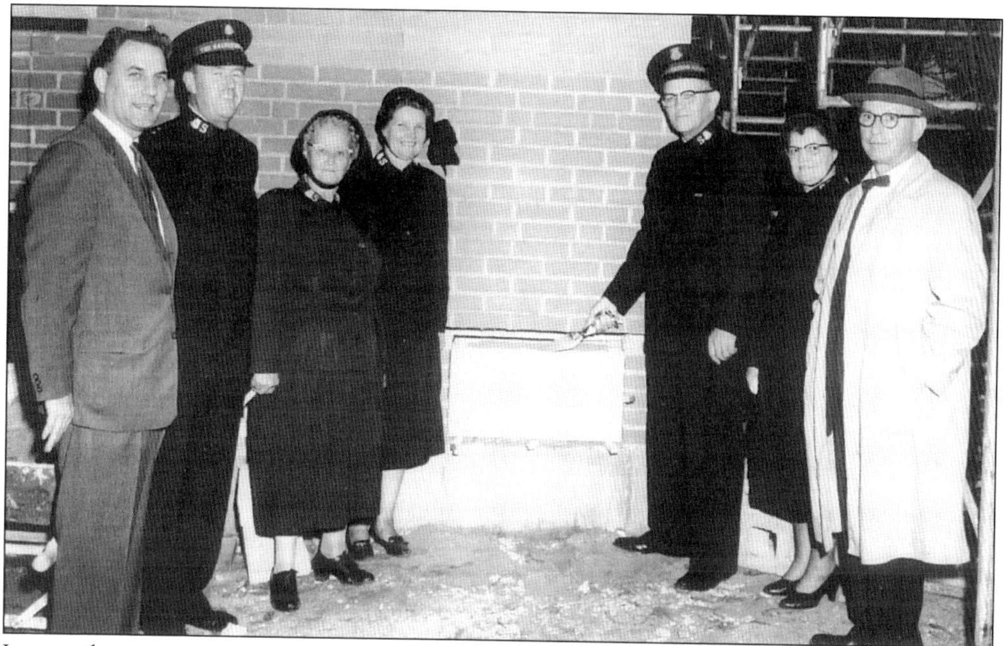

Laying the cornerstone of the Salvation Army Building in 1961. Opening its headquarters in February 1897, the Salvation Army has aided residents for almost one hundred years. Shown at the ceremony are, from left to right: Mayor Julius Kremski, Divisional Commander MacKennsie, Mrs. Frederickson, Brig. Alice Theleen, Colonel Johanson, and Atty. Carlos Richardson. (Salvation Army.)

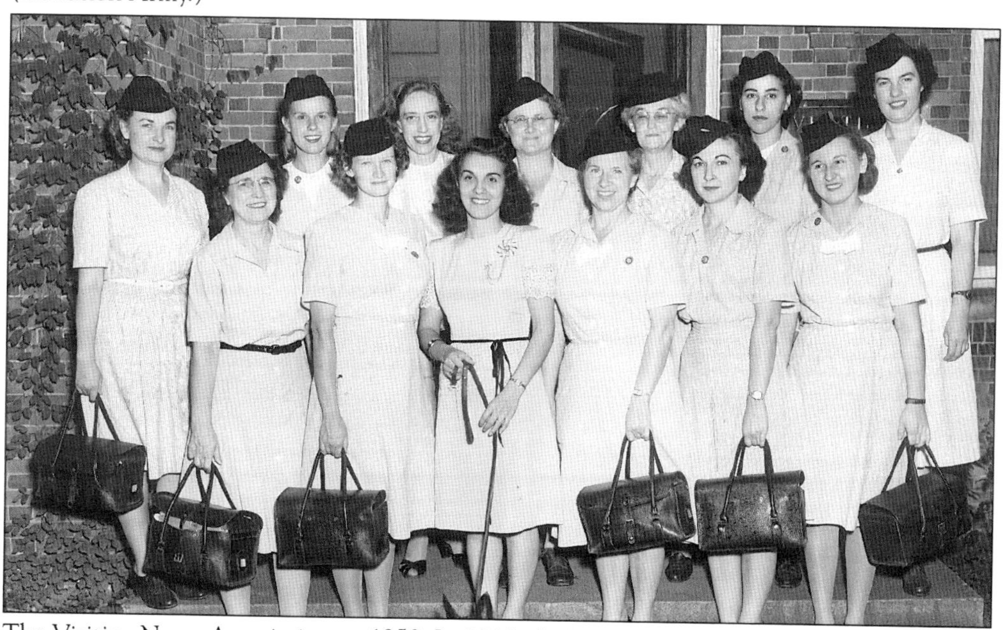

The Visiting Nurse Association, *c.* 1950. In 1915, the VNA began service in the city with only one nurse. By 1909, the all-male board of directors had been replaced with an all-female board. Incorporated in 1914, this agency has continued to grow. The year 1992 saw the Visiting Nurse and Home Care Services of Central Connecticut, Inc., become a subsidiary of CenConn, the parent company of New Britain General Hospital. (Fred Hedeler.)

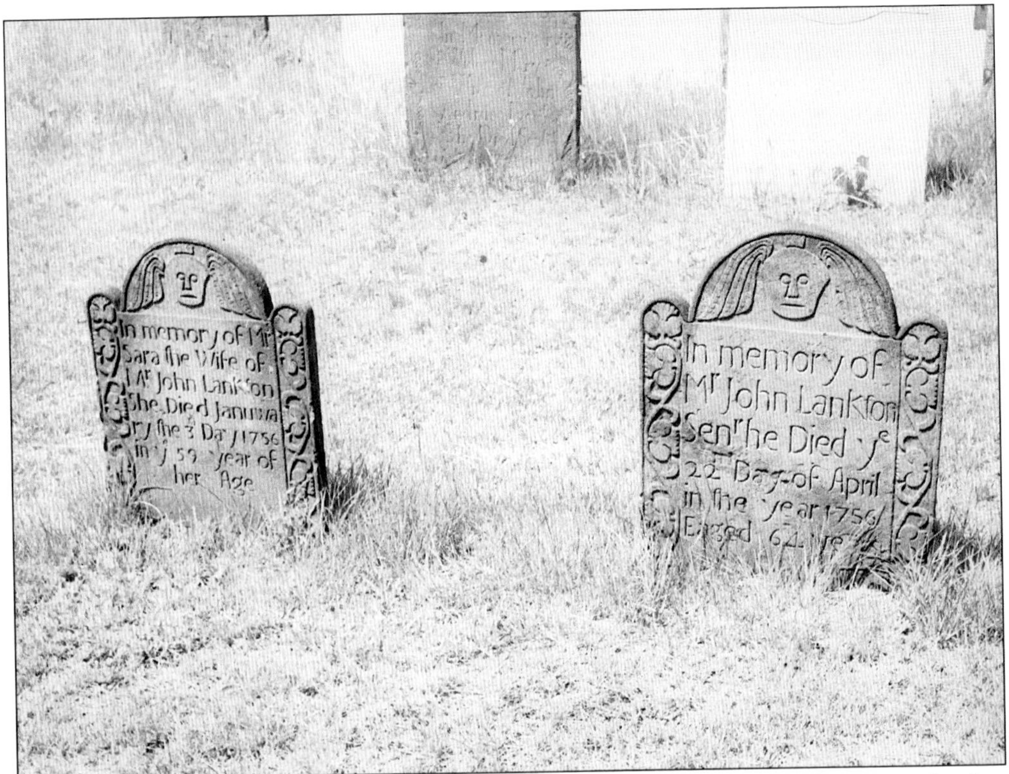

The graves of Sarah and John Lankton in Fairview Cemetery. Sarah Lankton was the first person buried in what would become the municipal cemetery, having died in 1756 at the age of fifty-nine. Her husband outlived her by only three months. Containing the graves of most of the city's founding fathers, notables such as Elihu Burritt and Dexter Fellows and veterans from every war, Fairview Cemetery has provided residents a final resting place for 240 years. (Local History Room, NBPL.)

Afterword

Like any urban center, New Britain has suffered setbacks, but recent years have also seen positive developments. The Hardware City Rock Cats, farm team of the Minnesota Twins, play in the newly constructed New Britain Stadium. The Tomasso Critical Care Tower puts New Britain General Hospital in the forefront of medical care, and the Arts Alliance of Greater New Britain is unifying the city's many cultural organizations. With Government Center opening this year, new jobs will be created. May this trend continue.